Poetry For Dummi

D0598885

Poetry Pop Quiz

1. Who was the first official U.S. Poet Laureate — Robert Penn Warren, Muriel Rukeyser, Ezra Pound, or Russell Edson?

2. Who was the first woman to win the Pulitzer Prize for poetry — Edna St. Vincent Millay, Sara Teasdale, or Mona Van Duyn?

3. What is said to be the longest poem in world history — *The Mahabharata; Howl* by Allen Ginsberg; *Paradise Lost* by John Milton; or Poem #312 by Emily Dickinson?

4. Who wrote the poem "Funeral Blues," which was recited in the movie *Four Weddings and A Funeral* — Victor Hugo, Amy Clampitt, Pablo Neruda, or W.H. Auden?

5. Which statement about Emily Dickinson is not true?

    a. She lived at her parents' house her entire life.

    b. She published fewer than a dozen poems during her lifetime.

    c. She was left at the altar.

    d. She was a bread judge at the local cattle show.

6. What did Robert Bridges, Thomas Campion, William Carlos Williams, and Henry Vaughan have in common?

7. Which one of these poets doesn't belong in this group and why?

    a. Amenhotep

    b. Léopold Sédar Senghor

    c. Jimmy Carter

    d. William Shakespeare

8. True or False: A line of iambic pentameter must have ten syllables.

9. Name the popular film from 1961 starring Natalie Wood and Warren Beatty that took its title from William Wordsworth's "Ode: Intimations of Immortality." Was it *Leaves of Grass, Love Canal, Splendor in the Grass,* or *The Grapes of Wrath?*

10. Connect the place on the left with the poet associated with that place on the right:

Lesbos	Charles Baudelaire
Martinique	Lorine Niedecker
New Hampshire	Sappho
Paris	Robert Frost
Wisconsin	Lawrence Ferlinghetti
Chicago	Aimé Césaire
San Francisco	Carl Sandburg

Answers: 1. Robert Penn Warren, in 1986; 2. Sara Teasdale, in 1918; 3. *The Mahabharata;* 4. W.H. Auden; 5. c; 6. They were all physicians; 7. d (Shakespeare was not a head of state); 8. False; 9. *Splendor in the Grass;* 10. Lesbos, Sappho; Martinique, Césaire; New Hampshire, Frost; Paris, Baudelaire; Wisconsin, Niedecker; Chicago, Sandburg; San Francisco, Ferlinghetti.

For Dummies: Bestselling Book Series for Beginners

Poetry For Dummies®

Cheat Sheet

How to Read a Poem Aloud

- ✔ Read silently first.
- ✔ Note surprises and unfamiliar words.
- ✔ Establish a positive, conversational tone.
- ✔ Follow the music.
- ✔ Don't rush.
- ✔ Pause for emphasis.
- ✔ Treat line endings with care, pausing briefly or raising your tone of voice.
- ✔ Repeat for best results.

Fifteen Poems: A Crash Course in Poetic History

- ✔ *The Odyssey* by Homer
- ✔ Rubaiyat XII by Omar Khayyam
- ✔ "Farewell" by Chao Li-hua
- ✔ *The Inferno* by Dante
- ✔ Sonnet 73 by William Shakespeare
- ✔ *Eugene Onegin* by Alexander Pushkin
- ✔ "Crossing Brooklyn Ferry" by Walt Whitman
- ✔ "A Narrow Fellow in the Grass" by Emily Dickinson
- ✔ "The Second Coming" by William Butler Yeats
- ✔ "Walking Around" by Pablo Neruda
- ✔ "Requiem: 1935–1940" by Anna Akhmatova
- ✔ "Song of the Initiate" by Léopold Sédar Senghor
- ✔ "Daddy" by Sylvia Plath
- ✔ "Under a Certain Little Star" by Wislawa Szymborska
- ✔ "Monster Mash" by David Trinidad

Copyright © 2001 Wiley Publishing, Inc.
All rights reserved.

Item 5272-4.

For more information about Wiley,
call 1-800-762-2974.

For Dummies: Bestselling Book Series for Beginners

Praise For Poetry For Dummies

"It might be easy to make the snide assumption that a book called *Poetry For Dummies* must be a dumbed-down waste of time—easy, but wrong. *Poetry For Dummies* turns out to be a great guide to reading and writing poems, not only for beginners but also for anyone interested in verse...The authors say one of their primary aims was to change the minds of those who 'don't get' or 'don't like' poetry. They've done more than that. *Poetry For Dummies* is fun even when it preaches to the choir."

> — John Mark Eberhart, books editor, *The Kansas City Star*

"...despite its title, this is an intelligent and accessible introductory guide that should prove useful and entertaining to both readers and poet wannabes. The authors discuss reading and interpreting poetry, tell about the history of poetry and various movements, offer advice about writing and publishing poetry and point you where to find out more...Talk about a poetry slam."

> — Nancy Pate, book editor, *The Orlando Sentinel*

"..fun, reliable and cool...[the] breezy, irreverent style will get you through that poetry unit and leave a smile on your face."

> — Tom Mayo, *Dallas Morning News*

"The book touches on all different kinds of poetry, with male and female authors from more than a dozen countries equally represented."

> — Susan Van Dongen, *TimeOff, Central New Jersey's Weekly Guide to Cultural Survival*

"As you would expect of anything written 'for dummies,' the tone here is down-to-earth, though also respectful."

> — Karen Sandstrom, book editor, *Plain Dealer,* Cleveland, Ohio

"If you were traumatized into prose by a 10th-grade English class in which you had to learn to tell a dactyl from an anapest and search out "hidden meanings" in Emily Dickinson, this may be the book for you."

> — Charles Matthews, book editor, *San Jose Mercury News*

"Does Robert Pinsky know about this?...It's one-stop shopping for the iambic pentameter crowd—from Angelou, Maya to the Objectivist poet Zukovsky, Louis and most everything in between...Need guidance on composing a ghazal (Arabic verse form), a tanka (Japanese), or a psalm? This is the book for you!"

> — Alex Beam, *The Boston Globe*

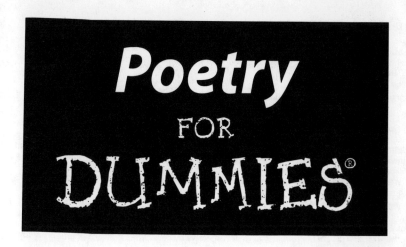

Poetry

FOR

DUMMIES®

by The Poetry Center and John Timpane
with Maureen Watts

Poetry For Dummies®

Published by
Wiley Publishing, Inc.
909 Third Avenue
New York, NY 10022
www.wiley.com

For general information on our other products and services or to obtain technical support, please contact our Customer Care Department within the U.S. at 800-762-2974, outside the U.S. at 317-572-3993, or fax 317-572-4002.

Wiley also publishes its books in a variety of electronic formats. Some content that appears in print may not be available in electronic books.

Library of Congress Cataloging-in-Publication Data:

Library of Congress Control Number: 00-110796

ISBN: 0-7645-5272-4

Manufactured in the United States of America

10 9 8 7 6

1B/SQ/QY/QS/IN

About the Authors

The Poetry Center & American Poetry Archives at San Francisco State University was founded in 1954 on the basis of a gift by W.H. Auden. The Poetry Center is one of the most long-lived, prestigious, and nationally renowned literary arts institutions in the United States. For almost 50 years, since Ruth Witt-Diamant, with esteemed poets Robert Duncan and Josephine Miles, initiated the Poetry Center's pioneering reading series, the Center has presented readings by poets, novelists, and other writers, in accord with the highest standards of literary excellence. The Poetry Center presents readings over two seasons annually, both on- and off-campus, open to the public.

The Poetry Center today operates under the aegis of San Francisco State University's Creative Writing Department, the largest in the country, and represents an irreplaceable collective record of the past half-century of American literary accomplishment. The Poetry Center's American Poetry Archives is a collection of over 2,000 original recordings of poets and writers reading from their work, recorded since the 1950s at Poetry Center readings. The collection includes rare readings by Allen Ginsberg, William Burroughs, Langston Hughes, William Carlos Williams, Marianne Moore, Alice Walker, Anne Sexton, Frank O'Hara, and many other great writers of the past 50 years.

John Timpane is the Commentary Page Editor of *The Philadelphia Inquirer.* How'd he get there — and how'd he get from there to *Poetry For Dummies?* John was graduated from Stanford University with an M.A. and Ph.D. in English and the Humanities in 1980. He taught English in colleges and universities for 20 years; wrote books on composition and poetry; published articles on Shakespeare, Spenser, and other great writers; and, on the side, did a nifty little freelance writing gig (scientific writing, industrial film scripts, and journalism). John has written poetry since he was very small, works at the craft, and is very much involved in the poetry scene. He won the Academy of American Poets Prize at Stanford in 1980 and was a Fulbright Scholar in 1983–1984. Poetry, with its demand for clarity of vision, concentration of feeling in a small space, and richness of language, helps John be a better editor and writer at the *Inquirer.* He is the eldest of nine children and is married to Maria-Christina Keller, copy manager of *Scientific American* and a fine writer herself. They have a daughter, Pilar, and a son, Conor. John also musicks about, as a flutist in a jazz band and a bassist in a zydeco outfit. You can e-mail him at jtimpane@aol.com.

Maureen Watts started her career as a receptionist at a small publishing company in Berkeley, California, after graduating from the University of California at San Diego. From there, she fell into the exciting world of book publicity. The idea for *Poetry For Dummies* came to Maureen while she was driving over the San Francisco Bay Bridge on a bright day in March. A long-time poetry activist, she is on the board of directors of the National Poetry Association and past president of Small Press Traffic Literary Arts Center. She attributes her love of poetry to long afternoons spent playing in the fields of Illinois as a child. Watts adds literary agent and writer to her job description as head of Watts Communications in San Francisco, California.

Dedication

To our families and to everyone — from Enheduanna to the pair of eyes on these very words — who loves reading and writing poetry. Let *Poetry For Dummies* declare our lifelong thanks.

Authors' Acknowledgments

Creating *Poetry For Dummies* has taught us that collaboration is the best part of writing. We'd be amiss not to thank all who helped us nose this project over the finish line.

First, thanks go to the Poetry Center at San Francisco State University. Frances Phillips and Professor Robert Glück, board members at the Poetry Center, played instrumental roles in getting this book written, commenting on the manuscript, suggesting poems, and, in many cases, rewriting things until they worked. Special thanks go to Robert Glück for his hard work, particularly with the section titled "Experimental poetry" in Chapter 7, and to Steve Dickison, executive director, and the staff at the Poetry Center, who opened the Center's resources to us. Special thanks go to Dr. Robert A. Corrigan, President of San Francisco State University, and Maxine Chernoff, chair of the Creative Writing Department at SFSU.

Our friends and editors at Hungry Minds, Inc., saved our necks at many a parlous turn. Elizabeth Kuball, our faithful and brilliant editor, teamed with Kathy Cox, Karen Young, Joyce Pepple, Roxane Cerda, Carmen Krikorian, and Susan Decker kept us on track all the way. Kathy Welton and Hollie McGuire first said "yes" and remained steadfast and enthusiastic from the very beginning. Our technical editor was Paul Hoover of Columbia College Chicago; his kind and patient comments made this a much better book.

Thanks also to Willis Barnstone, Damion Searls, Jerome Rothenberg, Pierre Joris, Dana Gioia, Laura Moriarty, and Chris Satullo for generous and indispensable assistance; Lawrence Ferlinghetti, Ed Taylor, and Michael Warr, for reading the manuscript; the Amherst College Archives and Special Collections; the Allen Ginsberg Trust; the National Poetry Association; Scott Tambert of PD Images.com; David Huang, Rob Lee, Chris Felver, and Emily Grossman for their photographs; Richard Linker, Brian Rowling, Marjorie Rauen; and Roberta Greifer and Lea Rude, librarians at the Noe Valley Library for their research assistance; Linda Jarkesy for the case study of her poem "The Bed"; Charles Bernstein, Maxine Chernoff, Kelly Holt, Daniel J. Langton, Bernadette Mayer, Brighde Mullins, and Eileen Myles for their permission to use their writing exercises. Watts thanks Timpane, and Timpane thanks Watts.

Special thanks goes to Elizabeth Vahlsing and Tom Southern of Boaz Press, who let Timpane out of his cage long enough to type up the book, and to Chris Van Buren and Nancy Webb for special guidance and never-ending support.

Publisher's Acknowledgments

We're proud of this book; please send us your comments through our online registration form located at www.dummies.com/register.

Some of the people who helped bring this book to market include the following:

Acquisitions, Editorial, and Media Development

Project Editor: Elizabeth Netedu Kuball

Acquisitions Editors: Susan Decker, Roxane Stanfield, Joyce Pepple, Holly McGuire

Technical Editor: Paul Hoover

Senior Permissions Editor: Carmen Krikorian

Editorial Manager: Jennifer Ehrlich

Media Development Manager: Laura Carpenter

Editorial Assistant: Carol Strickland

Reprint Editor: Michelle Hacker

Cover Photo: The Stock Market, © Chuck Keller, Jr./TSM

Production

Project Coordinator: Dale White

Layout and Graphics: Amy Adrian, LeAndra Johnson, Brian Massey, Jeremey Unger, Erin Zeltner

Proofreaders: Jennifer Mahern, Susan Moritz, Marianne Santy

Indexer: Joan Griffitts

Special Help
Kristin A. Cocks

Publishing and Editorial for Consumer Dummies

Diane Graves Steele, Vice President and Publisher, Consumer Dummies
Joyce Pepple, Acquisitions Director, Consumer Dummies
Kristin A. Cocks, Product Development Director, Consumer Dummies
Michael Spring, Vice President and Publisher, Travel
Brice Gosnell, Publishing Director, Travel
Suzanne Jannetta, Editorial Director, Travel

Publishing for Technology Dummies

Richard Swadley, Vice President and Executive Group Publisher
Andy Cummings, Vice President and Publisher

Composition Services

Gerry Fahey, Vice President of Production Services
Debbie Stailey, Director of Composition Services

Contents at a Glance

Cartoons at a Glance

By Rich Tennant

"I appreciate the poetry of Lewis Carroll's 'Jabberwocky' too. But could you not call the Offensive End a 'frumious Bandersnatch' every time he makes a touchdown?"

page 241

page 7

"This next poem is called, 'Never Try to Milk a Bull'."

page 213

"Stuart—would you like to come up and rap some 'Tennyson for us?"

page 91

"Yes, I think I can consider myself a published poet. I submitted all of my Personal Ads in the form of a Haiku."

page 139

Cartoon Information:
Fax: 978-546-7747
E-Mail: richtennant@the5thwave.com
World Wide Web: www.the5thwave.com

Table of Contents

Introduction

Suppose you invented a way to concentrate all the best things people ever thought and felt into a very few words. And suppose you *did* something to those words to make them pleasant, beautiful, unforgettable, and moving. Suppose this invention could get people to notice more of their own lives, sharpen their awareness, pay attention to things they'd never really considered before. Suppose it could make their lives — and them — better.

You'd really have something there.

Well, don't look now, but that invention has been around for at least 5,000 years — probably more. Millions of people love it and make it part of their lives. They turn to it when they need a smile, a lift, a moment of thoughtfulness. And millions of people write it, too.

What is this fantastic creation? Poetry. And it includes the work of Homer, Sappho, Kalidasa, Dante, Shakespeare, Ono no Komachi, Keats, Basho, Byron, Whitman, Dickinson, Frost, Yeats, Plath, Ginsberg, Amiri Imamu Baraka, Adrienne Rich, Gerald Stern, Lucille Clifton, and many others. It's been a great five millennia, and we're starting the sixth in better shape than ever.

Poetry saw a tremendous surge in popularity at the end of the 20th century — from Magnetic Poetry mania to the explosion of poetry slams across the country to an increased public appreciation of poets. And here in the 21st century, poetry continues to win more and more people over. And why not? It's great stuff.

We love poetry so much that we wrote this book. Most poets write poems for anyone willing to read and listen. But sometimes between the poet's notebook and the listening public a break occurs. Our hope and vision was to offer a book that gets past the things that sometimes divide poets and readers, things like technique, style, and school or genre, and the random distribution of books, poetry books, and journals.

Our goal in writing *Poetry For Dummies* was to bridge the literary gaps and throw open the doors of poetry — past, present, and future — to all. And, our hope is that if you say you "don't get" poetry or "don't like" poetry, this book just may change your mind.

Oh, and one promise: If you let poetry into your life — if you read aloud and read attentively, discover how to *interpret* poetry for yourself — you'll start seeing benefits, including a broader life, a more sensitive awareness, and a more flexible spirit.

If you are a poet or want to try your hand at poetry, welcome to an ancient and ever-changing craft with many traditions, rewards, and challenges.

About This Book

Poetry For Dummies is for everyone. In these pages, we serve as your guides in the art of reading and interpreting poetry. We hope you will discover poets you haven't heard of or read before, revisit some old favorites, and pick up some pointers on poetry that will bring you a new understanding and enjoyment of the art.

Besides being a good introduction to the history of world poetry, *Poetry For Dummies* also offers a lot of practical information, too. Not sure of a literary term? Check our glossary in Appendix A. Looking for poetry on the Web? Our resource guide in Appendix C will point you in the direction of a few good places to start. Have a poem you've written that you want to get out into the world? Read Chapter 13 for information and tips on how to get out and read your poem to an audience or send it out for publication.

You can use this book's many writing exercises to brush up on your writing skills, add structure to your writing life, or help you break out of writer's block. Have a broken heart and want to write a traditional poem to bring your loved one back? Check out the section on writing sonnets and traditional forms (we offer no guarantees, of course).

When you start thinking about poetry, you will notice it's all around you. We give you tips on where to find poetry, where to find poetry readings and other events, and which journals to pick up if you want to read the latest poetry being published.

These are just a few of the ways you can make use of this book. The rest, as they say, is up to you.

How This Book Is Organized

This book does four things at once:

- ✔ It introduces you to reading and interpreting poetry.
- ✔ It introduces you to writing poetry.
- ✔ It tells you about poetry history, movements, and techniques.
- ✔ It guides you to good ways to find out more about poetry (organizations and magazines devoted to poets and poetry, as well as Web sites and places to attend readings).

This book *does* have a logical organization, and we invite you to use it. But by all means, be your own guide. Go straight to the parts you find most interesting. Flip through. See what looks good. If a poem beckons you, stop and read it. We'll wait.

A good beginning is Chapter 1, our all-purpose introduction to the art. We lay a special emphasis on reading aloud, a skill many people haven't exercised since they left grade school. We help you get your reading muscles in shape and ready for any poem that comes your way. And we close with a writing exercise for readers who can't wait to start writing their own poetry.

The following sections explain how the book is broken down and lets you know what you can expect to find in each part.

Part 1: Reading and Understanding Poetry

What *is* poetry, anyway? Where does it come from and why is it important? In this part, we define poetry and discuss where it stands at the beginning of the 21st century. Here you also find a short course on the essential skill of reading aloud (the best way to get to know poetry).

Reading poems is fine. But thinking about what they mean and how the poets *got* to that meaning is even better. So in Chapters 2 and 3, we look at how poems work. We survey the elements that make up poetry, beginning with the ways poets work with language, including the many varieties of metaphor, symbol, speaker, and situation. Then we move to subject and tone.

Chapter 4 talks about interpretation — the best way to get the most out of the poems you read. Becoming a good interpreter of poetry means paying attention to what *you* think, becoming more alert and sensitive, and being very aware of detail and implication.

Some of the greatest poetry in history comes to us from poets of long ago. But we are readers of now, and most of us need a few special skills to get the most out of poems from the past. Those skills are the heart and soul of Chapter 5.

Part 11: In the Beginning Was a Poem

In this part, you get to flip through the family photos, so to speak. We figured you would want a little background on the whole endeavor, so we load everybody on a bus and roar, tilting from side to side, through a quick tour of the 5,000 years of poetry. It has been an *eventful* 5,000 years, we can tell you that. And of all these poetic centuries, the 20th may have been most poetic of all.

We look forward to an even more poetic 21st! Our tour of poetic history is global because poetry is global — so you'll read about the poetry of India, China, Japan, Africa, and South America and discover their greats and golden ages alongside Europe and the United States.

Part III: Writing Poetry: A Guide for Aspiring Poets

Everyone is waiting for the next Shakespeare or Emily Dickinson to appear on the literary horizon. Here we show you a sampling of techniques and good approaches, as well as suggest some standards for you to shoot for. Want to submit your poems for publication? Enter the performance scene? You'll find some advice on these endeavors, too. The writing exercises collected here should bring out the poet in just about anyone. Warning: Writing poetry can be habit-forming.

Part IV: The Part of Tens

This book wouldn't be a *For Dummies* book without a Part of Tens. The Part of Tens in this book gives you ten myths about poetry (true and untrue), ten great poems to memorize for life, and ten love poems for you to read and enjoy. This part is the perfect place to turn if you have just a few minutes here or there and want to soak up as much information and poetry as you can. Go to The Part of Tens for your regular quick poetry fix.

Part V: Appendixes

This part is where you can find a glossary of literary and poetic terms and a timeline for the whole history of world poetry.

You'll also find resources for ways to get even more poetry. We list Web sites that specialize in poetry, locations of poetry centers, and places around the country that offer poetry events of all kinds. We tell you about the big poetry festivals throughout the country (Cowboy poetry? You bet!), and steer you toward some of the major magazines and journals that publish poetry. We also include a brief list of books helpful to readers of poetry and especially aspiring poets.

And then we blow kisses, saddle the mules, cue the organist, and sprint madly around until we melt into the sunset.

Icons Used in This Book

Throughout the book, you will encounter *icons,* which are the pictures in the margin that alert you to a special feature, or a piece of information, advice, or instruction. They're meant to help direct you to the indispensable moments, the absolute honey of the book. We use the following seven icons:

This is one icon you see a lot of throughout this book. Whenever we quote a passage, we mean for you to read it aloud. Poetry is meant to be read aloud for the best and fullest effect. This is your opportunity to give your voice to poetry. And if you seize that opportunity, you'll get the most out of *Poetry For Dummies.*

When you see this icon, you can count on finding an essential bit of advice that will make you a better reader, interpreter, or writer of poetry.

This icon points to historical or technical information of great value. So open up your brain and get ready to get technical. But if you're just looking for the basics on a subject, you can skip over the information flagged by this icon and come back later when you have more time.

Some thoughts are simply essential, such as the sentence, "Poetry is meant to be read aloud." Because such sentences appear more than once, we tag them with this icon so you remember to put them in your brain for keeps.

When you see this icon, you know to avoid the idea or habit it highlights. Or at least handle the topic gently.

This icon alerts you to lists of sources for some of the greatest poetry in history. You don't have to read all these books — but if you're wondering, "What's so great about Homer?" or "Who is this Emily Dickinson anyway?" an excellent way to find the answer is to sit down and read a few lines. So fill your bookbag and fill your mind!

The gal in this icon is Calliope, one of the Greek muses of poetry and, fittingly enough, the head of *all* the muses. She pops up whenever we encounter something truly inspiring, when you can really see the insight and invigoration of poetry happening right before your eyes.

Where to Go from Here

Poetry is for everyone. Poets write for the world, which, last time we checked, is where you live. And knowing about poetry can make your world better.

The idea is not to know it *all;* nobody ever could. The idea is to get *started,* to discover a little about how poetry works and how writing poetry works, and then blaze your own path. Think of this book as your first step in forging your very own personal taste in poetry, or in exploring your own powers as a poet. Talk about the thrill of beginnings! So what are you waiting for? Turn the page and dive right in.

Part I

Reading and Understanding Poetry

The 5th Wave   By Rich Tennant

In this part . . .

*I*n the chapters in this part, we dissect poetry into its basic elements. Here you find out why attention to each element is essential if you want to fully appreciate and understand poetry. We take you on a tour through subject and tone and point out the essential tools of the story-teller's art. We give a short course on sound in poetry and how poets orchestrate the music of words. And then we get to the good stuff: the art of interpretation itself. You'll discover how to speculate about a poem's meaning and recognize the implications of that meaning. Finally, we give you a short course on reading poems of the past — and understanding language that may not be second nature to you. In these chapters, you get a sense of the poem's impact on you as a reader.

Chapter 1

Poetry 101

· ·

· ·

The word *poetry* sends chills down the spines of many otherwise strong and balanced people. Perhaps you have flashbacks of being called on in class to read a poem aloud — and not having a clue what the words you were reading meant. Or maybe you remember being required to write a poem, and even today you're still not exactly sure what sets a poem apart from any other bunch of words thrown onto a blank page. Or perhaps you're just curious about poetry, but you're intimidated by the huge number of poetry books in your local bookstore or library.

No matter what your past experiences with poetry have been, you can set your worries aside. To read and write poetry, you don't have to join some secret club, where you have to wear a moose hat with antlers, stand on one leg, and recite secret ritual formulas in Greek . . . although, goodness knows, that would be quite interesting, and we'd be happy to watch if you volunteer.

Poetry is something human beings have always done and always loved. If you want to be one of them, come along. In this chapter, we give you a working definition of what poetry is and fill you in on why people have been writing it for thousands of years. We also let you know about some great places to turn if you want to read more poetry — and while we're on the topic, we give you a quick guide for actually reading a poem. Finally, if all this talk about poetry has inspired you (and we sure hope it has!), you can dive right in and write a poem of your own.

What Is Poetry and Why Do People Write It?

Poetry is the practice of creating artworks using language. Sculptors use marble, steel, cardboard, goose liver pâté, whatever material they choose. Musicians use sound. Painters use paint. Furniture-makers use woods and fabrics. And poets use language.

So what makes poetry different from other uses of language? Here are five things almost all poetry has more of than other language (the non-poetic kind):

✔ **Attentiveness:** Poets are extremely careful with the way they use language. They pay attention to everything from spelling to the way the words sound and what they mean. They think about punctuation and the spaces between and around words. Most people simply don't pay as much attention to these elements of language — but paying attention is the poet's job. And poets want *you* to pay that sort of attention, too — to the language you read and use *and* to your life.

✔ **Concentration:** Poetry has more meaning, music, and emotion per word, per syllable, and per letter than other kinds of writing. Poets find ways to open up explosions of understanding and emotion — while using carefully selected combinations of words. More meaning, fewer words — a nice trick. Whenever you find language especially charged with passion, music, or significance, you're probably looking at poetry or something close to it.

✔ **Experiment:** Poets try to use language in as many new, surprising, and challenging ways as they can come up with. They use language in special ways to startle, awaken, or challenge you.

✔ **Originality:** Poetry says or does something new; it makes something new happen in the reader's mind. This new thing can be a totally original observation about life, or it can be a neat way of saying something many other people have already thought or said. Whatever it is, you can tell it's original because it doesn't try to echo someone else's way of saying it — it finds its own way.

✔ **Form:** Most people write from one margin across to the next. Sometimes they indent to show that a new paragraph is starting. But poetry is different: It's very often about *form* — the very shape or structure a particular group of words takes. The word *form* also refer to the way a poem is written (its *mode*). You can write a poem in the form of a prayer, a letter, a laundry list. And all forms carry their own worlds of meaning. So poets think a lot about form.

Poetry isn't the only way of using language to make art, of course — for example, short stories and novels are works of art, too. But poetry usually has a greater degree of attentiveness, concentration, experiment, and form than you find in most other uses of language.

Poets are interested in exploring experience through the written word. That includes any experience you can have, as well as the world of your dreams and fantasies — the story of civilization; the taste of a peach; dancing with your father; imaginary worlds with imaginary inhabitants; sending your daughter off to college; leaving someone you love; a full moon transfiguring a winter sky; explaining the ways of God to humanity. The poet takes all these kinds of experiences, and the emotions and feelings they bring with them, and makes them into art through the way he uses language. And that — because you use language, too — gives you an instant link to poetry as well.

So why do people write poetry? The reasons are as numerous as the poems themselves. Some people want to

- ✔ Make nice with the gods, as in the Psalms or the *Bhagavad Gita*.
- ✔ Tell the stories of their communities, as Homer did in *The Odyssey*.
- ✔ Record history, as Anna Akhmatova did in "Requiem, 1935–1940."
- ✔ Commemorate a moment of personal history, as Ben Jonson did in "On My First Son."
- ✔ Take an achingly clear snapshot of experience, as H.D. did in "Heat."
- ✔ Embody their feelings, as Theodore Roethke did in "I Knew a Woman."
- ✔ Create a state of feeling, as Stéphane Mallarmé did in "Afternoon of a Faun."
- ✔ Explore language, as John Ashbery did in "Corky's Car Keys."

If you haven't read some or all of these poems, consider this list a good place to start.

No formula can cover all these different motivations. But most poets are trying to do one or both of the following:

- ✔ Create an intense emotional experience.
- ✔ Draw attention to something that is true.

We delve a little deeper into both of these goals of poets in the following sections.

Creating an intense emotional experience

Poetry constantly presents its readers with bursts of concentrated emotion — the poem that makes your beloved fall in love with you; the poem that comforts a suffering friend; the poem that celebrates a day of joy or triumph; the poem that praises God, mourns the dead, or exults in the universe. The more attention you pay to poetry, the more you'll savor these surges of passion and understanding.

In his poem "On My First Son," Ben Jonson, a Renaissance poet who lived at the same time as Shakespeare, writes a poem of farewell to his son, who has died at just 7 years old. The poem contains a few examples of Renaissance English (words that you may trip over initially), but only a few. Read the poem silently, and then read it aloud:

> Farewell, thou child of my right hand, and joy;
> My sin was too much hope of thee, loved boy:
> Seven years thou wert leant to me, and I thee pay,
> Exacted by thy fate, on the just day.
> O could I lose all father now! For why
> Will man lament the state he should envy,
> To have so soon 'scaped world's and flesh's rage,
> And if no other misery, yet age?
> Rest in soft peace, and asked, say, "Here doth lie
> Ben Jonson his best piece of poetry."
> For whose sake henceforth all his vows be such
> As what he loved may never like too much.

Here's a brief list of the phrases you may find unfamiliar in this poem:

- **child of my right hand:** The name *Benjamin* means "son of the right hand" in Hebrew, so this phrase means both "son of whom I'm especially proud" and is a pun on the name of both the father and the son.

- **the just day:** The day on which payment is due on a debt. The boy was "lent" to the speaker for seven years, and then "fate" (the lender) "exacted" (required) repayment on the due date.

- **O could I lose all father now!:** This passage could mean, "Now I am no longer a father," or "After such pain, I never want to be a father again."

- **'scaped:** This is just the poetic way of saying "escaped."

- **And if no other misery, yet age:** Here the poet is saying that even if his son escaped no other misery, at least he escaped getting old.

- **Ben Jonson his:** This is a fancy way of saying "Ben Jonson's."

Across five centuries, this poem delivers the speaker's suffering to you. But notice that Jonson never refers directly to his own pain. The line "O could I lose all father now!" is the closest the poem comes to that. Instead, you can guess at the great suffering from the tender restraint in this poem: "Rest in soft peace" is one of the tenderest leave-takings in all poetry; the punning on "best piece of poetry" (the son is the best "poem" Ben Jonson ever created) and the name Benjamin (which in Hebrew means "son of my right hand") suggest, without dwelling on them, the father's fondness for his son; and the vow at the end — to love things in this world, but not to become attached to them — suggests the suffering of a father at the death of his child without speaking any of those words directly.

"On My First Son" is a quiet, dignified poem, but the concentrated emotion in it is unmistakable. Ben Jonson gives you a demonstration of what poets everywhere try to do: Lead you into an intense encounter with feeling.

Drawing attention to something that is true

Most people are so busy living their lives that they don't pay attention to what's around them. Poets are constantly beckoning their readers to stay alert to the things of this world — both the familiar things that become invisible to you through habit, and the miraculous things right in front of you that you're too busy to notice. Poetry can expand your awareness and keep you alert to truth and beauty — and to what they can both teach you.

The Japanese master-poet Issa captures an exquisite moment in this passage:

> morning:
> one deer licks
> snow from the other's
> coat

This poem presents a delicate, exquisite image of animals seemingly taking care of each other in the wild — and it also suggests that it is a cold morning, and the deer have spent the night out in the snow. The poet doesn't have to comment on this image; he simply lets its truth show and lets you marvel at it. You may find the words meaningful, or you may find no meaning beyond their beauty — but surely that was worth the poet writing it down.

In this poem, Li Po, a Chinese poet from the T'ang Dynasty, mistakes one thing for another and gives you a vivid experience that ends on a meditative note:

> Moonlight pools at the head of my bed —
> I mistook it for frost blanketing the earth!
> I look up: see the moon on the mountain;
> I look down: think long thoughts of home.

You have to change the image in your mind from *moonlight* to *frost* and back again. Then the speaker, after he realizes it *is* moonlight, follows it up to the source of the light itself. That would be neat enough — a call to be sensitive, just like Basho's poem earlier in this section — but then the speaker's eyes stray from the moon, and the speaker becomes nostalgic for home. Why does this moment make the speaker miss home? Good question. Maybe something about seeing the moon on the mountain reminded him of home. Sometimes that happens: An image out of nature unlocks old memories, unexpected feelings.

Poetry keeps telling you to pay attention. It's a way to expand your awareness, your understanding, your store of experience.

Bringing Poetry into Your Life

Although most people don't realize it, poetry is all around them. You may hang poems on your refrigerator or on the walls of your bedroom or office, just so you have your favorite inspiration nearby. A friend of ours has George Herbert's "Love (III)" on a scroll over her desk at work. City subways in London, Chicago, and New York run poems in the subway cars all the time. And although graffiti is a form of vandalism, it's also often a form of poetry.

You can also find poetry in the more traditional places, like books and magazines. In fact, poetry is easy to find — it certainly isn't hiding. And you don't actually need to go anywhere to get it. If you have access to the Internet, you can connect to poetry from all over the world, sampling the best poetry of all time for the cost of logging on.

In the following sections, we let you know where you can turn if you want to inject some more poetry into your life.

Checking out libraries

Your local library is a great source for poetry — and best of all, it's free! When you visit your library, ask the librarian where the poetry section is, go there, and pull a book out at random. We did, and we came upon these lines:

> Summer swallows spring and goes into September
> Like long division it is always there
> Autumn, fall we say, fruit releases itself
> You are new enough so the old catches up
> Cross this bridge come to that one
> You grow up and ancient history snaps back
> Rubber band and rake handle

The poem turns out to be "Vermont Apollinaire" by William Corbett. Not bad for a stab in the dark at a random shelf in a library.

When you read this poem, the first line tells you that it's about autumn: Corbett writes about summer "go[ing] into" September, an echo of long division (in the second line), in which things "go into" other things. The poem explores how the past comes back to you, snapping back like a rubber band or a rake handle when you step on the upturned part of the rake. But Corbett doesn't use the word *like;* instead, he gives you two things that snap back — a rubber band and a rake handle — and lets you make the connection. The way things "snap back" stings a little — as autumn does when it makes you think of summer days gone by.

Notice that Corbett is comparing the past with the rubber band and rake handle in an implicit, unspoken comparison — called a *metaphor.* Had Corbett said "ancient history snaps back *like* a rubber band or a rake handle," he would have been using a *simile.* Metaphors and similes are among the most important techniques in a poet's repertoire.

Try pulling a poetry book off a library shelf yourself, and if you like what you read, check out the book and sample more.

Browsing through bookstores

If you'd rather own your own books of poetry than check them out from the library, poetry won't bust your pocketbook. Go to your local bookstore and peruse the following list of inexpensive books of poetry. Select two or three and see what you think.

- ✔ *The Inferno of Dante: A New Verse Translation,* by Dante Alighieri. Translated by Robert Pinsky. (New York: Noonday Press, 1996.) $9.00

- ✔ *Selected Poems,* by Emily Dickinson. (New York: Dover, 1991.) $1.00

- ✔ *Eight American Poets: An Anthology,* edited by Joel Conarroe. (New York: Vintage Books, 1997.) $14.00

- ✔ *Twenty Love Poems: And a Song of Despair,* by Pablo Neruda. Translated by W.S. Merwin. (New York: Penguin, 1993.) $9.95

- ✔ *Favorite Poems,* by William Wordsworth. (New York: Dover, 1992.) $1.00

Note: The prices we provide here are the *list prices* of the books (the prices the publishers recommend selling them for). But you can usually find them for even less at major bookstores, used bookstores, and online booksellers.

Anthologies a go-go

A great way to begin a search for new poetry is to check your local library or bookstore for *anthologies* (collections of poems from different poets). An anthology (the word *anthology* means "collection of flowers" in Greek) is like a literary smorgasbord of writing: You can sample a variety of poets within the pages of one book. When you get a taste for certain poets, you can satisfy your hunger by finding books containing only poems written by them.

Thousands of poetry anthologies are in existence — many with specific themes — and many display the best a particular culture or group has to offer. A *very* brief list of titles suggests the range of what you can find: *1000 Years of Irish Poetry; A Book of Luminous Things: An International Anthology; A Book of Women*

Poets from Antiquity To Now, Americans' Favorite Poems; Canadian Poetry: From the Beginning through The First World War; Unleashed: Poems by Writers' Dogs; Listen Up! Spoken Word Poetry; Moving Borders: Three Decades of Innovative Writing by Women; What Book? Buddha Poems from Beat to Hip Hop; Spirit & Flame: An Anthology of Contemporary African American Poetry; The New Young American Poets; Cowboy Poetry Matters; Word of Mouth: An Anthology of Gay American Poetry; Literatures of Asia, Africa, and Latin America; In the Grip of Strange Thoughts: Russian Poetry in a New Era; The Defiant Muse: Hebrew Feminist Poems from Antiquity to the Present; and *100 Great Poems by Women.* Get out and start your personal flower collection today!

Attending readings

More likely than not, you can find a number of places near you where poetry readings, like the one shown in Figure 1-1, happen every week. Do you live near a college or university? A coffee shop? Does your local library have a reading series? Are there any reading groups in town? (If not, you could always start one.)

If you're not sure whether poetry readings are happening in your neighborhood, check your local newspaper. Most papers have entertainment sections that list things to do. Also, if your city has a Web site, check to see what's available. Call area bookstores to see if poetry readings take place there as well. Check bulletin boards at your local college or café.

Seeking cyber-poetry

You don't even need to leave your house to get your hands on some poetry. Thousands of Web sites feature poetry, and they're yours for the taking. Just type a poet's name into your favorite search engine, and you're sure to come up with numerous sites worth your perusal. We typed *Emily Dickinson* into a search engine and found 22,599 Web pages! Dickinson is one of many poets, including William Shakespeare, Dante, Homer, and Walt Whitman, whose work has a big presence on the Web.

So get out or stay in, and find some of this good stuff. Poetry takes many forms, is almost always a pleasant surprise, and can improve your world. Not bad for a few words in a small space.

Figure 1-1: A 1995 poetry reading at City Lights Bookstore in San Francisco, California, featuring poet Lawrence Ferlinghetti.

© Christopher Felver

Reading Poetry Aloud

If you're like most people, you haven't read aloud since the last time you read to a child or since you were in school. For many people, reading aloud just doesn't feel good — maybe it conjures up all those bad memories of being called on by a teacher to read in front of the rest of the class. But it's time to lose those fears. Because, after all, poetry is *meant* to be read aloud. That's right, aloud — as though you were delivering the poem to an attentive audience.

Why you should read poems aloud

Here are the three most important reasons you should read poetry aloud:

> ✔ **Poets design their poems to be read aloud.** The earliest poetry was *oral*. People chanted it, sang it, recited it — and they still do. From its earliest forms to the poems being written today, poetry has kept its

close alliance with speaking and singing. The *music* of poetry — that is, its sounds and rhythms — is not just for the eye and the mind, it's meant to be given voice. In fact, as they write, most poets imagine someone reading their poems aloud. Poetry is supposed to be a living thing, and poets write accordingly, with an audience in mind.

✔ **You'll experience the whole poem if you read it aloud.** Poems read aloud are different animals from poems read silently. A big part of poetry is sound and rhythm — and the best way to get the full impact of these important elements is to put them into action by pronouncing them with your own throat, lungs, teeth, lips, and tongue. Sound and rhythm don't exist just for their own sakes, either; they exist to give you pleasure (because humans naturally like music and rhythm in our poetry) and lead you to the poem's meanings. Commas, spaces between words, line endings, and other pauses may hint at melancholy, hesitancy, or passion. Punctuation has its traditional functions (exclamations! questions? wistfulness . . .), and it often also is used in unexpected ways — or not used at all. You may miss all these signals if you don't read aloud.

✔ **You'll understand and remember more if you read aloud.** Memory and understanding are everything. If you remember something *and* understand it, it takes up long-term residence inside your brain. And then you can use that knowledge as a building block to discover more and more about the world of poetry.

Don't believe us? Read these four sad lines (by the Greek poet Sappho) silently to yourself:

> The moon has set
> and the Pleiades. Middle of the
> night! Time passes,
> and I lie here alone.

Reading silently is a great way to make a poem's acquaintance. Here, you can instantly absorb the situation: The speaker is lying alone at night. The speaker can feel time pass, and she isn't thrilled, apparently, at being up this late.

Now read the lines aloud. Pause a little at the end of each line. Notice how each pause carries a little information, a little jolt of feeling with it.

> The moon has set
> and the Pleiades

If you look up the word *Pleiades* in your handy reference book, you'll find out that the Pleiades are that familiar cluster of stars at the top of the sky. So maybe the word *Pleiades* is just a time-reference: The moon goes down, and then this cluster of stars follows. That could take quite a while (depending on how the constellations are arranged that night) — it gives you the feeling that a good amount of time has passed.

Now you come to another pause:

> Middle of the [pause]
> night!

You can almost *hear* the speaker groan. Pausing helps emphasize how weary and restless the speaker is. You may even begin to wonder *why* the speaker is staying awake. Is she waiting for someone? You may spot an answer in the last two lines:

> Time passes, [pause]
> And I lie here alone.

This insomniac speaker is alone. You get a feeling (without being told) that she wishes she weren't. Where do you get it from? Her wakefulness, maybe, or her awareness of time passing and her solitude.

One more word about the Pleiades: In mythology, the Pleiades were the seven daughters of the Greek gods Atlas and Pleione. And the hunter Orion — also a constellation in the sky — was thought to be eternally chasing them (without ever catching them). So each time you looked at the Pleiades — at least, if you were Sappho — you may have thought of the chase of love, which would *not* help your insomnia or lonesomeness at all.

Keep your reference books handy when you're reading poetry!

Chances are, you understand Sappho's poem better for having read it aloud. And that's the way she would have wanted it.

The basic steps to good reading

We hope we convinced you in the previous section of the importance of reading poetry aloud. Now you need to know the best ways to do it. Check out the next sections — you don't have to take the suggestions below one by one. You can do them in different orders, and some you may do simultaneously. Think of all these steps below as components of good poetry reading.

Have the right tools handy

A firefighter who charged into flames without a hose wouldn't be very well prepared. And you wouldn't start painting your house, or shampooing your dog, or beginning any other activity without the right tools nearby, would you? Reading poetry isn't any different.

When it comes to poetry, the right tools include the following:

✔ **A dictionary.** A dictionary is a great help when you come across words you don't know. Don't be ashamed — they happen, such words. Looking up words you don't know (see the discussion of the word *Pleiades* in a previous section) helps you understand a bit more of the poem — and of the poet who wrote it. One of the many Webster's dictionaries (or similar ones) are excellent places to start.

✔ **A book about the history and forms of poetry.** Such a book can help answer questions that arise as you read — questions about kinds of poems, traditions, histories of poetry in different languages, and so on. We recommend *The New Princeton Encyclopedia of Poetry and Poetics,* edited by Alex Preminger and T.V.F. Brogan, as a great reference in this category.

✔ *Poetry For Dummies.* This, of course, is a fine book providing much good information on poetry. And we're not at all biased. Nope. Not one bit.

Read silently first

When you first look at a painting, you probably step back to take in the whole thing before you move closer to see the details. Follow the same approach with poetry:

1. **Scope out the poem.**

   Skim over it, noting its title, length, and overall structure. Do you see one big flow of words on the page? Or is the poem broken into groups of lines (often called *stanzas*)? Does the poem rhyme? Who wrote the poem? If the information is available, find out when the poet lived. This kind of background information could come in handy in understanding the poem's meaning.

2. **Read the poem silently, to yourself.**

   Enjoy yourself. Stay relaxed and open. No one's timing you. In fact, the slower you read, the better — because you can absorb more.

3. **Take notes as you read silently, if you want.**

   Taking notes isn't required, but it's a good idea — especially if the poem includes unfamiliar words, *allusions* (references to persons, places, things, or history, for example), or concepts you don't understand. If you own your book, you may even want to make notes in the margins, jotting down the meaning of this or that line, for example. The notes some people make in their poetry books become a sort of journal for them, a history of their reading and their thought processes over time.

Note surprises and unfamiliar words

As you read, you will most likely run across some words you're not familiar with or words whose impact (in the context of the poem) you aren't ready for. Even in the shortest poems, you get them.

Take a look at this Native American "Song of Naquali":

> I wonder what
>   my future life
> will do to me.

The first two lines are "normal" enough — but then "will do to me" is unexpected. You may expect the speaker to say, "I wonder what / my future life / will be like," or, "I wonder what / my future life / has in store." But instead, the speaker is wondering what the future will "do to me," as if the future was a force that could make things happen. What will the future cause to happen to the speaker? Good question: The speaker sets up the future almost as a malevolent force, and there's not much you can do about what it brings your way. What's going to happen is going to happen, and much of it won't be that great. The poem is wry — in the sense of being ironic or grimly humorous — and it is also fatalistic, meaning the speaker doesn't think you can do much about fate, besides wonder what it will do to you.

You don't ever have to plow top to bottom, all the way through, when you read a poem. Stop, repeat, go back, dwell. If you really like certain lines, reread and enjoy them again. If the poem is in a book you own, underline the part you like or note it in the margin. And keep your dictionary by your side so that you can look up words you're not familiar with.

Find an engaged, conversational tone

Every poem has a *speaker* — someone you imagine saying the poem. Sometimes the speaker is a disembodied voice, just saying the words. At other times, the speaker is a character you get to know in the poem. When you read aloud, you need to use the right tone of voice for that speaker. Here are some suggestions for the kind of tone you should shoot for:

- ✔ **Engaged.** Your tone of voice should show that you're really interested in what you have to say. You're leaning forward to tell someone else. If you're happy, you're *really* happy. If not, you're *really* not. Give the words a slight push; project.

- ✔ **Conversational.** Don't shout and don't whisper. True, you are performing the poem, but you can still remain close to the normal way in which you speak to people in everyday conversation. You're just reading as though you're engaged in *interesting* conversation, conversation with passion behind it.

Many poets and poetry fans like to work on their reading aloud. If you want to practice your reading, record yourself (this exercise can be humbling at first, but it's always instructive). Listen to how you read. Is your reading clear? Is it attentive to the poem? Are you pausing in the right places? Are you being expressive? Are you bringing your idea of the poem across? Attend readings and observe how other people read their poetry, too.

Don't rush

Read at a moderate, deliberate pace. Enjoy the words and phrases you're saying. *Enunciate* (pronounce the words clearly). You may come across very long sentences as you read. Just take your time, and you'll have an easier time understanding what the sentences are saying.

Use the following poem as a reading-aloud challenge. The passage is from the play *Antony and Cleopatra,* by William Shakespeare (see Figure 1-2 for a glimpse of what he looked like). Someone is describing Cleopatra, Queen of Egypt, as she sails down the Nile in her barge. *Remember:* This passage will be gobbledygook unless you relax and let it go at its own pace. When you read over the passage, you'll find a lot of commas and periods, which means you're meant to pause quite a bit. Consider what's being described: a queen in her private barge (a stately subject). So this is an excellent opportunity to observe that great piece of wisdom, "No need to rush."

The barge she sat in, like a burnish'd throne,
Burnt on the water. The poop was beaten gold,
Purple the sails, and so perfumed that
The winds were love-sick with them; the oars were silver,
Which to the tune of flutes kept stroke, and made
The water which they beat to follow faster,
As amorous of their strokes. For her own person,
It beggar'd all description: she did lie
In her pavilion — cloth of gold, of tissue —
O'er-picturing that Venus where we see
The fancy outwork nature.

Shakespeare lived in the 17th century, so the English he used is a bit different from the English you use today. Here are some definitions of words or phrases that may be unfamiliar to you:

- **poop:** Short for *poop deck,* which is a partial deck over the last half of a boat's main deck.

- **As amorous of their strokes:** This phrase means "as though the water were longing for the oars' strokes."

- **her own person:** Her physical self.

- ✔ **beggar'd all description:** The literal meaning is "made description go begging," a creative way of saying, "You really can't describe what she was like."

- ✔ **pavilion:** A big tent, underneath which Cleopatra is reclining.

- ✔ **O'er-picturing that Venus:** This phrase means "outdoing that famous picture of Venus." The speaker is imagining a very famous portrait of Venus, the Roman goddess of love and beauty, and then says Cleopatra was even more beautiful than *that*.

- ✔ **fancy:** Imagination.

You may not feel you "get" the entire passage from *Antony and Cleopatra* at first reading. Not to worry. The idea is to read poetry again and again, feeling your way in. Try breaking the passage down into sentences. This passage has three sentences, the first of which is

> The barge she sat in, like a burnish'd throne,
> Burnt on the water.

The word *Burnt* is a surprise: You may initially ask, "Why is Cleopatra's boat burning?" But the speaker doesn't mean it literally. The boat is so polished, so bright, that it's brilliant, fiery, sunlike. (You find out in the next lines that the poop deck is "beaten gold" and the oars silver.) So *Burnt* is a metaphor — without using *like* or *as*, the speaker is comparing a brilliant, golden boat to something aflame.

The word *Burnt* gives you a good opportunity for a pause, to register its full impact: "The barge she sat in, like a burnish'd throne, [pause] Burnt on the water." Do you hear the repeated *b* sounds in *barge, burnish'd*, and *Burnt*? That's called *alliteration* (the repetition of initial consonant sounds), and it's a hint to you, as the reader, to emphasize those three words a little more than the rest.

You can't rush the stately pace of Shakespeare's verse. Too much is going on; too many gorgeous images are presented to you. Yet the speaker here is enthusiastic, and that enthusiasm grows as the speaker warms to the description of the barge — which leads to a description of its beautiful passenger. Enjoy the imaginative images throughout this passage: The wind is "lovesick" for the sails, and the water is in love with the oars. The speaker is overwhelmed with the "burning" barge, the gold, the silver, and most of all with Cleopatra. As you get to know this passage, see whether you can read the passage with the same loving admiration that the speaker has for Cleopatra.

Figure 1-2:
William
Shake-
speare.

Pause for power

One of the reasons people read poetry over and over is to figure out how to read it aloud. The better you know a passage, the better you'll know what tone of voice to use as you read it, where to go quickly, and where to slow down.

One of the most powerful tools in any reader's arsenal is the pause. Where *do* pauses come? Wherever you see a powerful moment. Such moments include

- ✔ **Any punctuated pause, including dashes, commas, semicolons, or periods.** Poets use punctuation as carefully and meaningfully as they use any other part of language; it's always powerful.

- ✔ **Any surprise.** If you find yourself surprised by a word, phrase, or image when you read, dwell on it just a little bit, long enough to let that word, phrase, or image register in the mind of your audience (real or imagined).

- ✔ **The end of one stanza (or group of lines) and the beginning of another.**

- ✔ **The ends of lines.**

Pay attention to line endings

When you come to a line ending, pause slightly unless doing so is unnatural. Refer to the Sappho poem in the section called "Why you should read poems aloud," earlier in this chapter: "Middle of the [pause] night." Just a little pause bestows such power on the word *night*.

Here's a passage from "In What Manner the Body Is United with the Soule," by Jorie Graham. The speaker suddenly realizes how to listen to music, and the epiphany is magic. This poem really *needs* you to pause slightly at the ends of lines, to lend the images and feelings their full drama.

> Finally I heard
>   into music,
> that is, heard past
>   the surface tension
> which is pleasure, which holds
>   the self
>
> afloat, miraculous
>   waterstrider
> with no other home.
>   Not that I heard
> very deep,
>   but heard there was a depth

As you read aloud, you'll find yourself pausing at mid-sentence commas as well as at line endings: "which is pleasure [pause] which holds [pause] the self [pause] afloat." Isn't that gorgeous?

Keep in mind that there aren't any hard rules about exactly how long to pause, or whether to pause longer at commas or at line endings. Experiment. See what seems to fit. You can even decide not to pause if you feel the lines run strongly together — as some readers do with the words "heard past / the surface tension." But if there is more white space (where no words exist, as between "the self" and "afloat"), pause longer. Treat white space as time, and observe that time with silence. More space, more pause.

You'll find, as you reread and reread, that some words call for slightly more emphasis. For example, try emphasizing the words *into, surface, pleasure, waterstrider* (especially the *water* part of the word), and the word *was* in the last line. Those are just suggestions; you may choose to accent other words. Again, experiment. Although emphasizing the word *was* may seem trivial, it can actually lead you to a distinction the speaker finds important: She isn't claiming she was very sensitive, but she was learning there were depths to music she never dreamed of before.

A *waterstrider* is one of those long-legged bugs that walks on water (it actually walks on the surface tension of the water). What does the word *waterstrider* refer to in this poem? Our guess is the *self* (from the last line of the previous stanza). The self is just striding along, held aloft by pleasure.

This passage has a striding, loping rhythm. The many opportunities for subtle pauses in these lines set up a rhythm that allows room for the quiet depth of this passage. The poet is telling you that the self, that old waterstrider, has "no other home" than pleasure. What an interesting idea — your self is most at home when you are experiencing things that give you pleasure. Could be. And you may not have seen that meaning so clearly had you not paused at the ends of the lines.

Treat white space as time

Just as you pause a little at the ends of lines and pause more between stanzas and groups of lines, pause where you see *white space* (where no words exist). If you see a little break before another word, pause a little. If you see a lot of white space, pause more. (It's no accident that poems look the way they do on paper, with ragged edges, margin indents, single words appearing smack-dab in the middle of a line — the poet crafts the pauses as carefully as the words.)

"Silent Poem," by Robert Francis, is almost impossible to read silently. But if you read it aloud, with the right pauses, it turns into a striking, descriptive piece, with a sense of time passing.

backroad   leafmold   stonewall   chipmunk
underbrush   grapevine   woodchuck   shadblow

woodsmoke   cowbarn   honeysuckle   woodpile
sawhorse   bucksaw   outhouse   wellsweep

backdoor   flagstone   bulkhead   buttermilk
candlestick   ragrug   firedog   brownbread

hilltop   outcrop   cowbell   buttercup
whetstone   thunderstorm   pitchfork   steeplebush

gristmill   millstone   cornmeal   waterwheel
watercress   buckwheat   firefly   jewelweed

gravestone   groundpine   windbreak   bedrock
weathercock   snowfall   starlight   cockcrow

The short pauses between the words help you — perhaps even gently *force* you — to visualize each hard, concrete thing as you come to it, until, as the reader, you are in the midst of nature.

One poet known for his unusual punctuation (and use of lowercase letters) is e.e. cummings. Here is one of cummings's best poems, "in Just–." Try observing the white space as time. If words run together, runthemtogether.

in Just–
spring   when the world is mud-
luscious the little
lame balloonman

whistles   far   and wee

and eddieandbill come
running from marbles and
piracies and it's
spring

when the world is puddle-wonderful

the queer
old balloonman whistles
far   and   wee
and bettyandisbel come dancing

from hop-scotch and jump-rope and

it's
spring
and
    the

        goat-footed

balloonMan   whistles
far
and
wee

Read those last three words with great pauses between them. But earlier in the poem the kids (eddie and bill) should come running fast, as the words do.

Do it more than once

Ask anyone who likes poetry: When you find a poem you like, you keep reading it your whole life. As you change, it changes. And that changes you some more.

So whenever you read a poem aloud, read it aloud several times. Each time, you'll probably see something different. (Try using pauses differently each time, vary your tone of voice, add more or less drama to your reading.) You wouldn't date someone you like only once, would you? One poetry reading deserves another.

Writing Poetry

Millions of people have tried their hand at writing poetry. Often, people turn to writing verse at times of great emotion, insight, or need. And many people who always loved poetry think about writing it.

We could never cover everything about writing poetry in just one chapter (that's why we devote a whole part of this book to poetry writing). But here are some basic guidelines for you to consider right now, if you just can't wait to get your feet wet.

Becoming a poet

Writing poetry involves not just scribbling in a notebook, but also undertaking a way of life, one in which you value being creative and sensitive. To write good poetry, work to do the following:

- ✔ **Discover as much as you can about the poetic craft.** Read lots of poetry. Meet other poets. Become part of a poetic community. Get a mentor who will guide you. Attend readings and workshops. Take writing classes.

- ✔ **Become as sensitive as you can, both to life and to language.** Figure out your personal sense of what is beautiful — both in life and in poetry.

- ✔ **Think *divergently* (that is, keep your mind open and nimble, and be willing to think in different ways and new directions).** You never know when, where, or how inspiration will come to you, but you can prepare the way for it.

- ✔ **Make time for yourself to write.** After all, if you don't write, you're not a writer.

- ✔ **Be disciplined.** Rewrite your poetry again and again. Don't settle for using clichés or other people's language. The idea is to find out what kind of poetry only *you* can write.

Keeping a poetic journal

Many poets keep a *journal,* a repository containing ideas, images, subjects for poems, drafts of poems, other people's poetry, *found objects* (things you pick up that inspire you or that could become the basis for poems, such as someone else's grocery list). You can keep a journal in anything that's portable and easily accessible, such as a notebook, on a laptop, or on a microrecorder.

Many poets commit to writing in their journals each day. Their journals are, in a way, the "office" where the work of poetry takes place. Keeping a daily journal is a good idea, so we heartily recommend you go out and get a journal for your own use.

So what do you put in your journal when you have it? Some people keep a diary in their journals. Some write down their dreams, their meals, or scraps of personal or overheard conversation. Some poets have separate journals for individual topics (say, a journal exclusively dedicated to *Money and My Lack of It*.) But only you can decide the exact way in which you'll fill your journal.

Trying your hand at a writing exercise

Here's an exercise you can try in your journal. It's called the "Poetry Pentad." A *pentad* is a group of five things, and this exercise applies our five major poetic principles — attentiveness, concentration (of language, insight, and emotion), originality, experimentation, and form (all covered earlier in this chapter) — to seemingly mundane ideas. The pentad helps you do two things: generate material for poetry, and think about what makes poetry poetic.

Here's how it works:

1. **Write down a very mundane, straightforward prose statement about the outside world.**

   You could write about a cut on your hand, a kiss, awkward silences, a cash machine that won't give you any money, the death of a loved one, the lyrics of a song you can't stand but hear all the time, a painful memory you avoid, a car crash, what it feels like to sit at the bottom of a pool and look up, homeless people, Leonardo Da Vinci's *Mona Lisa,* the last movie you saw, a pet that makes you feel uncomfortable, or a sunset. Write something as simple as, "Sure is a nice sunset."

2. **Now pay closer *attention* to the thing you just wrote about.**

   Write down what you notice. Brainstorm. List as many aspects as you can — for example, "The color of the sunset is red in some places and a flat grayish-blue in others. The sky nearer to the sun is pretty, but farther away some of it is already dark and colorless."

3. ***Concentrate* on your subject and come up with a few new ways of presenting or describing the thing your *original* statement was about.**

   Try using some metaphors, images, turns of phrase. Don't write down anything you've ever heard or read before. Reject anything that seems familiar or secondhand. Using the sunset as your subject, you could write, "The sunset is like a bruise; it's like spilled stew on a rug; it's a molten core with a hard outer crust."

4. **Write at least two passages of poetry on this subject,** *experimenting* **with different** *forms.*

   Choose very different forms (say, two lines that rhyme with each other, or a passage of *free verse,* which doesn't have any rhyme). Use some of the material you generated under Step 3. For example, two rhyming lines about the sunset could be:

   > Blood-red, flat grey, the sunset colors fuse,
   > Spreading and growing dull green, like a bruise

   And free verse may be:

   > The sunset spilled over the rug of the sky   seeped into its fabric
   > A stain spread, a ravishing mess   will leave a
   >   mark   no way
   > I can cleanse it from my absorbent brain. It's running down
   >   the corners,
   > lava hardening, darkening, losing light. It's nighttime.

5. **Now rewrite one of the passages in as few words as you can.**

   Go for maximum meaning and emotion. For example:

   > Sunset spilled on the rug, stained
   >   the fabric, can't get it out
   > of my brain. It's lava, hardening
   > to darkness.

In this example, we started with a pretty common subject for poetry — a sunset — and then really observe one. We brainstormed a list of interesting observations. Then we generated some pretty divergent images (bruise, stew, lava) for what we saw the sunset doing. Then we tried a rhyming couplet and a free-verse passage. We rewrote the second one, working for greater concentration.

Did we come up with Shakespeare? We didn't have to — our aim was to find fresh ways of making our readers experience a sunset. "Sure is a pretty sunset" wasn't poetry, but in our final passage — with spills, stains, and hardening lava — we're much closer to something poetic. Notice how we don't explain what the "rug" is — it could be a metaphor for the sky, or it could be just a rug on which the day's fading light is falling. And "hardening / to darkness" conveys the last moments of a sunset in an unexpected way.

You can go through this process as often as you want for any one statement. If you get inspirations while working your way through, stop and work on them.

The whole idea is to get used to some of the distinguishing characteristics of the poetic craft — and to generate images, ideas, and forms that you can use later in building poems. If you don't come up with anything useful in one round, don't worry — you will *always* throw more away than you use. Keep trying, and watch what you come up with.

Chapter 2

Subject, Tone, and Narrative

• •

• •

*W*hen you read poetry, make sure you're open to what the poem is about and what the poet is communicating to you through his words. Your frame of mind is best when you're

✔ **Alert.** Pay close attention to the poem. Look for meaning — all the time, everywhere. Poems have meaning in every rhythm, every phrase.

✔ **Analytical.** Take poems apart and look at their different elements — this image, that sound, this suggestion.

✔ **Comfortable with ambiguities and difficulties.** Be open to actually *enjoying,* as the English poet John Keats once wrote, "being in uncertainties, mysteries, doubts," without trying to solve them immediately. Who ever "solved" *Hamlet?* Who can claim they "understand" the *Mahabharata?* Probably very few people. But many people just *love* to be in the midst of that poetry, to keep experiencing what's perplexing, what's beautiful, what's true.

✔ **Sensual.** Allow your mind to look for *pleasure.* Poetry pleases the mind (in the things it says and means) and the body (in its appeals to the senses and to experience). Pleasure can exist for its own sake, or it may have a crucial role in the poem's larger meaning.

The more you know about poetry, the more you find to like. A few simple tools — including a sharpened awareness of some of the basics, like subject, tone, and narrative — can enhance the way you read poetry. Paying attention to details makes life, and the person living it (that's you!), better and richer. Being aware of the details is simply good for you, in the same way poetry is good for you.

In this chapter, we take a look at three things you should always try to determine when you approach a new poem — subject, tone, and narrative — and show you how to identify them.

Understanding Subject and Tone

The *subject* of a poem is the idea or thing that the poem concerns or represents. The *tone* of a poem is the attitude you feel in it — the writer's attitude toward the subject or toward the audience. In a poem of praise, you feel approval. In a satire, you feel irony. In an antiwar poem, you may feel protest or moral indignation. Tone can be playful, humorous, regretful, anything — and it can change as the poem goes along.

Subject: A natural starting-point

Looking for the poem's subject is natural. Almost all poetry has messages to deliver — lots of them, profound and diverse as stars. But these messages are sometimes hidden, and you have to read attentively to make them out.

Notice that we specifically avoid saying, "The subject is what a poem's about" — because that implies that what a poem *says* is all there is to a poem. If that were so, why would people go to the trouble of writing poetry? Instead, people go to the trouble because poems sound a certain way, are built in certain shapes, and have certain beauties in sound and meaning — all of which accompanies the meaning and goes beyond it. (For more on those aspects of poetry, consult Chapters 3 and 4.)

Not all poems have a single subject. Some poems have many subjects, and some have subjects that aren't clear. Sometimes a poem's subject is simply *itself* — the words in it and their relationships to one another. The point is to be alert for the subject (or subjects) of any poem as you read.

Tone: It's got attitude

When you speak, your tone of voice suggests your attitude. In fact, it suggests two attitudes: one concerning the people you're addressing (your audience) and one concerning the thing you're talking about (your subject). That's what the term *tone* means when it's applied to poetry as well. *Tone* can also mean the general emotional weather of the poem.

Sometimes tone is fairly obvious. You can, for example, find poems that are absolutely furious. The Scots poet Hugh MacDiarmid did not care for *mercenary soldiers* (men who fight not because they believe in a cause, but because someone is paying them to fight). Here is MacDiarmid's very angry "Another Epitaph on an Army of Mercenaries":

It is a God-damned lie to say that these
Saved, or knew, anything worth any man's pride.
They were professional murderers and they took
Their blood money and impious risks and died.
In spite of all their kind some elements of worth
With difficulty persist here and there on earth.

Poetry is already so packed with emotion that seeing a poet swearing right at the start may be a shock, but MacDiarmid does exactly that. He makes the disturbing move of *insulting* the dead soldiers, calling them "professional murderers." Usually, people try not to speak ill of the dead, but evidently MacDiarmid thinks so little of the mercenaries that he feels justified in insulting them. In the last two lines, he implies that, with such evil men in existence, human goodness persists only "with difficulty." These clues lead you to MacDiarmid's tone and his attitude toward his subject: contempt.

If poems could spit

What was the *angriest* poem ever written? One contender for that dubious distinction may be "To Edward FitzGerald" by the Victorian poet Robert Browning. FitzGerald (like Browning, a fine poet) had died in 1883, and when some of his unpublished papers were published six years later, Browning read a passage in which FitzGerald spoke of the death of Browning's beloved wife, Elizabeth Barrett Browning (1806–1831), as "rather a relief to me."

In one of the strangest of poems, Browning wrote in white-hot anger to the dead poet about Browning's dead wife. "How to return you thanks would task my wits," Browning wrote (with heavy irony on *thanks*). He concluded with four lines that illustrate both the concept of tone and how you determine what a poem's tone is:

Kicking you seems the common lot of
    curs —
While more appropriate greeting lends
    you grace,
Surely to spit there glorifies your face —
    Spitting from lips once sanctified by hers.

So where is tone in this poem? Well, the poet first wants to kick FitzGerald — but that's "the common lot of curs," a punishment that's too ordinary. FitzGerald is so low he isn't *worth* kicking. He's not even a "cur" (which is a mongrel or a worthless dog). Browning can't even spit in FitzGerald's face, because Browning's lips once kissed his wife's lips and therefore were "sanctified," or made holy. FitzGerald doesn't deserve such a favor. Kicking is too ordinary; and spitting on him would make him holy. There's no way to thank such a man — by which Browning really means "punish"). That's *irony* — saying one thing ("thank") when you really mean another ("punish"). All these clues lead you to the tone of outrage in this poem. And if Browning is so outraged at FitzGerald, he must *really* have loved his wife, as the word "sanctified" implies.

Sometimes you can pick up tone from *clues* in what a person says or writes, as in this untitled poem from the classic Chinese poet Liu Tsung-yüan:

> From one thousand mountains the birds' flights are gone;
> From ten thousand byways the human track has vanished.
> In a single boat, an aged man, straw cloak and hat,
> Fishes alone; snow falls, cold in the river.

This poem conveys a tone of melancholy. How can you tell? The birds have abandoned the mountains, and the footprints of human beings (which are signs of human presence) have "vanished" from thousands of roads. The old fisherman you see at the end is all alone, and the word "single," used for his boat, conveys loneliness. The last image is wintry indeed, with snow falling all around him. Taken together, all these elements create an atmosphere of melancholy.

Often, poets simply allow their speakers or the stories they tell to *imply* their attitude. In this poem, "Résumé" by American poet Dorothy Parker, you can determine tone from the speaker:

> Razors pain you;
> Rivers are damp;
> Acids stain you;
> And drugs cause cramp.
> Guns aren't lawful;
> Nooses give;
> Gas smells awful;
> You might as well live.

What is this a résumé of? The poem doesn't tell you, but you can figure it out by filling in the blanks: The speaker is talking about suicide. So you may expect the tone to be tortured or full of fear, but not in this poem. Instead, you get a speaker who rejects each option for fairly trivial reasons. The implication: Suicide isn't worth it unless it's easy, painless, and neat. That attitude suggests that both living and suicide are trivial pursuits — and that is ironic.

Irony is a common tone in poetry. *Verbal irony* is the practice of saying one thing when you mean another. Such forms of irony include *understatement,* in which the speaker says less than he means, as in these lines from "Mr. Brodsky" by Charles Tomlinson. Tomlinson meets a man who brings him home to have supper — and afterward plays the bagpipe in the living room. Tomlinson writes,

> A bagpipe in a dwelling is
> a resonant instrument

Bagpipes are loud — and bagpipes indoors are *extremely* loud. Tomlinson says only "resonant" — which tells the truth with so much restraint that you can guess just *how* loud Mr. Brodsky's bagpipes really are. Tomlinson is *understating* the case — yet still leading his readers to the humorous truth. You could well imagine Tomlinson reading the word *resonant* with an ironic smile.

Verbal irony also includes *overstatement* (as in telling someone "Oh, you're the *best* poet who ever existed on the face of the earth," when it's clear you don't mean it). The term *situational irony* refers to events that happen contrary to your expectations, often with a fatal overtone, as when Oedipus Rex declares he will find out who killed his father — only to discover it must have been himself. Sharpen your awareness of tone. You'll see it in direct statement, to be sure (as when MacDiarmid cries, "They were professional murderers"), but tone can also reside in:

✔ Images and how they are presented, as in Liu Tsung-yüan's poem.

✔ The implications of a statement or story, as in "Résumé."

✔ The very music and rhythms of a poem. Think of the singsong rhythms of "Résumé," grating against the dark topic.

Reading for subject and tone

Two things you want to know right away when you're reading a poem are what's being discussed and what the poet thinks about it. Those two concerns translate to *subject* (the center of discussion; the thing being regarded or portrayed) and *tone* (the author's attitude toward the subject or toward the audience). Paying attention to these elements helps familiarize you with the poem in front of you and suggests new ways to explore the poem.

Here is a poem called "The Death of the Ball Turret Gunner," by Randall Jarrell, based on his observations as a control tower operator for the Army Air Corps in World War II. It contains some shocks, but therein lies its beauty.

From my mother's sleep I fell into the State,
And I hunched in its belly till my wet fur froze.
Six miles from earth, loosed from its dream of life,
I woke to black flak and the nightmare fighters.
When I died they washed me out of the turret with a hose.

You can find plenty of metaphors here — the "sleep" of the mother (possibly a metaphor for her contented unawareness of the horrors of war), the "belly" of the State (possibly a metaphor for the way society protects young men, who stay "hunched in its belly" like growing fetuses, until it sends them off to war), the "wet fur" of the young gunner (young mammals have wet fur when they are born, so this may be a metaphor for the youth and naiveté of the speaker), and the "dream of life" on earth (a peaceful dream for civilians far away from the horrors of war). You may also sense an implicit metaphor between the mother's womb (not directly referred to, but as part of the birth of the gunner) and the ball turret in which the gunner hunches. These lines reveal a series of births and awakenings, transitions between dreams of safety and the perils of reality. The shocks of each line lead us to the final horror of the last.

The subject of the poem is probably pretty clear to you: war and its terrible effects on the people who fight it. But what separates this poem from other war poems is its *tone*. Much about this poem may make you feel uneasy (after all, how often do you hear a dead person narrating his own death?), fearful, aware of the inevitability of fate. You're feeling the penetrating irony for which this poem is famous. What makes you feel the irony? The metaphors and their implications. The matter-of-fact language of the last line. The story the poem tells.

Figuring Out a Poem's Narrative

Many poets are also storytellers, and as storytellers, they, too, use all the elements of narration. These narrative elements include:

- ✓ **Speaker (also known as *persona*):** This is the imaginary person who "speaks" the words in a poem. Some poems feature speakers as full-fledged characters with names and histories. But for the sake of discussion, imagine *all* poems as having speakers.

- ✓ **Setting:** This is the time, location, and physical environment in which a story takes place.

- ✓ **Situation:** This word refers to the circumstances or state of affairs at a given moment in a poem or story. It can also refer to the circumstances a character finds himself in at a given moment.

- ✓ **Plot:** This term refers to the deeds and events in the story, which are organized toward a particular emotional or moral end.

- ✓ **Character:** This word refers to the fictional representation of an imaginary person. A character is really a bunch of words that spurs us to have a mental image of a person.

We cover each of these narrative elements in the following sections, and throughout our discussion we refer to "The Death of the Ball Turret Gunner" (which you can find in the preceding section), so you can see how to identify all these elements in one poem.

Speaker: The person we're listening to

In "The Death of the Ball Turret Gunner," the *speaker* (the imaginary person who "speaks" the words in the poem) is the gunner himself. He's also the main character in the poem. Another word for the main character's role is *protagonist,* the character to whom all the important events happen.

The speaker isn't a straightforward element of any poem. Some readers make the mistake of assuming that the poet himself is always the speaker of the poem unless otherwise specified. But the speaker is very often *different* from the poet. So avoid this mistake at all costs. In "The Death of the Ball Turret Gunner," Randall Jarrell was obviously a living human being when he wrote the poem, and the speaker of the poem is a young man who dies in an air war, illustrating how the speaker is a fictional creation of the poet.

One of the big questions to ponder is, "Who is the speaker and what is he like?" Speakers have personalities. They also have a *point of view* from which they see the events they narrate.

Speakers are not always perfect. In fact, they're quite often flawed in interesting ways. They may not know the whole truth, or they may be mistaken, or they may have prejudices that color what they tell you. Be sure to always evaluate what they're telling you. Consider what the poem tells you about the speaker (his or her background, biographical facts), and what you can see from what the speaker does and says (hints about his or her personality and motivation). Consider the atmosphere the poet weaves around the speaker. And remember: Speakers are like people — most are reliable, but a few aren't. That's good reason to pay close attention to what you know about any speaker you encounter in a poem — and you'll find that attention adds to the richness of your reading experience.

In "The Death of the Ball Turret Gunner," you can see that:

✔ **The speaker is not the poet, Randall Jarrell.**

✔ **The speaker is narrating his death and events beyond that death.** That lends irony and horror to the poem. Such a narration literally could never happen. It has the calm, detached quality of a voice of the dead. Even though he speaks of terrible, ugly things, the things he himself does are passive: He falls, hunches, wakes, and dies — which lends his character a submissive, obedient quality. And he never raises his voice, never protests — anger or pain are absent from his language.

✔ **The speaker's personality has an innocence you may associate with young men caught in the terrifying machinery of war.** His "wet fur" is an image usually used to describe just-born mammals. The way he wakes up implies he hasn't understood (until it's too late) what's actually happening to him.

Setting: Knowing where you are

Setting (the time, location, or physical environment in which a story takes place) can involve history and locale. Knowing the setting of a poem as well as you can is important, because poets and their characters alike are creatures of their setting. Read carefully for clues about the time, place, and situation the poem presents. Most of the time, poems give you this information straightforwardly. Some poems may mention the time of year ("It was the merry month of May,"), describe part of an exterior scene ("the humming forest," "crawling traffic," and so on), or name a place ("welcome to Miami"). But sometimes you may need to do some research — another good reason to have your reference books always near at hand.

When poets describe a scene for you, or even mention one in passing, be sure to stop and imagine the scene in detail. In his poem "La Belle Dame Sans Merci," the English Romantic poet John Keats writes

> The sedge has withered from the lake,
>   and no birds sing.

Stop and imagine it. *Sedge* is a marsh plant often growing thickly around the margins of lakes and rivers. But here, all the sedge has withered — an ominous scene, especially when combined with the absence of singing birds. Now perhaps you start wondering why these ominous things have happened. Imagining setting in full will bring you forcefully into the poem.

In "The Death of the Ball Turret Gunner," the setting is the 1940s, during World War II, in the skies above Europe (at least, that's where the planes of the Eighth Air Force, planes Randall Jarrell helped guide, were going). Thousands of airmen and civilians were killed in the air war. It was a theater of terror, with new technologies, including radar, long-range *flak* (anti-aircraft) guns, and fighter planes, increasing the death and destruction.

Situation: Circumstances and their victims

Situation is the circumstances or state of affairs at a given moment in a poem or story. Most poems begin telling the story with the first words. So pay close attention to clues about the circumstances of the poem, the speaker, and the main characters as a poem opens. What characters do or say usually relates directly to the situation they're in.

The speaker, or protagonist, of "The Death of the Ball Turret Gunner" goes through a series of situations, from birth to the nightmare of war and death, all in this one poem.

Plot: Stuff that happens

Plot refer to the deeds and events in the story, which the storyteller organizes toward a particular emotional or moral purpose. Poems tell stories, but they may not always tell them straight. They may tell events out of sequence, imply important events, or leave out whole steps in a story (to be supplied by you, the attentive reader). Keep track of the plot as you read — ask yourself what you know and what you don't.

Sometimes, the speaker may want to hide something from you or lie to you. So you need to be on your guard and compare what you're being told happened to what you *think* actually happened.

"The Death of the Ball Turret Gunner" tells a tale in straightforward chronological order — but it has a slight and all-important twist. One thing the speaker of the poem does not narrate is the death itself. One moment he is waking up from the "dream of life," and the next he is being washed out of the turret. You are, therefore, forced to imagine what happened, which involves you more deeply in that event.

Character: What kind of person would do a thing like that?

The word *character*, as in "the character of King Arthur," refers to the fictional representation of an imaginary person. Character is important to poetry. Every character in a poem has a different point of view, a different motive, a different goal. When you put characters together, you get tension and drama.

Consider the people in "The Death of the Ball Turret Gunner" other than the protagonist: the mother, the men who operate the enemy guns and planes, and the faceless "they" who have to hose out the turret at the end. Think of how different they are from the gunner and from one another. You're told that the mother was in a "sleep," a metaphor for many things, including the civilian unawareness of the loss and pain of war. The enemy guns and planes are part of a "nightmare," however — the nightmare that human savagery is real and unrelenting when released. The scrubs who do the hosing belong to the obedient young who, like the speaker, have to do what they're told.

You may also think of the "State" as a character. Because the fur freezes in the belly of the State, you presume that it's cold. The shocking last image, the hosing-out, is also cold and wet, unceremonious and without feeling.

Note this irony: If the ball turret is a kind of womb, what is the hose? After the gunner's death comes a sickening reenactment of the sexual act that led to his conception.

The speaker is also a character, which brings up a neat trick Jarrell turns with the point of view here: The speaker never pities himself — yet you feel the pity. The speaker never says anything against war — yet you get the anger and *pathos* (the evocation of pity or compassion). How? From the events, not from any protest from the speaker.

Although the poem is ironic, the speaker is *not* ironic about what happens to him. As a gunner, he is definitely a warrior, a dispenser of death, yet he seems nevertheless innocent. Perhaps the mother should have known better; perhaps the State is at fault, in its impersonality, its coldness, and its unleashing of the nightmare. But one person remains beyond blame: the gunner himself.

"The Death of the Ball Turret Gunner" operates through both language (its metaphors and its irony) and storytelling (plot, character, speaker, situation, and setting). In this chapter, we run this little poem through the machinery of narration to show you what a little attention can lend to even the shortest poem.

Considering subject, tone, and narrative — following them in detail, keeping track of them, imagining them in all dimensions — can open up a poem and reveal the true extent of a poet's craftsmanship. If you want to be a poet, reading with such attention can help you see what's possible, if you work at it.

Chapter 3

Tuning In to Language

. . . .

. . . .

To appreciate poetry, and to write it, you need to cultivate your knowledge and appreciation of the poet's material, which is *language*. In this chapter, we provide a short course on some of the ways poets mine this mother lode of human expression. We divide our tour of language into tools of significance (including similes, metaphors, and other figures of speech), *music* (sounds and rhythms), and *visual rhythm* (the shape of words and lines). But first we let you know why language is important.

Why You Need to Snuggle Up to Language

At times, language seems spiritual, as insubstantial as breath on a winter's day. Everything seems slathered and permeated with language — it's how we think and how we see. Yet language is also a *physical* thing, with characteristics and oddities — in sound and shape. To get closer to poetry, you need to fine-tune your sensitivity to language and to its histories, overtones, rhythms, meanings, and suggestions.

Noticing the beauty of language

Language is what successful poets are good with. Whether they're born or made, poets are language people. If you have a long relationship with poetry, you become more sensitive to language. You start spotting moments of beauty, start feeling the burst of meanings in a single phrase, the punch in a well-turned line. And poetry can show you how to pay attention — both to poems and to life in general. You may start noticing the details, the surprises, the unforgettable images.

Whenever you want to speak vividly or imaginatively, you can use language in special ways. When you're hungry, you may say, "I could eat a horse." Now, you couldn't actually eat a horse, and you know it. Somehow you and the people you're talking to recognize that you're being imaginative (not literal) in your language. Your audience switches into that imaginative gear and sees that you're really just saying that you're very, very hungry. In saying you could eat a horse, you're using a *figure of speech* (that is, any statement or turn of phrase that is not to be taken literally yet has a meaning you and your audience can recognize). These include *metaphors* (comparisons poets make without using *like* or *as* — in fact, *any* imaginative treatment of one thing as if it were another), *similes* (comparisons that use *like* or *as*, as in "he came in riding *like* a hurricane"), understatement, overstatement, and other unusual uses of language that poets use to stretch your imagination.

Another word you'll hear often in reference to poetry is *image,* which has many meanings. It can mean simply a vivid picture, or it can mean an especially powerful appeal to the senses.

Packing in more meaning with every word

With so many special uses of language, poetry can sometimes seem to be nonsense at first reading. But in fact, poets are trying to pack in more meaning per word than people pack in ordinary language. When you say, "Please give me a hamburger and a vanilla milkshake," you usually have one meaning and that's it. You want to be taken *literally.* But that's not always so with poetry. Poets set up words to resonate with many meanings at once — and often the only judge of all that is *you,* the reader.

How to judge? By paying close attention — but pay attention with an open, playful mind. Look for different possibilities in the words and phrases you're reading. If you find an *implication* (that is, something the poem *suggests* without coming out and saying it), great.

Try reading this poem, "About Face," by Fanny Howe. At first glance, it may seem close to nonsense, but stay with it, and you'll see that its unusual uses of language pack more possibilities of meaning per word than normal uses of language. You *could* say that the apparent "nonsense" ends up being *super*sense!:

> I wrap my bones around my head
> Speak through the holes
>
> It sounds like math
> is rounding the curves
>
> or a mouth is light years
> ahead of words.

Fanny Howe is using words differently from the way people normally use them. People usually speak literally, trying to limit their words to a single meaning. This poem is a tricky one, because so much of it has more than one possible meaning. Look at the title: "About Face." It *could* mean "a turnaround or reversal." Or, it could indicate that this poem concerns having a face.

None of the words in this poem is difficult or unusual. But everything that happens in it is *very* unusual, starting with the startling first line: "I wrap my bones around my head." The poet *can't* mean it literally — so you know you're in the presence of a metaphor. But a metaphor for what? Well, if the poem is about having a face, the line "Speak through the holes" makes sense, because holes (eyes, noses, and mouths) are what people speak through.

Think about *speaking* for a moment — just the act of using your mouth to make words. (**Remember:** This is just our guess, not a certain statement, about what Fanny Howe intends.) People are always speaking through the bones around their heads — they use their teeth, their jaws, and their facial bones to make the sounds of words. So "About Face" may be toying with the notion of what speaking involves.

Move on to the next stanza: When I speak, "It sounds like math / is rounding the curves" — two more simple and yet *very* tough lines. In math, you do a lot of rounding off of numbers, to the nearest tenth and so on. But then instead of rounding off of numbers, Howe gives you "rounding the curves." So speaking can "sound like math" (our guess) because it's always *approximating* the things people want to say or the things they want to point to in the world. People are always rounding things off — words are often insufficient, so people never actually say the exact thing they want, but they get close: They round things off.

"About Face" *seems* to be pointing out the way speaking doesn't quite do everything people pretend it does. Language does a good job, but it's approximate. So maybe that's how "a mouth is light years / ahead of words" — a mouth is something real, and words are only a bumbling attempt to get at it. No word could ever get all the way. All the word *mouth* can do is *refer to* a real mouth — it can't *be* a mouth or *give* you one. So a mouth always will remain "light years / ahead of words." (Yet another possible pun: We all are "ahead of words," and we have a *head* of words — we're thinking words all the time.)

Howe has us thinking about having bones in our faces, about mouths, about words, and about what words can and can't do. This witty, quizzical poet has brought together figures of speech to release numerous possibilities about the poem's meaning after you give it just a few moments' consideration.

We hope we've sold you on the value of snuggling up to language. In the rest of this chapter, we turn to the basic tools of the poet's art: symbols, similes, metaphors, and allusions.

Tools of Significance: Symbols, Similes, Metaphors, and Allusions

People use symbols to *stand for* things, they use similes and metaphors to *compare* things, and they use other figures of speech to make their words powerful and moving. Successful poets are masters of *all* these tools.

Symbols: When A stands for B, which brings in C

People use symbols all the time. Symbols are central to the way our minds and worlds function. Think of all the symbols you see every day: Stop signs, for example, which *stand* for your legal obligation to stop and drive safely. There's no police force, judge, and jury waiting at every stop sign — there's just the sign itself, standing for the whole machinery of safety, social obligation, and law. Words themselves are symbols: They *stand* for the things they refer to. Instead of lugging a horse into the room each time I want to discuss a horse, I can say a word — *horse* — that *stands* for that animal. Even the letters in words are symbols: They *stand* for the sounds you'd make if you spoke the word aloud. We just couldn't function as human beings without symbols.

A *symbol* stands for something else — which in turn brings with it an intense world of meaning. It's an A that "stands for" a B, which results in a C (a greater meaning). Symbols unite a concrete thing with an idea or concept greater than that thing. Here are a couple symbols and how this pattern works with each one:

✔ **Money:** A dollar (or a pound or a ruble) is a symbol. Money is really just a piece of paper or metal. That paper or metal is the A (the real element). But it *symbolizes* (or stands for) a certain economic value, which is the B. So what's the significance that B results in? Buying power. (That's the C. So A — the hard currency — is a symbol for B — the economic value — that results in C: purchase power.) Everyone agrees to abide by that symbolism. If they didn't, you wouldn't be so reluctant to part with your money, or so pleased to discover some in your jeans pocket.

✔ **A wedding ring:** A wedding ring is really just a piece of gold, molded into a certain shape. That gold is the A. But it symbolizes (stands for) a marriage, which is the B. And what's the significance that B (marriage) brings with it? Lifelong commitment and unending love, all symbolized by that never-ending line of the wedding ring (and that's the C).

Identifying symbols

So how can you tell whether something is a symbol? You can be relatively sure something is a symbol if:

✔ **You already recognize the symbol as a symbol.** A lot of literature and other art contains common symbols you probably recognize: flowers, storms, sunrises. These symbols come ready-made with their own meanings (storms, for example, usually symbolize trouble, but sunrises often symbolize hope). If you see such things in a poem, try looking at it as a symbol and see what that does for your understanding of the poem.

✔ **The poet leaves indicators (including your own feelings) that the poem represents a much larger world than its images normally would by themselves.** For example, in Robert Frost's poem "The Road Less Traveled," a hiker comes to a crossroads and must decide which road to take. That event is not, in and of itself, too meaningful. But later, the speaker says his choice of road has made "all the difference." That statement invests the choice of road with a big (and unexplained) importance, leading you to wonder about all such choices, all such "crossroads." And that makes it a symbol.

✔ **The poet has created an unusually highly-charged *setting* around these objects or events — a place or time or circumstance in which everything takes on a heightened meaning.** A familiar kind of heightened setting is the horror movie, in which almost everything symbolizes good, evil, devils, spirits, and so forth.

✔ **The possible symbol takes on a great deal of importance within the poem itself.** For example, think of the sword in the stone in many King Arthur tales. Swords are symbolic already, of course: They often stand for war, or for political power (such as in kingship). But when the little boy draws the sword out of the stone, something none of the great warriors of the world have been able to do, the sword comes to *stand for* the child's glittering future as the powerful king of Camelot, as well as his close alliance with magic.

✔ **You think it's a symbol.** If something strikes you as symbolic, go with that feeling. Apply it to the rest of the poem and see how it works. Trust your powers of reading.

Figuring out what symbols stand for

You can find symbols everywhere in poetry, as in this poem. "The Sick Rose," by English poet William Blake:

> O rose, thou art sick.
> The invisible worm
> That flies in the night
> In the howling storm
>
> Has found out thy bed
> Of crimson joy,
> And his dark secret love
> Does thy life destroy.

You *can* read this poem literally (a flying worm destroys a flower) — which is what probably happens with a quick review of the words on the page. But you'll appreciate the poem more — and understand it better — if you dig deeper and try to figure out what the symbols mean. Here are some clues:

- ✔ **You get a sense that the events in the poem *transcend* themselves.** That is, these events don't stand only for themselves, a *particular* rose being savaged by a *particular* worm. If that were all, you could easily say, "Who cares? Worms eat plants. Big deal." But these events suggest a larger world of meaning. How do you know? In this case, both the rose and the worm are well-established symbols: Roses often signify love or beauty, and the worm is often used to signify death and decay. So here, you see one famous symbol (which you know as a symbol for death) destroy another famous symbol (which you're familiar with as a symbol for beauty). Although literally all you read about is a worm destroying a flower, you *feel* a great weight of significance, pulling you to think of *other* kinds of destruction, and how other beautiful things lose their beauty or their lives.

- ✔ **The *setting* of the poem is gruesome and frightening.** You feel the setting in the words the "howling storm," the night, and the invisible, flying worm that destroys the rose with its "dark, secret love" — all scary notions. These words invest everything that happens with a heightened character, as in a melodrama or frightening story. That heightened character helps suggest that the action is symbolic.

- ✔ **This poem seems to create its own universe, in which the death of a rose involves sickness, love, and sorrow.** The worm is "invisible" and its love "secret." Secrecy and invisibility imply stealth and furtiveness, as though fate or some malevolent entity were ensuring the rose's death.

- ✔ **The speaker addresses the rose as "thou," an unfamiliar way to talk to a plant.** Blake is using *personification*, giving human attributes to something not human. The rose had a prior life of "crimson joy" that it is now losing, and you may feel sympathy for the rose. The worm is also characterized as destructive, inescapable, and scary — all human characteristics placed onto something not human.

We hope we've convinced you that the rose and the worm are symbols. So what do they stand for? The poem doesn't exactly say, so you may have to do a little guesswork and digging here.

Traditionally, red roses symbolize beauty and love, and worms symbolize death. So is this poem about death destroying beauty? That's definitely a possibility. The rose also seems innocent and vulnerable; it doesn't stand much of a chance, what with a howling storm carrying lethal worms. The rose is bright red, and the worm is invisible and comes from the darkness. As a reader, you may feel not only the death of innocence (symbolized by the death of the rose) but also the inescapability of that death. Some readers see the rose's "bed / Of crimson joy" as a symbol for sexual innocence, which gives the worm a sexual significance, too, representing a man deflowering a woman.

Watch for indicators (including your own feelings) that the poem represents a much larger world than its images normally would alone. In "The Sick Rose," Blake shows you the larger universe, in the play of love, life, joy, sickness, and the storm. Many poems, possibly most, have a moment when you feel the poem indicate a larger universe. That's when you know you're in the presence of symbols.

Digging deeper to uncover private symbols

With some symbols, the poet gives you an obvious A, but you get few clues as to B or C — that is, what the symbol stands for and what it means. These are known as *private symbols*. Clues in the poem — sometimes just the emotion with which the poem is written — tell you that they *are* symbols, but you just don't know what they stand for. The French poets called the *Symbolists* created an entire poetic technique from this kind of symbolism, and it dominates much poetry written today.

One of the most famous of private symbols is from Arthur Rimbaud's "Bateau Ivre" ("The Drunken Boat"):

> If I desire one water in Europe, it's the pond,
> Black and cold, where, against the perfumed twilight,
> A crouching child, full of sadness, launches
> A boat, frail as a butterfly in May.

Here, the A is achingly clear and detailed: the cold pond, the sad child, the boat, the butterfly. Our guess is that this image is packed with the sadness, loneliness, and fragility of childhood. Maybe this symbol is from Rimbaud's childhood, but maybe not. Either way, the setting is definitely emotionally charged. Everything seems to take on a larger meaning than you'd expect in the simple image of a child playing with a boat on a pond. That heightened setting, suggesting a larger meaning, is why many readers think this seemingly private moment stands for all childhoods, not just Rimbaud's.

How do you know when a symbol *is* a symbol? In general, whenever an image seems to evoke meanings that extend far beyond itself, you can call it a symbol — even when you can't work out the B and C for sure.

Similes and metaphors: My love is like a can of tuna; no, he is a can of tuna

With symbols, one thing represents another. Similes and metaphors, however, work differently. Both of these figures of speech are forms of imaginative comparison.

Similes

A simile is an explicit comparison — it is directly stated, often using the words *like* or *as*. If a poet writes, "My love is like a can of tuna," that silly poet would be coming right out and saying, "He resembles that can of tuna in many ways." (Cold and hard on the outside, soft and nourishing and a bit fishy on the inside?)

You can find similes everywhere. In Homer's *The Iliad,* the great warrior Achilles changes a battle simply by letting loose a great shout:

> Infinite terror wracked the foe:
> Like the piercing shrill of a trumpet
> The lucid voice of Achilles rang —
> And when the Trojans heard his brassy cry
> Their hearts hurt, their thick-maned horses
> Bucked, knowing agony was near

The shout was *like* "the piercing shrill of a trumpet," which is a simile.

Notice how the word *brassy* continues the comparison of Achilles's voice to a trumpet.

When Byron wants to describe the savage attack of the Assyrian army in "The Destruction of Sennacherib," he compares it to a wolf attacking a flock or "fold" of sheep:

> The Assyrian came down like a wolf on the fold

Notice that Byron says the Assyrian was *like* "a wolf on the fold."

Similes help make an image or state of feeling more precise. You can feel the reverberant shout of Achilles in Homer's writing and the attack of the Assyrians in Byron's.

Metaphors

Metaphor makes a comparison *without* using *like* or *as.* Instead, the poet talks as though thing A really *were* thing B. (My love isn't *like* a can of tuna; he *is* a can of tuna.)

Where simile works with similarity, *metaphor* is a claim of exact equivalence or identity. It's far more intimate and packs a greater emotional punch. When in his poem "The Search" Ghanaian poet Kwesi Brew writes that "The past / Is but the cinders / Of the present," the unspoken comparison between the passage of time and the destructiveness of fire drives home the way time erases what used to be (much stronger than if he had written, "The past / Is *like* the cinders / of the present").

Because metaphor works with an unspoken comparison, it challenges you to think of all the ways two things are alike — for example, the passage of time and the destructiveness of fire. Those ways that the two things being compared are alike are called the *grounds* of the metaphor.

How do you know when you're seeing metaphors? When poets speak of one thing as being another, even though literally those two things *aren't the same.* My love is not *literally* a can of tuna, but I *call* him one to bring out the similarities between him and that foodstuff. In *The Iliad,* Homer writes of war-spears "stuck in the ground, longing for their fill of flesh." Spears can't long for bloodshed; only warriors can. But Homer speaks as if the spears *can* thirst for blood, as if the spears were *literally* warriors. This is definitely a metaphor (actually, *personification,* which is a kind of metaphor that speaks of a nonhuman thing as if it were human). It rams home the all-penetrating rage of war.

Shakespeare seemed to *think* in metaphors. When Hamlet feels he has done something wrong, he cries, "O, my offense is rank; it smells to heaven," implicitly comparing his misdeed to something rotten. When a servant in *Timon of Athens* wants to say a rich man has no money, he declares, "'Tis deepest winter in Lord Timon's purse," comparing the emptiness of winter to the lack of money in Timon's purse. These images have greater power for *not* using *like* or *as.*

In most metaphors, we can sort out the *vehicle* (the thing being compared) from the *tenor* (the thing to which it is being compared):

Piece of Writing	Vehicle	Tenor
Brew's "The Search"	Fire	Time
Homer's *The Iliad*	Spears	Warriors
Shakespeare's *Hamlet*	Hamlet's offense	Something rotten
Shakespeare's *Timon of Athens*	Lord Timon's finances	Winter

Sometimes you get only the vehicle, with the tenor being strongly implied. That happens in Christopher Marlowe's *Doctor Faustus,* when Faustus cries, "Fair Nature's eye, rise, rise again, and make / Perpetual day." Marlowe doesn't tell you that the tenor is "the sun," but you can dig deeper and see that the thing that is rising and making day is the sun.

Metaphors come in different varieties. In *metonymy,* the poet replaces the name of a thing with the name of something closely associated with that thing. (People do this all the time, as when they speak of the *White House* when they mean the *President,* or when they use the word *suits* when they mean *bosses.*) In *synecdoche,* people take a part of a thing and use it to stand for the whole thing, as when people use the word *wheels* when they mean *car.* In "The Love Song of J. Alfred Prufrock," T.S. Eliot has his speaker say, "I should have been a pair of ragged claws / Scuttling across the floors of silent seas." The speaker doesn't mean that he should be just claws, of course, but instead some lowly, crablike animal, an excellent metaphor for Prufrock's dissatisfaction with himself.

Knowing the names of these tools of language is not as important as being aware of all the ways poets can create them. When you come upon a metaphor, try to sort out vehicle and tenor, and think about the grounds. The poet's art, and much of its psychological magic, will become a little clearer and all the more impressive.

Allusions: Names and places you just have to know

An *allusion* is a reference to something — a person, place, story, historical event — outside the poem. Poets allude to these things to create metaphors and intensify the message of their poetry.

In his poem "Epithalamion," which is about his wedding day, the Renaissance poet Edmund Spenser describes his bride-to-be, who approaches "Like Phoebe from her chamber in the east." Who's Phoebe? A brief consultation with your reference books will tell you that Spenser is alluding to Phoebe, the Greek goddess of the moon, a virgin goddess. The moon rises in the east. So his bride is coming like the rising moon, a virgin goddess. His allusion creates a simile that praises his fiancée for her beauty and chastity.

In the case of Spenser's poem, if you know about Phoebe, you're off to a great start; if not, you owe it to yourself to find out who she is and why he alludes to her.

Writers of all periods make allusions — none more than contemporary writers. The lyrics of hip-hop, rap, and metal music are full of allusions. A brief perusal of Rage Against the Machine's album *Evil Empire* reveals references to Jacqueline Onassis, NBC, ABC, General Electric, Disney, and Aztec mythology. Rap artists refer constantly to one another, to the names of cities, TV shows, films, and pop stars and celebrities.

Here is the distinguished chemist and poet Roald Hoffman, in a passage from his list poem "Deceptively Like a Solid." Even the title is an allusion, because the poem concerns glass, which is a liquid deceptively like a solid. The poem ends in a spasm of allusions, all having to do with glass:

Optical fibers   Crystal Palace
                 The Worshipful Company of Glass Sellers
recycled   Millefiori
prone to shattering   Prince Rupert's drops
Chartres, Rouen, Amiens   float
Pyrex   Vycor   glass wool
network modifiers   the Palomar mirror

If you really want to know this poem, you'll get busy tracking down these allusions. "Chartres, Rouen, Amiens" is a list of three great Gothic cathedrals in France; each one has a magnificent stained-glass window. And "the Palomar mirror" refers to a huge reflecting mirror created for a giant telescope at Hale Observatory on Mt. Palomar in California. Like the cathedrals' windows, the Palomar mirror is an astonishing thing done with glass.

Tracking down allusions makes the experience richer, and you'll be that much better informed about glass, about this poem, and about the world if you do the legwork.

Music: What You Hear, Feel, and See

When people talk about poetry, they use some of the same terminology that they use when they talk about music. For example, a *line* of poetry is a group of words printed as a unit on the page — usually on the same physical level. Here's one line from Shakespeare:

> Farewell — thou art too dear for my possessing

And two lines from Jack Spicer:

>   Poet,
> Be like God.

People also speak of numbers of lines as units. Two lines are a *couplet;* usually we use this word to refer to two lines in the same form, like these two from John Milton's "L'Allegro":

> Come and trip it as ye go
> On the light fantastic toe

They also speak of *tercets* (three lines), *quatrains* (four), *cinquains* (five), *sestets* (six), *septets* (seven), and *octaves* (eight).

Just as in music, a *stanza* is a group of lines arranged as a unit. The most familiar kinds of stanzas are those the poet repeats in exactly the same form again and again, as in Robert Herrick's "To the Virgins, to Make Much of Time":

> Gather ye rosebuds while ye may,
>   Old time is still a-flying;
> And this same flower that smiles today
>   Tomorrow will be dying.
>
> The glorious lamp of heaven, the sun,
>   The higher he's a-getting,
> The sooner will his race be run,
>   And nearer he's to setting.

But the word *stanza* can also refer to any group of lines considered as a unit — not just those that have a repeated form.

Finally, the word *music* is used to denote the sounds and rhythms in a poem. In the following sections, we separate music into these elements:

- ✔ The sounds of words
- ✔ *Rhyme* (which is the echoing or repetition of sounds)
- ✔ The rhythms of lines

Orchestrating sound

Poets are supremely conscious of the physical properties of words — their length in letters and syllables, and even their length in time (how long it takes to say them); their vowels, consonants, and ease or difficulty of pronunciation. Poets know what sorts of sounds are smooth and sweet, and which are clotted and ugly. When sounds are pleasant together, it is referred to as *euphony;* when they are uncomfortable, rough, or ugly, it is called *dissonance.*

Poets are famous for writing beautiful, sweet-sounding verse — and they should be. Here are six lines of pleasing sounds from "The Garden" by the 17th-century English poet Andrew Marvell. The speaker finds himself in a beautiful garden:

What wondrous life is this I lead!
Ripe apples drop about my head;
The luscious clusters of the vine
Upon my mouth do crush their wine;

Listen for the vowels in the first line: "What wondrous life is this I lead!" Many readers find the vowels light and delightful. This line is a good example of euphony. Marvell chose the vowels on purpose to create this lovely scene of a rich garden offering itself to the inhabitant. The phrase "luscious clusters of the vine," with its *u* and *s* and *sh* sounds, is truly luscious!

Here are three lines of very ugly sounds from Jonathan Swift's "Description of a City Shower." Swfit is describing all the garbage swept up in a flood that washes through London:

Sweepings from butchers' stalls, dung, guts, and blood,
Drowned puppies, stinking sprats, all drenched in mud,
Dead cats, and turnip tops, come tumbling down the flood.

Can you hear the crowded, ugly pile of consonants *(ng, g, bl)* in phrases such as "dung, guts, and blood"? Swift wants you to be disgusted, and he uses these sounds to reinforce that effect. Poets sometimes actually *want* poems to sound ugly when ugliness is appropriate — as, for example, in describing war, suffering . . . or city trash. These three lines are a great example of dissonance.

The poet's challenge is to orchestrate the sound properties of words. So in a poem, you'll find patterns of sounds, repetitions, or combinations — all of which are there because the poet brought them together in that specific way.

Alliteration

When a particular consonant sound is repeated in a passage of verse, it's called *alliteration*. (Some people use this word to mean repetition of the same sound at the *beginnings* of neighboring words, but we use it more generally.)

Read the following lines from Jackson Mac Low's poem "Antic Quatrains":

Granados labeled a gateleg table stable
As droll goaltenders tensed at tenebrist rites

See and hear all the *l* and *t* sounds in this passage? That's alliteration (the repetition of the same sounds).

Assonance

When the same *vowel* sound is repeated in a group of neighboring words, it's called *assonance.* Listen for the assonance in Barbara Guest's poem "Red Lilies":

> snow erupts from thistle
> to toe; the snow pours out of you.

Repeat Guest's lines and feel and hear — especially in the second line — the deep vowels roll slowly over and over.

How alliteration and assonance work together

Just *seeing* alliteration and assonance is one step; the next is seeing how these patterns connect to the poem's meaning and its impact on you. The English Romantic poet Percy Bysshe Shelley's poem "Ode to the West Wind" portrays the wildness of the spring wind, largely through its use of sound. Listen to these lines, in which he addresses the wind:

> Thou, on whose stream, 'mid the steep sky's commotion,
> Loose clouds like earth's decaying leaves are shed,
> Shook from the tangled boughs of heaven and ocean

Spectacular pictures of the clouds, the sky, the storms, and winds. But what makes those images *physical* are the alliteration and assonance. Hear all those *s* and *sh* sounds? Those sounds are like the ones the wind makes. And different *o* sounds seem to dominate, although the second line gives a spasm of long *e* noises. Shelley adores this wind as a worshiper would adore a wild god, and the wildness and divinity come through in wind noises to accompany his ecstatic images.

The whole poem is available in hundreds of anthologies of poetry.

Recognizing the varieties of rhyme

Rhyme is the repetition of a sound; it's an echo. In English, the most familiar kind of rhyme is called *perfect rhyme,* in which the echo is fairly exact, as in *moose* and *noose, floss* and *moss,* and *sting* and *ring.* The most familiar place for the occurrence of rhyme is at the ends of lines, which is called *end rhyme.*

End rhyme is what you hear in the Elizabethan poet Thomas Campion's "When to Her Lute Corinna Sings":

> When to her lute Corinna sings,
> Her voice revives the leaden strings,
> And doth in highest notes appear
> As any challenged echo clear

End rhyme helps organize poetry. It helps make it musical, songlike, and memorable. But there's more: Rhyme very often helps carry out what the verse is doing. Corinna sings; we hear the strings revive. The *ing* sound that was in *sings* comes back around in the *ing* sound of *strings,* so the poem is doing exactly what it's describing: Corinna's voice really *is* reviving the strings. In the last two lines, her voice is made to *appear,* and it is like an echo, *clear,* just like the rhyme. Was Campion just lucky? No, he wrote the poem to have these effects.

Rhyme isn't just an echo. Often it's how the poet gives a physical impact to the pictures he is trying to create in your mind.

Many kinds of rhyme are not as exact as perfect rhyme. They tease and tickle the ear with almost-likeness. Many varieties of rhymes almost echo, but not quite. Poets can rhyme only the final consonant sounds in the accented syllable of a word, as in *amaze* and *freeze;* this technique is often called *slant, near,* or *partial rhyme.* Poets may rhyme *only* the vowel of two words, as in *nose* and *mope;* this technique is called *vowel rhyme.* And in English, which has wacky spelling, poets can rhyme words that *look* as though they should rhyme even though in fact they don't, like *bough* and *tough;* this technique is called *sight rhyme.*

The names of these techniques are less important than the effects the poets use them to achieve. Good readers look for those effects and watch how poets achieve them. And good writers master the sounds of their chosen language to have full mastery of rhyme.

Emily Dickinson was quite an experimenter with rhyme:

> I taste a liquor never brewed —
> From Tankards scooped in Pearl —
> Not all the Frankfort Berries
> Yield such an Alcohol!

Alcohol and *pearl* share that final *l* sound, and their final vowel sounds, although not the *same,* are close enough for a very interesting effect.

Rhyme is an echo. And such echoes can come anywhere in a line of poetry; they don't have to come only at the end of the line. Edgar Allen Poe's poem "The Raven" features several lines in which there is *internal rhyme* — that is, rhyme occurring *within* lines, as well as at the ends: "Once upon a midnight dreary, while I pondered, weak and weary. . . ."

When reading poetry, watch for the poet's use of echoing sounds. In Poe's line, the rhyme is there for more than just pretty noise. The adjective modifying *midnight* rhymes with the adjective modifying *I,* which links the dreary night with the weary speaker.

Feeling rhythm and measuring meter

Rhythm is the patterns of stresses in a line of verse. When you speak, you *stress* some syllables and leave others *unstressed.* When you string a lot of words together, you start seeing patterns. Even in that last sentence, you can hear them:

> When you *string* a *lot* of *words* together, you *start see*ing *pat*terns.

Rhythm is a natural thing. It's in everything you say and write, even if you don't intend for it to be.

Traditional forms of verse use preestablished rhythmic patterns called *meters.*

The word *meter* means *measure* in Greek, and that's what meters are — premeasured patterns of stressed and unstressed syllables.

Much of English poetry is written in lines that string together one or more *feet* (individual rhythmical units). Feet are the individual building blocks of meter. Here are the most common feet, the rhythms they represent, and an example of that rhythm.

- ✔ **Anapest:** duh-duh-DUH, as in *but of course!*
- ✔ **Dactyl:** DUH-duh-duh, as in *honestly*
- ✔ **Iamb:** duh-DUH, as in *collapse*
- ✔ **Trochee:** DUH-duh, as in *pizza*

To build a line of verse, poets can string together repetitions of one of these feet. Such repetitions are named as follows:

- ✔ 1 foot: monometer
- ✔ 2 feet: dimeter
- ✔ 3 feet: trimeter
- ✔ 4 feet: tetrameter
- ✔ 5 feet: pentameter
- ✔ 6 feet: hexameter

So the famous *iambic pentameter* is a string of five iambs, as in Christopher Marlowe's line from *Dr. Faustus:*

> Was this the face that launched a thousand ships
>
> Duh-DUH-duh-DUH-duh-DUH-duh-DUH-duh-DUH

Here you'll notice that there are five unstressed syllables alternating with five stressed — in other words, five duh-DUHs. As you read more poetry, you'll start to recognize feet and meters.

Rhythm is not the same as meter. The difference between rhythm and meter is the difference between the beat of a song and the rhythms played over that beat.

To see the difference between rhythm and meter, take a look at Sonnet 43 from *Sonnets from the Portuguese* by Elizabeth Barrett Browning:

How do I love thee? Let me count the ways.	(A)
I love thee to the depth and breadth and height	(B)
My soul can reach, when feeling out of sight	(B)
For the ends of Being and ideal Grace.	(A)
I love thee to the level of everyday's	(A)
Most quiet need, by sun and candle light.	(B)
I love thee freely, as men strive for Right;	(B)
I love thee purely, as they turn from Praise.	(A)
I love thee with the passion put to use	(C)
In my old griefs, and with my childhood's faith.	(D)
I love thee with a love I seemed to lose	(C)
With my lost saints — I love thee with the breath,	(D)
Smiles, tears, of all my life! — and, if God choose,	(C)
I shall but love thee better after death.	(D)

This is a *sonnet* — 14 lines written in iambic pentameter. It also has an interesting *rhyme scheme,* which we've marked out at the end of every line. The poem has two quatrains in an ABBA rhyme scheme, and a sestet rhyming CDCDCD. Writing a poem like this is hard, because the poet has to come up with four rhymes for two of her chosen sounds. A couple of the rhymes — *grace* and *ways; faith* and *breath* — are inexact. Browning is playing with your ear, inviting you to delight in the difference between what you expect (perfect rhyme) and what she gives you (just this side of perfect).

Now take a look at the *meter* and how it compares to the *rhythm.* Iambic pentameter goes like this:

Duh-DUH, duh-DUH, duh-DUH, duh-DUH, duh-DUH

Apply that to the very first line of the poem:

How *do* I *love* thee *let* me *count* the *ways*

A robot may say it that way. But reading it like this is more natural:

> *How* do I *love* thee? *Let* me *count* the *ways*

The first foot, which we expect to be duh-DUH, gets reversed into DUH-duh. You can do that; there's no rule against it. In fact, poets make substitutions like that throughout a metered line. What Browning is doing is *varying the rhythm*. Iambic pentameter is in the background, as steady as the beat in a song, but Browning is playing natural rhythms over the meter, just as a jazz soloist will play all sorts of different riffs and rhythms over a steady beat.

Certainly, this poem has lines that adhere closely to the iambic pentameter, such as this one:

> I *love* thee *to* the *depth* and *breadth* and *height*

Although, you *could* read that line like this:

> I *love thee* to the *depth* and *breadth* and *height*

Can you feel the emotional difference between the two? Those two strong stresses in *love thee* truly sell the notion that the speaker loves the beloved.

Consider this way of reading line 4:

> For the *ends* of *being* *and* ideal *grace*

It's still an iambic pentameter line. You can't read it

> For *the* ends *of* be*ing* and *i*deal *grace*

The first way is more natural. That first foot is actually an *anapest* (duh-duh-DUH) substituted for the iamb. You don't necessarily need to know that — only hear the beat of the iambic pentameter meter behind the spoken rhythms of the poem.

Browning ends some of her lines with commas or periods, which we call *end-stopped lines,* but she also runs some sentences right over into the next line without intervening punctuation, as in:

> I love thee with a love I seemed to lose
> With my lost saints

That is called *enjambment* — the practice of continuing a phrase or clause from one line to the next without intervening punctuation. You expect to pause at the end of each line, but Browning tugs you irresistibly into the next.

Poets use enjambment to pull you into all manner of surprises — for example, the echo of *lose* with *lost*. Enjambment is a way to emphasize words and phrases, create tension, or lead the reader around the end of one line to a realization or discovery in the next one — as in "With my lost saints."

Browning is working with rhyme and rhythm *along with* the words and images she's orchestrating. The music is part of the words but also a world, so to speak, *underneath* the words, a physical world of sound and stress. Browning knows what rhythm and music do to you, and she uses them to elicit certain feelings and responses in you.

As a reader, sharpen your sensitivity to music and rhythm. Watch how poets use the words as well as the world under the words.

The Shape of the Poem: Visual Rhythm

Visual rhythm is a poem's shape and the physical length of its lines. Much of the way you *feel* about a poem has to do with that shape, the ins and outs of its lines. So in reading a poem, you're not only trying to figure out its *sense* (what it's saying), and not only taking account the music and rhythm and how they contribute to the meaning, you're also taking into account the *visual aspects* of the poem — the way it looks, its shape, the way lines and words are arranged on the page. That, too, has a lot to contribute to the poem's impact on you.

Consider these lines from "Death" by George Herbert:

> Death, thou wast once an uncouth, hideous thing,
> Nothing but bones,
> The sad effect of sadder groans:
> Thy mouth was open, but thou couldst not sing.

A long line contracts to a shorter line, which opens to a slightly longer line, a little less indented, and then back to a long line. The two shorter lines seem enclosed in the longer ones, and you're invited to expand and contract your attention along with the lines.

See how the first line, containing the "uncouth, hideous thing," contracts to "Nothing but bones," as though it were a body decomposing?

Visual rhythm is *supremely* important in open-form verse, in which the poet sculpts each line to its perfect length. George Oppen, one of the finest of the Objectivist poets, handles the visual rhythms of these lines from "Psalm" with almost unbearable sensitivity. His theme is deer and the natural world:

> Their paths
> Nibbled thru the fields, the leaves that shade them
> Hang in the distances
> Of sun
>
> The small nouns
> Crying faith
> In this in which the wild deer
> Startle, and stare out.

Oppen, a master of white space, goes from a very short line, much indented, to a much longer one, perhaps giving the sense of how deer paths wander through the fields. (Note the motion of the enjambment in "Their paths / Nibbled thru the fields," which makes you follow the clause around the end of the line all the way back to the word *Nibbled,* as if *you* were following a path, too.) The stanza contracts to "Of sun," concentrating your imagination on the sun (he actually makes you look right at it) and how it illuminates distance. *The small nouns,* three small words, are isolated away from the other lines, again redirecting your attention to the words of which this poem is made. Again and again, the shape of the poem guides your understanding and experience, both of what the words are saying, and of the very words as objects in and of themselves.

Oppen uses enjambment to keep you unraveling the sentence all the way to the end and the final image. Constantly, he moves you in and out, left and right. That visual rhythm lends dramatic wonder to the poem.

We give you an arsenal of new terms, new ways into poetry, in this chapter. You'll get better at using them — as both a reader and a writer — the more you practice.

Chapter 4

The Art of Interpretation

In This Chapter

▶ Understanding the elements of interpretation

▶ Getting comfortable with speculating (as opposed to knowing for sure) about a poem's meaning

▶ Understanding what is explicit in a poem and what is implied

▶ Practicing informed speculation

▶ Using subject, tone, language, music, and narrative elements to help you interpret a poem

*P*oems are meaningful things. In fact, poetry is famous for having more meaning per word than other kinds of writing. Poetry is supposed to *burst* with meaning.

Ah, but when you start asking "What does this poem *mean?*" all too often it's like walking onto a battleground. How often have you been told, "No! You're wrong!" when discussing a poem or a song lyric in a classroom? How often have you decided, "Well, this is too hard. I won't like this stuff"?

Interpretation is the act of accounting for the feelings the poem gives you when you read it. When you look closely at a poem and see how it works, you find a way into it; you discover feelings, meanings, and richness, some of which the poet creates, some of which you make for yourself.

So interpretation is in part the discovery of how a poem makes meaning and feeling. You ask: Why does this poem make me feel the way I do? What is the poem doing, and how does the poet do it?

In this chapter, we give you guidelines and pointers to become a good interpreter. And we look at different approaches to this tricky and rewarding activity.

Reading at a Deeper Level

The first place to start when it comes to interpreting poetry is reading it at a deeper level than you read other things. When you pay closer attention to poetry, you're rewarded with an understanding of it that goes much deeper — and lasts much longer — than a quick read gives you. In fact, poetry, as the poet Robert Creeley once said, is "an act of attention." Reading (and writing) poetry is a great way to learn how to pay attention to the world.

Reading poetry means you pay attention to at least two things at once: *what* a poem is doing and *how* the poem accomplishes it. This assignment is a tricky one — kind of like making bread while riding a unicycle — but it's worth it. The question is, what do you pay attention *to?*

Start by paying attention to two general aspects of poetry, and focus on those:

- ✔ **Sense:** What the poem is saying or appears to be exploring.
- ✔ **Music:** The total of the poem's sounds and rhythms.

We cover sense and music in more detail in the following sections.

Sense: Determining what a poem is saying

Many people think of poetry as being full of profound statements and insights. And it is! You need to pay attention to those statements and insights when they occur. But not *all* poems make statements. Some poems simply present a picture, ask a question, or plunge the reader into an experience. Almost all poems have a *sense,* something they mean to express, to do, or to call your attention to.

Poems that make you feel (instead of making a statement)

Take a look at this poem, "The Solitary Reaper" by the English Romantic poet William Wordsworth. Notice how it gives you an experience but doesn't offer much in the way of bold statements or insights:

Behold her, single in the field,
Yon solitary Highland Lass!
Reaping and singing by herself;
Stop here, or gently pass!
Alone she cuts and binds the grain,
And sings a melancholy strain;
O listen! for the Vale profound
Is overflowing with the sound.

No Nightingale did ever chaunt
More welcome notes to weary bands
Of travellers in some shady haunt,
Among Arabian sands:
A voice so thrilling ne'er was heard
In spring-time from the Cuckoo-bird,
Breaking the silence of the seas
Among the furthest Hebrides.

Will no one tell me what she sings? —
Perhaps the plaintive numbers flow
For old, unhappy, far-off things,
And battles long ago:
Or is it some more humble lay,
Familiar matter of to-day?
Some natural sorrow, loss, or pain,
That has been, and may be again?

Whate'er the theme, the Maiden sang
As if her song could have no ending;
I saw her singing at her work,
And o'er the sickle bending; —
I listened, motionless and still;
And, as I mounted up the hill,
The music in my heart I bore,
Long after it was heard no more.

Here is a short list of words in this poem that may be unfamiliar to you:

- ✔ **Highland:** An area of Scotland with elevated hills and moors.
- ✔ **the Vale profound:** Another way of saying "the profound (deep) valley."
- ✔ **chaunt:** A different spelling of the word *chant*.
- ✔ **ne'er:** The poetic way of saying the word *never*.
- ✔ **Hebrides:** A group of islands in the west of Scotland.
- ✔ **plaintive numbers:** Melancholy rhythms.
- ✔ **lay:** Song.
- ✔ **Whate'er:** The poetic way of saying the word *whatever*.
- ✔ **o'er:** Another way of saying *over*.
- ✔ **mounted:** Climbed.

Wordsworth's poem plunges you into the midst of an experience. The speaker of the poem sees a girl working in the fields and hears the melancholy song she sings. The picture is vivid: the highlands, the deep valley, the girl's work as she reaps the grain. And you get a general feeling about her song: The speaker says it is beautiful and melancholy, and that it echoes throughout the valley. He compares her song to that of two birds: the nightingale and the cuckoo. (Both the nightingale and the cuckoo are mentioned in poems throughout history. If you consult your reference books, you'll find that the nightingale is famous for its melodious warble, and the song of the cuckoo usually announces the coming of spring, with all the joy and rebirth that season brings.) Yet this girl's song outdoes them both. Clearly, the speaker (evidently just a traveler passing through) is charmed and maybe a little intoxicated by the tune. The girl sings as if "her song could have no ending." The speaker stops for a moment, then climbs up the next hill and leaves the scene, with the memorable song in his heart.

Nice poem — but what does it mean? The speaker tells you everything but the meaning of it all. Notice he doesn't even know what the song is about. He asks whether anyone will tell him, but there's no answer (certainly not from the girl, who keeps working). He speculates: Is it a song of war? Or something more humble? An old song? Or something new? He gets no answers to these questions, either, and neither do you, the reader. The speaker doesn't know what her song means or says, but when he leaves, it stays with him "long after it was heard no more."

Many poems, like this one, simply present an experience without explaining it. They leave you to interpret it — or perhaps no interpretation is possible or necessary. Maybe Wordsworth simply wants you to enjoy the picture here: the girl in the midst of nature, singing a song that is the loveliest thing in a lovely environment.

What should you do with such poems? Let yourself have the experience. Envision the landscape of the Highlands; sense the rhythm of the girl's scything; hear the echo of her song throughout the deep valley. There's a mystery to the scene. You can't get to the bottom of it — but then, you can't get to the bottom of music either. You may find yourself thinking about how some songs stay with you long after you hear them, and how you can get the feeling from the melody of a song even though you can't understand the words. There is a sweetness to this momentary encounter. Neither girl nor traveler have anything to do with each other directly, but something pretty has happened — to the traveler and to you.

This poem does not make a statement — although it leads you into a singular, compelling experience. Many experiences are like this: They simply *are* and resist further explanation. What's interesting is how you respond to them. The poem is like the song: You can't really tell what it means, but it is lovely, melancholy, and stays with you long after you've read (or heard) it.

Poems that have a point to make (or a statement to convey)

Many poems *do* make outright statements. The poet has something to say about life, a judgment to make, a truth to reveal.

Here's an example, by the Arabian poet Abū-l-`Alâ' al-Ma'arrî:

> Friend, this world is like an unburied corpse,
> And we're the dogs barking round it.
> If you go in and eat, you're a loser;
> If you stay out, and hunger, you gain.
> Anyone the night doesn't mug
> Gets rolled: Time's disasters at dawn.

Even though this poem's statements are bold, reading a poem isn't just a matter of dragging your eyes over it. It's a way of *paying attention.* But just as you can listen to a friend talk while you're watching TV, or you can sit across the table and stare into that friend's eyes while she talks and really hear every word she says, you can pay attention to a poem on several different levels as well. Here are three different levels of attention you can pay to the poem by Abū-l-`Alâ' al-Ma'arrî. You can apply this to any other poem as well:

- ✔ **Base-level attention:** *Base-level attention* is what you do when you quickly scan the poem's length, the name of the poet, the title, and the structure. With this poem, you may notice that it is short and doesn't rhyme. It is written by an Arabian poet of the 10th and 11th centuries A.D. (The poet's name may suggest that the poet is Arabian — or, if it suggests nothing to you, consult your reference books. As for the date, if you didn't know that bit of information, you could turn to an encyclopedia and look it up.) The speaker doesn't see the world as a happy place.

- ✔ **Mid-level attention:** *Mid-level attention* is a little deeper — you read the poem through once and pick up anything that jumps out at you. You may notice the simile in the first line of the Abū-l-`Alâ' al-Ma'arrî poem: "[T]his world is like an unburied corpse." This simile is followed by a metaphor: "And we're the dogs barking round it." The world (human experience) is like a corpse that "we" (all people) feed on like scavengers with nothing better to eat. These sentiments don't exactly speak well for people — but think about that metaphor for a minute. It seems to imply a few things about people in general. Exactly what does it imply, though? Asking such a question will lead you to the next level of attention.

- ✔ **High-level attention:** *High-level attention* is what you do when you dig deeper, applying the experiences you get in poems in powerful and transcendent ways. Follow the sense of the metaphor, and you find that Abū actually has a little philosophical advice: Don't get too involved with "this world." ("If you stay out," he says, "you gain.") That way, when you suffer (and everybody either gets "mugged" by night or "rolled" by daylight, which brings "disasters"), you can at least control your own behavior.

High-level attention is a wonderful place. We can't tell you how much we enjoy going there. Don't be afraid of such intense attention. It means you care and are involved in what happens to you and around you.

Paying attention brings many rewards. We proposed a main message in Abū's poem: Don't get too involved in the world, and your sufferings will be less. But then we read this line: "If you stay out, and hunger, you gain." This line is a *paradox* (where two things appear to conflict, or even contradict, and yet coexist as if they were both true). You gain if you stay out — but staying out also leaves you hungry. We *love* that moment of realization. It's one of those moments poetry can give you. A weary speaker advises you to stay apart from the world — but then admits, to some degree, that it will be hard. Feel all the complicated experience behind those words?

High-level attention is what you do all the time. Bring it to poetry sometimes — after bringing it to your job, your favorite TV show, your loved ones, the purchase of underwear, skateboarding — and you may gain, and *not* be hungry.

To follow the sense of a poem, pay close attention. Watch both *what* a poem is doing and *how* it does it — and later, pay close attention to your conclusions and how you draw them.

Music: Hearing a poem's sounds and rhythms

We use the word *music* to mean the total of the sounds and rhythms in a poem. That means the rhymes, the chimes, the line endings, the pauses, just to name a few. But you don't have to know the labels to enjoy the sounds, any more than you have to know the number of a symphony to appreciate the music. (If you absolutely *have* to know the sound and rhythm jargon, we explain much of it in Chapter 3.)

Related to the *aural* (heard) music is the *visual rhythm* of the poem — how it looks, its shape, the line lengths, and the impact of all that word-sculpture on you.

The term *form* refers to the mode, shape, or structure in which a poem is written (ballad, sonnet, epic), its rhyme scheme (or lack of one), the way it sounds, and even the way a poem looks — its physical body. The way a poem *looks* is part of its message. Shape conveys feelings, just as sounds do. A poem written in bursts of brief lines strikes you differently from a poem that sprawls across the page in long lines.

In poetry, the form and the *content* (what the poem contains — images, message, viewpoint) are mixed up in each other. Form is content and content is form. Remember that as you read.

Here's a passage from W.S. Merwin's poem "Leviathan" with a lot of luscious music in it. This fact for free: It concerns a whale. Pay attention to the sounds and rhythms you hear as you read.

This is the black sea-brute bulling through wave-wrack,
Ancient as ocean's shifting hills, who in sea-toils
Travelling, who furrowing the salt acres
Heavily, his wake hoary behind him,
Shoulders spouting, the fist of his forehead
Over wastes gray-green crashing, among horses unbroken
From bellowing fields, past bone-wreck of vessels,
Tide-ruin, wash of lost bodies bobbing
No longer sought for, and islands of ice gleaming,
Who ravening the rank flood, wave-marshalling,
Overmastering the dark sea-marches, finds home
And harvest.

Do you feel the hugeness of the whale? If so, part of what's bringing that hugeness across is the poem's music, its sounds, its rolling rhythms. You can't really read these lines quickly. How quickly can you even say, "This is the black sea-brute bulling through wave-wrack"? The words force you to go slowly: The repeated *b*s and *r*s give your mouth a lot to do.

Read that first line again:

This is the black sea-brute bulling through wave-wrack

Your mouth is working like a whale's jaw in a squid school! And W.S. Merwin, one of America's most honored poets, wants it that way. He has put slow, solid, heavy music in there to weigh down the lines so you move like a . . . well, like a whale. The lines are *describing* a whale, but they're doing more: They're *embodying* a whale.

Music is never there only for its own sake. It can reinforce, represent, or even *be* the meaning of the poem. It's never just pretty, just window-dressing. Why not? Because poetry is *dense* (intense and compressed, like a really good cheesecake) and hasn't a syllable to spare.

Rhyme is an instrument that leads us to meanings as well. Here is "Nothing Gold Can Stay," by Robert Frost, a poet whose work has beckoned millions of readers with its descriptions of the New England way of life, its sensitive depictions of nature and the ways of the human beings Frost writes about.

Nature's first green is gold,
Her hardest hue to hold.
Her early leaf's a flower;
But only so an hour.
Then leaf subsides to leaf.
So Eden sank to grief,
So dawn goes down to day.
Nothing gold can stay.

How does Frost write this tiny poem, which doesn't seem to be much, and say what he manages to say? First, the lines are short, and they rhyme in *couplets* (pairs of lines). Each rhyme is part of the meaning. *Gold* is what nature can't seem to *hold* for very long. The *flower* of gold lasts only for an *hour,* reinforcing the message of the poem. And then the magic: Frost shifts from the *leaf,* which is what became of the flower, to Eden, the fall of humanity, and how things can't seem to stay at their best state for very long. He fits all of this in a tight, deceptively simple poem.

Rhythm can be *visual* (seen) as well as *aural* (heard). That's because poetry is as much sculpture as it is music. Poets build their poems in specific shapes for specific reasons, and those shapes become part of the poem's message and impact. A good example is Poem 15 from a series titled "A Coney Island of the Mind," by Lawrence Ferlinghetti, which is about poets themselves:

Constantly risking absurdity
                                  and death
        whenever he performs
                              above the heads
                                          of his audience
        the poet like an acrobat
                      climbs on rime
                                    to a high wire of his own making
        and balancing on eyebeams
                                above a sea of faces
              paces his way
                            to the other side of day
        performing entrechats
                          and sleight-of-foot tricks
        and other high theatrics
                            and all without mistaking
                      any thing
                                  for what it may not be

When reading this poem, slow down between lines, take your time, communicate Ferlinghetti's delicate, humorous tone. Notice the rhymes. And look up *entrechats* if you need to (we'll save you a step: it means an athletic ballet move in which the dancer leaps in the air and crosses his legs [or beats them together] several times).

You can apply the three levels of attention to the music of poetry as well:

- ✔ **Base-level attention:** What kind of music is there? Vowels? Consonants? Rhyme? Rhythms? Free verse? Do you see any interesting shapes?

- ✔ **Mid-level attention:** What is the music accomplishing? What's it doing in the poem? What are the big effects?

✔ **High-level attention:** This part is tricky but worth it. Ask, "What does the music add to the poem? How does the poem's form contribute to its content?"

Ferlinghetti's poem certainly does contain a lot of music. Read these lines aloud again:

> and balancing on eyebeams
>   above a sea of faces
>   paces his way
>   to the other side of day

In these few brief lines, you can notice the following based on the three levels of attention:

✔ **Base-level attention:** The lines have several long *a* and *i* sounds. And some very interesting shape-building is going on — the interspersed lines, the spaces between them, the lack of punctuation.

✔ **Mid-level attention:** Why the long *a* and long *i* sounds? Well, as a reader you have to guess. Perhaps to establish a little tension (the high-wire walker may fall any second). Or maybe to recall the sounds a crowd makes as a high-wire walker performs. As for the visual rhythms, the poet is said to be performing on a high wire, and the freewheeling lines, hanging mobile-like in the air, reinforce the risk and daring of it all.

In fact, Ferlinghetti once said that he was influenced by the artist Alexander Calder, who is famous for his many modernist mobiles. Ferlinghetti actually was trying to write word-mobiles!

✔ **High-level attention:** Now you get to balance on the high wire of your own imagination. How does this poem's form contribute to its content? The spacious, jagged arrangement of the lines recalls the height and depth and risk surrounding the poet, which reinforces the excitement (and a little of the fear) in the poet's heart, and the anticipation in the reader's heart, when a poem begins. And how is the poem's content reflected in its form? The poem's content is playful and profound at the same time. It's an example of the risk a poet takes each time he writes a poem.

Speculating as You Read

The trick about interpreting poetry is that most poems have different levels of meaning. There is a *literal* or *explicit* level, on which things are stated straight out, they happen, and no one can argue about it. In Robert Browning's poem "The Pied Piper of Hamelin," the guy with the pipe leads the kids out of town, and they're never seen or heard from again. That's the literal, explicit event in that poem, and if someone who has read the poem says, "No, he was playing a saxophone," or, "No, they all return as investment bankers," we can say, "Er, no. Says here they left and didn't come back."

But poetry has another world of meaning — one that isn't certain. You feel it and know it's there, but it takes some work to say *how* you know or exactly *what* you're feeling. So you *speculate* — you speak, not in certainties, but in a provisional way about what you *think* you see. You start from concrete evidence (that's crucial), but you soon branch out from that evidence to build *theories* to account for your feelings. When you speculate, you never know for sure if your interpretation is right, but you're building on clues and intuitions to make an educated guess.

People speculate constantly in their daily lives: They speculate about people, about love and courtship, about music. They interpret street signs: "ROAD WORK LANE ENDS 17 FT MERGE LEFT NOW." They interpret telephone schedules at hotels: "Local calls touch 8 plus area code plus local number. Hotel surcharge of $0.75 per call, for calls up to 20 minutes. $0.10 charge for each additional minute after the first 20 minutes (per call)." And poetry cries out for interpretation, too.

How do you know when an interpretation is "right"? Right answers sometimes do exist. (For example, if you said "Homer's *Iliad* is not set in 1956 Brooklyn," you'd be right.) But much of the time in the world of poetry, right answers either don't exist or aren't that interesting. So set aside the notion of "right" for a moment. Instead, think about interpretations that really say something useful, interpretations that are attentive to the poem. When coming up with an interpretation, shoot for an interpretation that is

- ✔ **Comprehensive:** It takes in as much of the poem as possible — its form; the speaker, theme, plot, problem, or character(s); the implications of the metaphors and figures of speech; the music (sound, rhythms, and so on); and visual aspects.

- ✔ **Accurate:** It tries to say nothing that is contradicted by something else in the poem, including its meaning, its form, or the historical and biographical facts surrounding the poem and its writer.

Mastering Three Steps to Interpretation

Some people think that when you're interpreting, you're trying to figure out what the poet intended in the poem. Others say that you can't ever be sure what the poet intended. But we recommend coming up with intelligent ways to account for the feelings the poem gives you when you read it. Try to explain what you think the poem is doing and how the poem does it.

When you interpret poetry, you do the same thing you do when you interpret anything:

✔ Understand the explicit, literal meaning.

✔ Consider what's implied, unsaid, or suggested — often by asking attentive questions about the poem.

✔ Build an interpretation based on your speculations about what's implied.

You may not take these steps in this order, and you may do some steps more times and other steps fewer, but all these steps are involved in the interpretation of poetry.

Understanding the literal

If the poem in front of you tells a story or seems to have a fairly explicit topic (one that's *given* to you), take note. A poem's literal meaning is its body, and you need to know it. That literal meaning, however, may be pretty complicated. But that's what's beautiful and worthwhile about poetry.

Here is the poem "Richard Cory," by Edward Arlington Robinson, one of the finest poets in U.S. history. Watch what the poem explicitly lays out for you.

Whenever Richard Cory went down town,
We people on the pavement looked at him:
He was a gentleman from sole to crown,
Clean favored, and imperially slim.

And he was always quietly arrayed,
And he was always human when he talked;
But still he fluttered pulses when he said,
"Good-morning," and he glittered when he walked.

And he was rich — yes, richer than a king —
And admirably schooled in every grace:
In fine, we thought that he was everything
To make us wish that we were in his place.

So on we worked, and waited for the light,
And went without the meat, and cursed the bread;
And Richard Cory, one calm summer night,
Went home and put a bullet through his head.

On the explicit or literal level, this poem tells the story of a high-class, rich, much-admired man who, contrary to all expectations, commits suicide. But that isn't all: The *speaker* in this poem, the voice telling it to us, is "We people on the pavement," and the people have a story, too, which Robinson explicitly lays out: They admire Richard Cory, they "wish that [they] were in his place," and they have lives filled with work and disappointment, which is fairly explicit in that line "went without the meat, and cursed the bread," an echo of a biblical image of misery.

Getting at what's implied

The literal part of a poem is important, but it's not all there is. Refer to "Richard Cory" by Edward Arlington Robinson in the preceding section. There's a further feeling in the poem, emanating from the words. The feeling isn't explicit, but it's pretty strong nevertheless.

When you have strong feelings as you read a poem, start *interrogating* the poem. Step back and ask global questions about things like setting, speaker, character, and situation:

- ✔ **Where does the poem take place?** In this poem, the setting is an American town.

- ✔ **What kind of town?** Some of the people are ordinary ("people on the pavement") and others aren't (Cory is "imperially" slim, which has overtones of royalty, picked up in the phrase "richer than a king").

- ✔ **What's the problem or conflict here?** The ordinary people wish they were like the richer, extraordinary ones. They find their lives hard and disappointing (implied in the phrase "went without the meat," as if meat were something they expected to have and didn't get, to be replaced by "bread," a second-best food that is "cursed"). Yet one of the extraordinary people, one of the most admired, kills himself. That gives you an unexpected, uneasy feeling, a feeling of surprise, of anxiety related to the workings of fate. Maybe you can identify a source for that feeling later.

You see some interesting things in "Richard Cory." The poem suggests a whole world of class divisions, based on wealth. Cory isn't a king, but he is *like* one. People look at him and think he's simply different, and they want to be in his place. Nowhere does the poem contain the phrase *class divisions* or *envy,* but you can feel these forces at work nevertheless.

Speculating on what's implied

In the previous two sections, we uncover many things that are *implied* or *suggested* in the poem "Richard Cory" by Edward Arlington Robinson. You're looking for ideas about class and social life in general. So you need to keep asking questions. What questions you ask depends on the poem. Often, you'll be asking about what isn't there, what doesn't happen, what is surprising or confusing.

For example, you may ask, "How well do the 'people of the pavement' know Richard Cory?" Not well, it seems. Almost all the adjectives describe his *outward* behavior and appearance. He glitters when he walks and is "admirably schooled." He is "imperially slim," "quietly arrayed," "human." The last two descriptions have a little overtone of surprise, as if the "people of the pavement" expect him to be a showoff in his dress and condescending when he speaks to them. Instead, he dresses "quietly" and speaks in a "human" way.

Maybe you feel less than satisfied with all this description. Ask yourself why. What *aren't* you getting here? Possibly this: None of these words really penetrate to Cory's personality or intimate concerns. Cory keeps to himself. He is civil to people but not self-revealing. He is known to be rich and have everything that everyone wants. And did you notice what you *aren't* told about him? He doesn't appear to work for a living. Somebody "schooled" him, but there is no mention of parents, a mate, children, or any emotion or love in his life. Cory's life is so apart from the other people that they can't guess what's going on inside him. They are concerned with their own hard lives, which arouse resentments in them. Meanwhile, Cory has a life that somehow leads to suicide.

The last line of the poem comes as a shock. And notice, the speaker doesn't say, "He shot himself." The speaker is more explicit, which increases the shock: Cory "put a bullet through his head" — a violent moment. In fact, the moment is *so* violent that you may want to go back over the poem looking for clues that led up to that point. And when you do, you realize that the poem gets *darker* as it goes on, until you reach the final stanza, with its working, cursing, and suicide. Cory is all the things that make the people wish they had his life and not their own. He is a reminder of the class system, a sign of everything these people want and can't get. Maybe they're looking at him not as a person, but as a symbol of what they want and can't have.

Many people have taken away this implication from "Richard Cory": All his riches couldn't buy happiness. This is a perfectly good moral to the story, if you're looking for one. But see how much more our *speculations* have revealed: the frustrations of class, the deceptive nature of social life, the way people can hide great suffering from others, the brute facts that we envy other people and sometimes hate our own lives. That speculation brings you a lot more than a simple moral to the story.

When interpreting poems, start with what's explicit. Then begin to consider what's suggested or implied and speculate on those suggestions. Try to build up an account of why you feel the way you do.

Good interpreters also watch out for the elements of poetry and take them into account when building interpretations. In the following sections, we discuss some of these elements of poetry, including subject, tone, language, music, and narrative elements, and how you can use them as clues when interpreting a poem.

Paying Attention to Subject and Tone

Your mind looks for certain things (like subject and tone) automatically when you're interpreting a poem. But you can help your interpretation along by being aware of them.

Searching for the subject

With the poem "Richard Cory" (earlier in this chapter), you can nominate any of several subjects: social life, class, alienation (the feeling of being apart from people). When you've said, "I think the subject of this poem is X," you now have a direction to take in your speculations — that is, what does the poem *do* with that subject? Where does the poem take it?

Some poems don't have subjects. Some are just wild howls of happiness or playful games with words. But it's hard to use words (even if they're flung all over the page) and not involve some aspect of the world and human life.

Tuning in to tone

Tone is the emotional atmosphere of the poem. Is it happy, sad, satirical, something else? Tone tells you a lot about the poet's feelings about the poem's subject and about his attitude toward the audience and life in general.

How do you figure out the tone of a poem? Watch your own responses. Many readers are obedient. If a poet says they should be happy, they'll be happy. If a poet is angry, readers will feel that anger as well.

The tone of "Richard Cory" (discussed earlier in this chapter) is *ironic*. How do we know that? In three ways:

- ✔ **Many readers get a fatal, surprised feeling, at the end of the poem.** This kind of feeling is a common response to irony.

- ✔ **The poem presents things that are contrary to expectation (one of the definitions of irony).** Readers see what the townspeople expect of Richard Cory and his very different reality. They assume that Cory is happier than they are — partly because they themselves are not happy. His suicide suggests that he is even *un*happier than they are — and that's ironic.

- ✔ **Readers may spot the trouble with Cory before the townspeople do.** They may realize that the townspeople assume that Cory is happy — but the poem gives readers little reason to think so. If you're paying attention, you may feel trouble far in advance of anyone else in the poem. That's called *dramatic irony,* in which the reader guesses a truth that the characters in a poem or story are unaware of.

Note, in the midst of the last, very eventful stanza, the "one calm summer night." This is even more irony. You may expect that a night of suicide somehow would be a violent night — but it isn't. The night of Cory's suicide recalls the "quiet" way he dressed and the "human" way he talked. Cory kept himself in reserve. There was no sign of trouble about him. And the night he kills himself is quiet as well.

How does all this irony help you interpret the poem? It makes you realize how little you know about people, how deceiving their exterior self-presentation may be. All may be quiet and calm on the surface but desperate and raging beneath. You realize the extent of human unhappiness — even in the midst of wealth. In the end, you get a profound sense of how human life works: The message is sad, but it is much larger than the scope of this short poem.

Looking at Language

Stay alert for symbols, metaphors, images, and surprising turns of speech as you read poems. These elements of language are all opportunities for interpretation, and you should take advantage of such opportunities when you find them.

In a graveyard, Hamlet lifts up the skull of Yorick, a jester who used to carry young Hamlet around on his back. That's a symbol, an invitation to *interpret:* Skulls often symbolize death or the passage of time, two things Hamlet is worried about.

When in "Coal," American poet Audre Lorde writes, "Some words live in my throat / breeding like adders," you see a metaphor (the words living in the throat) followed by a simile ("breeding *like* adders"). Right away, you can start to interpret: If a word "lives" in a throat, it grows, but maybe it never gets out, always stays in the throat, is never expressed. And the unpleasant image of snakes breeding — especially poisonous snakes like adders — suggests danger and ugliness. Connect that with never being expressed, and you may begin to think of the speaker as frustrated, angry, with dangerous things to say.

Listening to the Music in a Poem

Very often, a poem's music is a direct guide to interpretation. The music helps establish a poem's emotional weather.

First, listen to some smooth, ravishing music, from Alfred, Lord Tennyson's poem "Now Sleeps the Crimson Petal":

> Now sleeps the crimson petal, now the white;
> Nor waves the cypress in the palace walk;
> Nor winks the gold fin in the porphyry font.
> The firefly wakens; waken thou with me.

Tennyson's lines are liquid and whispery, with plenty of *s, l,* and *f* sounds. Those sounds are physical things and are partly responsible for the poem's impact on you. As the melody and harmony in a song spur certain feelings, so do the sounds in a poem. The setting is the fall of evening, and the speaker calls to someone else to wake up. If you feel as though Tennyson's lines are slow, quiet, perhaps sensuous, the whispering music can help you account for that feeling.

Rhythm, too, can be a clue to interpretation. Elizabethan poet John Donne's Holy Sonnet 14 begins with four lines that assault you with their insistent rhythms:

> Batter my heart, three-personed God; for You
> As yet but knock, breathe, shine, and seek to mend;
> That I may rise and stand, o'erthrow me, and bend
> Your force to break, blow, burn, and make me new.

The lines stop and start, as the speaker calls on God to intervene decisively in his life. You can connect this jerky rhythm with the speaker's agonized, desperate call. The rhythm is a strong clue to the speaker's emotional state.

Rhythm also informs these lines from Lucille Clifton. Listen as the words tumble forth from a speaker trying to explain her poetic gift:

> i don't know how to do
> what i do in the way
> that i do it. it happens
> despite me and i pretend
>
> to deserve it.
>
> but i don't know how to do it.
> only sometimes when
> something is singing
> i listen and so far
>
> i hear.

The rolling, tumbling lines lead you to feel the speaker's excitement at her gift for writing poetry. But notice the three strong *pauses* after the fourth, fifth, and ninth lines. (Pauses are part of rhythm, too!) That pause between "pretend" and "to deserve it" emphasizes the speaker's awareness that she *can't* deserve such a gift. It's a pause suggesting *humility*. She knows it may not be a permanent gift, as the pause between "so far" and "i hear" suggests. I hear *so far*, but it could change at any moment.

In traditional forms and free verse alike, you can use a poem's rhythms to figure out a poem's message, or at least your *reactions* to the poem.

Using Narrative Elements as You Interpret

Many poems tell a story, in which case, suddenly, all the aspects of narration — speaker, setting, situation, plot, and character among them — come into play.

Try paying attention to the narrative elements in this poem, "The Honey Bear," by Eileen Myles.

Billie Holiday was on the radio
I was standing in the kitchen
smoking my cigarette of this
pack I plan to finish tonight
last night of smoking youth.
I made a cup of this funny
kind of tea I've had hanging
around. A little too sweet
an odd mix. My only impulse
was to make it sweeter.
Ivy Anderson was singing
pretty late tonight
in my very bright kitchen.
I'm standing by the tub
feeling a little older
nearly thirty in my very
bright kitchen tonight.
I'm not a bad looking woman
I suppose   O it's very quiet
in my kitchen tonight   I'm squeezing
the plastic honey bear   a noodle
of honey dripping into the odd sweet
tea. It's pretty late
Honey bear's cover was loose
and somehow honey   dripping down
the bear's face   catching
in the crevices beneath
the bear's eyes   O very sad and sweet
I'm standing in my kitchen   O honey
I'm staring at the honey bear's face.

This poem certainly has a *speaker,* an "I" who makes the tea and tries to pour the honey into it. Whenever you see speakers, ask questions. What kind of person is this, and how do you know? You may see signs of loneliness (the repetition of the phrase "my very bright kitchen"), insecurity or perhaps self-mockery ("I'm not a bad-looking woman / I suppose"), dissatisfaction with herself.

The poem has a clear *setting* also — a bright kitchen in a woman's residence. Now, is this residence a house or an apartment? You may have a sense that her personal space is small. The tub is in the kitchen, so you can imagine it's a small place, maybe a studio apartment in a big city like New York.

The poem has at least two *allusions* as well — to Billie Holiday and Ivy Anderson, two great jazz singers of the mid-20th century. If you research those names — or even listen to some of their music — you'll see they often sang sad or bluesy songs, which may fit this scene.

The speaker is straightforward and conversational, which hides some clever metaphors. Note a few statements that could have more than one meaning. "It's pretty late" could refer to the time of night *or* the time in the speaker's life. And when the speaker tells you of her impulse "to make it sweeter," the word "it" could refer to the tea or to her life in a more general way. And "O honey" could be an exclamation at the potential mess she's making — or a call to an absent lover (or reader).

Ask, too, exactly how it is that the cover gets loose and honey "somehow" drips over the bear's face. Note the spaces in these lines:

> and somehow honey   dripping down
> the bear's face   catching

Those spaces suggest that you're watching the slow drip of the thick honey. Is the speaker being careful and attentive as she pours the honey? What may be distracting her? Consider her state of mind. Honey dripping all over the bear's face (What else drips down a face? How about tears?) may be a metaphor for the speaker's sadness and self-pity. It's a sweet sadness.

With this poem, as with any other, interpret by paying attention to what the poem says and your responses to it. And then the fun begins — building a bridge of speculation between the poet's words and suggestions and your reaction. Interpretation is the best part of reading poetry.

You may feel insecure at first, but you'll get to like the feeling. A good poem can be as sweet as a honey bear with the cover loose.

Chapter 5

Connecting with Poems from the Past

In This Chapter
▶ Getting the tools you need to understand older poetry
▶ Recognizing the importance of knowing about the poet's life and historical background
▶ Mastering unfamiliar language

*I*f you close your mind to all the great poetry written before your own time, you're missing out on a lot. And more important, you have only a *partial* idea of what poetry is. So why not be open to the poetry of all ages and peoples? Reaching out to the great poetry of the past is a fine way to educate yourself about the history of the human spirit. What you'll find, with just a little work, is that what's human is *always* interesting. Much of what's in ancient Sumerian, Hebrew, Greek, Egyptian, Chinese, and Indian poetry will speak to you. You'll have much to laugh and cry with in the poems of the Italian Renaissance and the English Romantic Period.

In this chapter, we offer guidelines on working with older poetry. After all, the 20th century represents only one of the 50 centuries from which we possess poetry, and each one of those centuries has wonderful things to offer. Keep an open mind, and you'll find greatness before you.

Gathering the Tools You Need

When reading poetry, try to have the following resources by your side:

- ✔ **Anthologies of literature.** Many publishers offer good anthologies of various cultures, periods, and genres. Historical surveys have good introductions and give background information on certain periods as well.

- ✔ **An encyclopedia.** You don't have to buy a set of multiple volumes; you can get an encyclopedia on CD-ROM or a one-volume book instead.

✔ **A good dictionary.** Many readers have both a modern dictionary and an *etymological* dictionary — one that traces the history of words. Both can come in handy when reading older poetry.

You may also want to have several of these helpmates nearby, especially if you want to dig a little deeper into the poems you read:

✔ **A dictionary of classical *allusions*,** references based on the literature and mythology of the ancient world.

✔ **A companion to literary study,** such as the *Oxford Companion to English Literature* or the *Cambridge History of Literature*.

✔ **A dictionary of poetic biography,** which offer short biographies of poets throughout the ages. One good example is the *Oxford Companion to Twentieth Century Poetry.*

What about the poet's times? What about his or her life? What about this unfamiliar language? We visit each of these questions separately in the following sections.

Facing the Challenges of Older Poetry

Older poetry poses special challenges for you in three areas, each of which we can state as a question for you, the reader:

✔ **Biographical background:** Who was this poet?

✔ **Historical context:** What was the world the poet lived in and referred to in his poems?

✔ **Language:** What are these unfamiliar words, allusions, and turns of phrase?

These are interesting questions for poetry of *any* period. So be methodical as you read. Before reading older poetry, till the field a little. Get to know the poet and his or her world. And dig for this kind of information every single time, because it always helps.

Discovering the historical context behind a poem

The more you find out about history and how it affects poetry, the more you'll become interested in it. And the more you'll probably want to discover. Kenneth Fields, a fine poet and teacher, is fond of telling his students that "poets and readers of poetry have to know more about more than ever before." Poetry is about life, and life includes lots of things: language, botany (have to know the names of those plants!), fashion (dost thou know what a *wimple* is? or a *buskin*? or *chopines, jodhpurs,* or *cravats*?), architecture (*naves, buttresses, Doric columns?),* mythology (Eros, meet Cupid; Zeus, meet Jove), science, and just about everything else.

When you read poetry of the past, you are reaching out to the past itself. So, when you're reading a piece of older poetry, find out immediately:

- ✔ **When the poem was written and when it was published.** The two dates could be quite different. Poems tend to be written at one time and not published until later — sometimes *much* later.

- ✔ **What was happening in the world when the poem was written.** This includes the historical currents, the politics, anything that could shed light on the poem. If you're reading some of Walt Whitman's Civil War poetry, reviewing what you know of the Civil War makes sense. If you're reading Dante's *Divine Comedy,* knowing the background of politics in Florence, Dante's native city-state, and why he was kicked out would make sense.

This information helps you appreciate the poem better, because poems are very much influenced by the times in which they're written.

Finding out about the poet

When reading older poetry, do everything you can to lessen the difference between you and the poet. You are likely to have less in common with a poet who wrote many years ago than you are with a poet of your own time. So because the poet you're reading can't make the introductions, reach out yourself and offer a hearty, "Howdy, neighbor!"

For example, if you're interested in reading one of Shakespeare's plays or a poem by Emily Dickinson, know the birth and death dates of these poets: Shakespeare, 1564–1616; Dickinson, 1830–1886. If the books you own don't already have good introductions to these poets and their lives, go out and find one at your local library — they'll be there.

When you do your research, you find out that Shakespeare was an Englishman of the Elizabethan and Jacobean era, that he moved from his provincial town of Stratford to London, that he was a playwright and a stock-holder in a theater company called The Globe. If you research Dickinson, you'll find that she lived in Amherst, Massachusetts, in the mid- to late-19th century, that she was well educated, she never married, she lived her whole life in her father's house, and she was somewhat reclusive (though a witty and passionate letter-writer) and a big reader.

When you're reading Shakespeare or Dickinson, you also need to know that both were Christians (rather original Christians) well-versed in their religion. A detail like that may explain why Hamlet hesitates to commit suicide (his life is pretty painful — why not end it all?), or why, at the end of Dickinson's poem "Because I Could Not Stop for Death," the "Horses' heads / Were toward Eternity." A Buddhist reader might be puzzled, but a Christian (or a reader prepared for Christianity by reading up) would feel some resonance.

Practicing what we preach

Here's a piece of older poetry, "To Lucasta, Going to the Wars," written by the 17th-century poet Richard Lovelace. Here's a tip: It's not Lucasta going to the wars — it's the speaker.

Tell me not, Sweet, I am unkind
That from the nunnery
Of thy chaste breast and quiet mind,
To war and arms I fly.

True, a new mistress now I chase,
The first foe in the field;
And with a stronger faith embrace
A sword, a horse, a shield.

Yet this inconstancy is such
As you too shall adore;
I could not love thee, Dear, so much,
Loved I not honor more.

The differences between the language of Lovelace and modern English are gentle and slight. *Tell me not* means *Don't tell me.* And *that* means *because* (as it still does sometimes today).

Now you have to rearrange words a little. In modern English, this would be, "Don't tell me, Sweet, that I am unkind because. . . ." Why? Look for the verb — there it is, at the end of the stanza. Now rearrange it: "Don't tell me, Sweet, that I am unkind because I fly." And you may already know that *fly* can mean *leave.* What is the speaker leaving? "The nunnery / Of your chaste breast and quiet mind." But what's a nunnery? *Nunnery* was a word with various meanings, including "an abode for nuns," or more generally, "a place of retreat." So he calls his beloved's "chaste breast and quiet mind" a place of retreat. *That's* what he's leaving to go to war. He's asking her not to call him unkind.

Nunnery may have rhymed with the word *fly* in 1649; or Lovelace may just be using a *sight rhyme* on the *y* in the two words.

In the next line, slide *I chase* next to *True,* and you'll get the thoroughly modern "True, I chase a new mistress now." The speaker is toying with the notion of war as his new beloved, so the "first foe in the field" is his new mistress. That's why you get "And with a stronger faith embrace" in line 7. "Stronger than what other faith?" you may ask. What other faith does the poem deal with? The faith between the speaker and his "Sweet." In leaving her and going to the wars, he (the poet pretends) is changing one faith (one pledge of love) for another. Now he loves his horse and shield more than his Sweet.

This, by the way, is called a *conceit* — a comparison that runs throughout the whole poem. Lovelace's conceit compares a man's faithfulness to a woman with his faithfulness to the demands of honor.

Look up *inconstancy* in line 9, and you'll find out it means *faithlessness*. The speaker is inconstant because he is leaving his human mistress for his new mistress of war. Yet he claims that his human mistress, too, will "adore" this inconstancy. Not many people like "inconstancy" in their lovers, so why would Lucasta? Lovelace, clever poet, has brought us right up against a paradox. The answer lies in the last two lines. "I could not love thee, Dear, so much" is easy. But the next line — "Loved I not honor more" — may seem confusing. *Loved I not* is the same as *If I didn't love* or *Unless I loved*. Now try it:

> I could not love you, Dear, so much,
> Unless I loved honor more.

The meaning is clever, and full of paradoxes. This little poem also measures the difference between Lovelace's world and the reader's. His speaker loves honor more than he loves his Sweet, and furthermore, he expects her to *adore* that fact. And, most likely, she would. After all, honor was the measure of a man in Lovelace's time. If he showed cowardice by not going to the wars, he wouldn't be worth loving. His love of honor is what gives value to his love of her. He expects her to know this, and to realize that he goes, partly, to *prove* that his love for her is worthwhile.

Taking it up a notch

After spending some time with this poem, you can see that it's a well-turned piece, with unexpected elements. But don't stop there. Reach out. Hit that encyclopedia and find out what was happening in England in 1649. You'll find out that "To Lucasta" was published at the end of the great Civil War in England (1641–1649), which overthrew King Charles I (he was beheaded) and led to rule by the Puritans (1649–1660). So war was *definitely* in the air.

Knowing something about the poet definitely pays off as well. Seek, and ye shall find that Lovelace was the son of a wealthy family in the county of Kent. He supported the King against the rebels, and he was indeed a brave soldier, being wounded, captured, imprisoned, and exiled. The sad thing is that Lovelace fought on the side of the King — and Lovelace's side lost. By the time he was released, he was a ruined man. This poem was published eight years before Lovelace's death.

Hit your friendly anthology or history of English literature, and you'll discover that Lovelace, as a poet, is said to belong to a group called the *Cavalier Poets,* who strove to write short, compressed poems of a glittering clarity — both of which "To Lucasta" certainly has.

And what can you make of the name Lucasta? There's a story even there. Lovelace was engaged to a woman named Lucy Sacheverell. His pet name for her was *Lux Casta,* which means "chaste light." (Aha! Remember "thy chaste breast"?) Alas, when a rumor got out that Lovelace had been killed, Lucy married someone else. While he was in prison, Lovelace wrote a series of poems to Lucy, giving her the name of Lucasta; this poem is one of them.

Now the poem has a great deal more meaning than it did when you first read it. You understand that Lovelace personally experienced the hardships of war and personally upheld the honor of which this poem speaks. At first, "Lucasta" may have appeared to be a slight poem — but now you see more tenderness, resolve, and nobility in it because you know that Lovelace suffered for his ideals.

Is this poem autobiographical? Apparently — but it also could stand for many men's departures for war. Its brevity, its elegance, its wit, and the burst of clarity at the end, are an affecting package. The extra work, we hope you agree, is more than worth it.

Know the poet, and you'll get to know the poem better.

Mastering unfamiliar language

Poets of the past write in the traditions of their times, which may differ from the traditions of our own time. They may also write in older language. And, because the *poets* aren't going to change, *we* must reach out to them and master their language as well as we can. This task usually isn't that difficult, and lots of nice people (known as editors) have done the work for you. Your book of Homer, Dante, Shakespeare, or Dickinson probably contains:

- ✔ **Introductions** written by the editors of these books, offering biographical information, historical background, and evaluations of the poets' work.

- ✔ **Glosses** (translations of unfamiliar words) in the margins.

- ✔ **Notes** either at the bottom of the page or in the back of the book. The notes explain historical or biographical issues arising in the text.

Use these guides well; they'll help you as you journey through the poem. If a note in the back of the book is interesting — for example, if you want to learn more about the English Civil War — follow your interests and read up on the subject. You may also consider taking a class to increase your mastery.

Older language poses three kinds of challenges: allusions, inversions, and vocabulary. In the following sections, we take a look at each.

Allusions: Have you heard the one about. . . .

Poets *allude* (make references) to things outside the poem all the time — things in the world, in history, in other literature, in popular culture, anything that will help them create metaphors or vivify their work. But they were then, and you are now, which means you have to do a little work to find out what their allusions are about and how they work.

Looking it up: When poets want you to do a little legwork

In his epic poem *Paradise Lost,* John Milton wanted his readers to feel the gentle sweetness of Adam's words to Eve. So he wrote that Adam spoke

> with voice
> Mild, as when *Zephyrus* on *Flora* breathes

A little research will tell you that *Zephyrus* is the Western wind, which blows in spring and brings long-dormant nature to life. *Flora* is the goddess of the world of flowers and plants; she often stands for flowers in general. The poem has, fittingly enough, a male god breathing on a female god. Adam breathes sweetly on Eve, and she comes to life — a gorgeous moment, and ambiguous, too, because of what happens later between Adam and Eve!

Tying one work to another

Allusions also can be shorthand for larger stories and contexts the poets' readers may know; they help set the material of the poem on a larger stage. Here's a passage from William Shakespeare's *The Merchant of Venice.* Lorenzo, a young Christian man from Venice, is wooing Jessica, who is a Jew and by law not allowed to marry him unless she converts to Christianity. It's a forbidden, thrilling love. Lorenzo says:

> The moon shines bright. In such a night as this,
> When the sweet wind did gently kiss the trees
> And they did make no noise, in such a night
> Troilus methinks mounted the Troyan walls
> And sigh'd his soul toward the Grecian tents,
> Where Cressid lay that night.

Shakespeare obviously thought his allusion to Troilus and Cressid would help his audience enjoy this moment between the two lovers. But *you* won't enjoy it until you find out who Troilus and Cressid are! Their names appear in many classical and mythological dictionaries. *Cressid* is the short form of the name *Cressida,* belonging to a widow living in the city of Troy during the Trojan War, which lasted nine years. The Greeks were attacking Troy because Paris, the son of Priam, King of Troy, had stolen Helen, the wife of Greek King Menelaus.

Cressida, in this story, falls in love with Troilus, a brave knight of Troy. They have a secret, passionate affair, all while the Trojan War grinds on. For the Renaissance, these two were the defining type of the passionate, doomed lovers. You think of Romeo and Juliet; the Renaissance audience thought of Troilus and Cressida.

At one point in the story, Troy trades Cressida to the Greeks, in return for some prisoners. Poor Troilus can't say anything about it. All he can do is pine away, after his beloved, whom he'll never see again. Why won't he? Ever heard of the Trojan horse? Troilus will die as his city falls, and Cressida will be taken away by the Greeks. Their story is awfully sad and beautiful. Geoffrey Chaucer wrote a wonderful poem (and Shakespeare an equally wonderful play) about it.

Now you can see why Lorenzo and Jessica, a Christian and a Jew, may see Troilus (a Trojan) and Cressida (now with the Greeks) as a fitting comparison. And, knowing the hopeless frustration of Troilus, you can sympathize and empathize more closely with Lorenzo as he pictures Troilus climbing the walls of Troy and sighing at the Greek tents where his beloved is being kept. Knowing this allusion makes this passage much richer and binds you more closely to the characters because you better understand their feelings — which is what allusions are supposed to do!

The same kind of reference to stories or characters from the past is happening in this, the first stanza of John Keats's "The Eve of St. Agnes":

> St. Agnes' Eve — Ah, bitter chill it was!
> The owl, for all his feathers, was a-cold;
> The hare limped trembling through the frozen grass,
> And silent was the flock in woolly fold:
> Numb were the Beadsman's fingers, while he told
> His rosary, and while his frosted breath,
> Like pious incense from a censer old,
> Seemed taking flight for heaven, without a death,
> Past the sweet Virgin's picture, while his prayers he saith.

After dealing with a few old-time turns of phrase — *a-cold* for *cold,* the inversion *censer old* for *old censer* (and you may look up *censer,* to find out that it is an implement of the Church from which incense is dispensed), and *saith* for *says* — you have three things to figure out: who St. Agnes is, what a beadsman is, and who the Virgin is.

Most books containing this poem will have a note telling you the following:

✔ **St. Agnes is a saint of the Roman Catholic Church.**

✔ **She was a martyr who died at age 13 in the fourth century A.D.**

✔ **Her feast day is January 21, so "St. Agnes' Eve" would be January 20, usually a fairly cold time.** That explains the trembling hare and the chilly owl.

✔ **St. Agnes was the patron saint of virgins.** If a virgin performed the correct rituals on St. Agnes's Eve, tradition had it, she would dream of the man she would marry. That may make St. Agnes a fairly popular saint.

The dictionary will tell you that a *beadsman* is a person paid to pray for someone else's soul. That's what this fellow is doing. The word *Virgin*, when capitalized, usually refers to Mary, the mother of Jesus Christ. She is often called the Blessed Virgin Mary, and it is her picture the beadsman's breath wafts past.

These references help set the stage for a superbly strange poem. You know the time of year in which the poem is set. And the mystical environment, of martyrs, incense, rosaries, and blessed virgins, is brought to intense life. See how important chasing down allusions can be?

Inversions: Confused you are?

Older poetry was comparatively forgiving when it came to word order. The *conventions* of the time (the generally agreed upon rules for writing poetry) allowed poets to bend sentences so they'd fit the poetic line. Consider this anonymous line from the English Renaissance:

My mind to me a kingdom is

Now, you may ask yourself, "Why didn't the poet just write, 'My mind is a kingdom to me'?" Excellent question. Here are a couple of answers:

✔ **The poet has chosen to write in *iambic tetrameter*, in which each line rolls out in four iambs.** An *iamb* is a rhythmic unit that goes duh-DUH, so four of them are duh-DUH, duh-DUH, duh-DUH, duh-DUH. The second line has no such regular rhythm: "My mind is a kingdom to me" rolls out duh-DUH duh-duh-DUH-DUH-duh-DUH. It's nice — and clear enough — but it won't fit the form.

✔ **The inversion allows the word *kingdom* to get a special stress, which the "straightened out" version doesn't have.**

✔ **You're dealing with differences in poetic taste and convention.** Renaissance readers apparently liked a little inversion. They found inversion a mark of the poet's ingenuity as a craftsman. A plain English line like "My mind is a kingdom to me" appeals to readers today, but it may not have struck many Renaissance readers as poetic.

Straightening out a phrase like "My mind to me a kingdom is" certainly isn't very difficult. Your mind to you not too twisted by it is — is it? That's about how hard it is to straighten out most inversions.

Vocabulary: Methinks thou doth protest too much

When languages change, vocabulary changes. New words are created (such as *Internet* or *wannabe*), old ones fall into disuse (like *rumble-seat*), and some words change meaning (the word *perspective* was used to mean *telescope* in Shakespeare's time). So older poetry in your own language may challenge you to uncover unfamiliar words — or older meanings of familiar ones — and create your own understanding of the poetry as you move along. Discovering new words makes reading a poem a little slower — but *much* more rewarding.

Three Steps to Reading Older Poetry

When you approach poems from the past, if you use the right tools, the poems open their worlds to you. We recommend three steps for reading older poetry. It's not necessarily a 1-2-3 affair — you can and will take these steps in any order, and repeat all of them as you get to know a poem. But they are phases in the process of understanding a poem from the past:

1. **Do a cold reading of the poem.**

   Sit down and read what's in front of you. Read it aloud (because poetry is meant to be read aloud). Reading aloud tends to slow you down (which is always good), revealing answers to quandaries and other difficulties.

2. **Translate the poem's meaning.**

   As you read the poem the first time, take into account any glosses or notes. What you're doing here is creating your own version of the poem, one you can understand. Translation involves three activities:

   • Mapping the poem: Here, you determine the parts you *do* understand and identify the parts you don't. We refer to the parts you don't understand as the *blanks*.

   • Filling in the blanks: When you've identified the words, phrases, or facts you need to uncover, go find the definitions, the information, the understanding, and apply what you find out to each blank in the poem until every blank is filled.

   • Creating your own version of the poem: You've made unfamiliar language familiar, and you've discovered enough about the poet's life and times to illuminate the poem. Now you un-invert the inversions and put unfamiliar material into your own words. *Note:* This is just an interim, provisional version. When you've created *this* version, you're better able to return to the original and experience it for itself.

3. **Reread the original aloud in its original form.**

   You now let the original words snap back into place, so to speak. Returning to the poem and rereading it in its original glory is crucial, because that, and only that, is the poem itself.

Here are six lines of Middle English poetry, from "Complaint to His Purse," written by Geoffrey Chaucer around 1400. Try reading the poem at one go.

> To you, my purs, and to noon other wight,
> Complaine I, for ye be my lady dere.
> I am so sory, now that ye be light,
> For certes, but if ye make me hevy cheere,
> Me were as lief be laid upon my beere;
> For which unto youre mercy thus I crye:
> Beeth hevy again, or elles moot I die.

When you map these lines more closely, you see that they contain exactly eight words a modern speaker probably couldn't figure out; the rest are simply spelled a little differently. If you "blank out" the passage (and replace unfamiliar spellings with modern-day ones), you might get:

> To you, my BLANK, and to BLANK other BLANK,
> Complain I, for you are my lady dear.
> I am so sorry, now that you are light,
> For BLANK, but if you make me heavy cheer,
> I were as BLANK be laid upon my BLANK;
> For which unto your mercy thus I cry:
> Be heavy again, or BLANK BLANK I die.

Not bad. Out of 57 words, you're probably unfamiliar with only 8. (***Note:*** We changed "ye be" to "you are.") Some of the blanks fill in fairly easily.

Chaucer's English was pronounced *very* differently from modern English. Mastering the pronunciation of older forms of language may require a teacher. What we're trying to do here is to help you piece together an understanding of the passage as well as we can.

You can navigate most of the first line with a little imagination. *Purs* is simply the word *purse* without an *e*. *Noon other* is just *no other* in a slight disguise. But what is *wight?* That's the first blank for which you may need a dictionary or some other help. And that's what we're here for: It means *man* or *person.*

You're halfway through, and here's what you have so far:

> To you, my purse, and to no other person
> I complain, for you are my lady dear.
> I am so sorry, now that you are light

Wouldn't *you* be sorry if your purse didn't have anything in it? Notice that the word *light* is being used playfully. The speaker is pretending his purse is his lady. In Chaucer's day, women were called "light" if they were unfaithful, promiscuous, or hurtful. And his purse, having nothing in it, is definitely causing him pain.

Look up *Certes,* and you'll find it means *Certainly* or *surely.* And *but if* means *unless:*

> For surely, unless you make me heavy cheer

Chaucer continues his fun with the light/heavy idea. The purse is light, causing him pain. So now he wants his purse to make him *heavy cheer* — cheer him up, so to speak, by getting heavier.

The next line — "Me were as lief be laid upon my beere" — is tough: You'll find that *Me were as lief be laid* means "I'd just as soon be laid," and *beere* is an unfamiliar spelling of the word *bier,* meaning the platform on which a coffin is laid for a funeral. In other words, unless his purse gets heavy, he'd just as soon die.

The next line is almost modern — "For which unto your mercy thus I crye." And the word *Beeth* means *Be.* It's a command, hurled pleadingly at his purse — "Be heavy again!" A little imagination may reveal that *elles* is our modern *else.* But *moot* is a tough one: It means *must.*

You've now made your own version of Chaucer's stanza:

> To you, my purse, and to no other person
> I complain, for you are my lady dear.
> I am so sorry, now that you are light,
> For surely, unless you make me heavy cheer,
> I'd just as soon be laid upon my bier,
> For which, unto your mercy now I cry:
> Be heavy again, or else I must die.

And you can more easily understand what the poem *says.* But the stanza you've created isn't Chaucer. It's *your* version of Chaucer (or the one we helped you create). Now, knowing his stanza much better, return to the original and reread it. Your understanding will (we hope) be much greater than it was after your initial reading.

If you reach out, you can connect with poets across many centuries. Cultivate your skills with older poetry, and the emotions, insights, and stories in that verse will strike you as fresh as this morning's news.

Part II
In the Beginning Was a Poem

"Stuart—would you like to come up and rap some Tennyson for us?"

In this part . . .

Here we take a look at poetry's history and heritage. Putting on our running shoes, we sprint through the 5,000 years of recorded poetry — taking you with us every step of the way. En route we discuss some of the most important movements and poets during each period and around the world. Our time travel ends in the 20th century with a discussion of ten important Modernist poets, as well as a glimpse at some of the movements that made this the Century of Poetry.

Chapter 6

An Intelligent Hustle through Poetic History: From the Earliest Poetry to the 1700s

- -

In This Chapter

▶ Identifying the different periods of poetry

▶ Knowing the great poets from each period

▶ Figuring out where to find great poetry from every era

- -

*I*n this chapter and the next, we tell the story of 5,000 years of poetry in about 7,000 words. In this chapter, we take on the first 4,700 years — a tough job, so we have to move fast. But we at least want to give you the general idea of where poetry has been and where it's going. We divided the past 5,000 years into 11 periods of poetry — somewhat of an arbitrary division, but one that helps explain where poetry has been and where it's going. We define each period and recommend some of the finest poets of each era.

Your assignment, should you choose to accept it: Pick one poet or poem mentioned in each era — and read! These writers were speaking to their own times, but they all have something to say to you today.

The Pre-Homeric Period (3,000 B.C.– 1,000 B.C.)

Some scholars say the oldest poetry was sung. Some think it grew out of religious rituals. Still others think it grew out of the work life. Whatever its source, poetry bore a close connection with music, an imprint it still bears today.

If you're interested in reading poetry from the Pre-Homeric Period, check out the following:

- *Ancient Egyptian Poetry and Prose,* edited by Adolf Erman, translated by Aylward M. Blackman
- *Gilgamesh: A New Rendering in English Verse,* translated by David Ferry
- *Gilgamesh: A Verse Narrative,* translated by Herbert Mason

Mesopotamian poetry

The earliest poetry we know of comes from around 5,000 years ago, from the Mesopotamian culture. The Mesopotamian people are the ones who invented cities, the wheel, the circular clock, and writing. They developed the *cuneiform script,* triangular indentations made in rolls of clay. Only in the last 150 years or so did we discover and learn to translate this poetry, which concerns mostly the gods and myths of the Mesopotamian people. These poems were probably already ancient when they were set down in writing, so you are seeing even further into the past than 3,000 B.C.

Mesopotamian poetry apparently was meant to be sung to a harp or a lyre. The earliest poet for whom we have a name is Enheduanna, high priestess of Nanna, the moon goddess of Mesopotamian religion. Enheduanna was a powerful, astonishing poet. Reading her words is exciting because they are the earliest we can trace (so far!) to a person with a name.

Here is a passage in which Enheduanna praises the daughter of Ishtar:

You are lofty like Heaven.   Let the world know!
You are wide like the earth.   Let the world know!
You devastate the rebellious land.   Let the world know!
You roar over the land.   Let the world know!

Listen for the songlike qualities — the repetitions ("You are . . . You are . . . You . . . You . . ."), the *parallelisms* (thoughts expressed in the same grammatical form, as "You are lofty . . .," "You are wide . . .," "You devastate . . .," and "You roar . . ."), the refrain ("Let the world know!"). Such clues suggest that this poetry may have been sung by bards or choirs.

The Greats: *Gilgamesh* is a series of epic tales about a real-life king who founds the city of Uruk. The two most famous episodes of this first of all epics concern Gilgamesh's descent into the underworld, in search of his dead friend Enkidu, and an episode in which the world is covered by a flood.

Egyptian poetry

The poets of ancient Egypt kept going for a long time. Their poetry (3100–30 B.C.) spans about three millennia, and it comes in many forms. It covers myths and gods and adds something new: personal poetry about attraction and courtship. Egyptian poetry is full of playful, flirtatious, desirous speakers longing for the objects of their affections, as in the following example:

> Only one, matchless sister,
> Prettier than anyone —
> Look: like the Star-Girl rising
> To begin a blessed year.
> Walks in the glow of her skin.
> Lovely eyes she looks through;
> Lovely lips she speaks with
> And not a word too much.
> Long neck, glowing
> Nipple, sapphire hair,
> Arms honey-gold;
> Her fingers, lotus blossoms;
> Firm midriff, dulcet bottom,
> Her legs a book of her beauty;
> Walks earth with pretty step
> And her hug snares my heart.
> Men turn their necks away,
> Dazzled with her countenance.
> Man who clasps her, happy
> As the richest, readiest boy.
> Watch her: she's going somewhere
> Like a goddess, the Only One.

The Greats: *The Book of the Dead,* a profound meditation on death and what happens afterward. Also the astonishing *Hymn to the Sun* by King Amenhotep IV.

The beginnings of poetry in India

Around 1,500 B.C., Sanskrit-writing scribes in what is now called India began to set down the Vedas, epic religious hymns concerning the deities and religious ideas of the Aryans, a tribe that invaded the Indian subcontinent around 2,000 B.C. These epics were called *Vedas,* from the word *veda,* meaning "knowledge." Over almost 1,000 years, a series of Vedas grew that became the great foundation of both Hinduism and the Buddhist tradition.

Mouth-to-mouth poetification

How did poetry get passed along before there was writing? By the human memory and the human voice. Folklorists and anthropologists call this process *oral transmission*. Poetic history is full of incredible feats of memory. The *Mahabharata,* the sacred epic of India, is perhaps the longest poem ever, yet it was not published until the 19th century, some 3,500 years after its composition! Millions of people simply *remembered* all or parts of it. To qualify for the position of scribe to some of the potentates of India, you had to be able to recite thousands of lines from the ancient Vedas by memory. Many scholars believe that several of the world's great epic poems — including *The Iliad* and *The Odyssey* by Homer, *The Song of Roland* (the French national epic), and *The Poem of the Cid* (the Spanish national epic) — were originally orally composed and passed along.

In the 19th century, two scholars heroically rescued orally-transmitted epics from oblivion. The Serbian epic known as *The Battle of Kosovo* memorializes a terrible battle on the Field of Blackbirds in 1389, when the Turks overwhelmed the Serbs. Thanks to Vuk Stefanovic Karadzic, who collected scraps and shards of the epic by interviewing monks, shepherds, and traditional singers known as *guslari,* the epic cycle was collected and published. The Finnish doctor and poet Elias Lönnrot roamed throughout Finland for 20 years, collecting remembered scraps of Finnish epic and lyric poetry, which he finally published as the *Kalevala* (1849).

There's still a lot of orally transmitted poetry in Asia, Africa, and elsewhere — even though some of it is printed, rap music is essentially an oral form. (And don't forget American Cowboy poetry, much of the earliest of which was sung on the range.) In the early 20th century, scholars discovered Balkan shepherds who were able to recite thousands of lines of poetry from memory while they tended their sheep — a clue to the way *The Odyssey* and much other great poetry survived the ages.

Here are a few lines from the Vedic account of creation:

There were no things;
There was no nothing;
There was no atmosphere
Nor the heavens beyond the air.
What was concealed?
Where was it hidden?
Who guarded it?
Was it hidden beneath the waters?
Was it the unfathomable deep?

The last and latest parts of the Vedas are called the *Aranyaka* and the *Upanishads.* Together, they are known as the *Vedanta* ("the end of the Veda"). The Vedas are the beginning and the bedrock of all Indian poetry.

Alongside the Vedas and probably just as old is the *Mahabharata*. The tales and precepts in this poem are the basis for Hinduism This vast epic concerns a war between the Kurus (forces of good) and the Pandus (forces of evil). (Yes, they're relatives.) All Indians know stories from the *Mahabharata*. It contains tales of the most familiar figures in ancient Indian mythology, including the god Vishnu, the creator/destroyer Shiva, and the hero Rama. Within this mega-epic are two super-epics:

  ✔ ***Bhagavad-Gita (Song of the Blessed One):*** Its main figures are the hero-warrior Arjuna and his chariot-driver, who is really the god Krishna. (Make sure you tip that man!)

  ✔ ***Ramayana:*** This epic tells the story of Rama, his wife Sita, and their battles against the forces of evil.

Sanskrit became the basis of Indian literature, philosophy, law, and culture. Poetry in Sanskrit was written for 2,500 years. Much poetry in Sanskrit is philosophical and scholarly, but there is some luscious love poetry as well and a strong tradition of poetry by women.

The Biblical/Homeric Period (1,000 B.C.–400 B.C.)

The poetry from the Biblical/Homeric Period is well-known around the world — but you may not have ever thought of it as poetry before. Read on to find out more.

If you're interested in reading more poetry from this era, check out the following books.

  ✔ The authorized King James Bible is the traditional source for the poetry of the Old Testament. Try to find an edition that renders the poetry in lines.

  ✔ *The Bhagavad-Gita,* translated by Juan Mascaró.

  ✔ *The Iliad,* by Homer, translated by Robert Fagles.

  ✔ *The Odyssey,* by Homer, translated by Robert Fagles.

  ✔ *The Psalms,* translated by Nicholas de Lange and edited by Peter Levi.

Biblical poetry

Poetry from this period, comprising maybe the best-known of all ancient poetry, makes up a good part of the Old Testament. This rich poetic culture was at its height for 600 years (1000–400 B.C.).

Most English-speaking people know the Psalms from the King James Bible. Here is a passage from the book called Ecclesiastes (3:1–5) or Koheleth.

> For everything there is a season
> > and a time for every matter under heaven:
> A time to be born, and a time to die;
> A time to plant, and a time to pluck up what is planted;
> A time to kill, and a time to heal;
> A time to break down, and a time to build up;
> A time to weep, and a time to laugh;
> A time to mourn, and a time to dance;
> A time to cast away stones,
> > And a time to gather stones together.

So *that's* where that song came from. . . .

Notice the sober grandeur, balance, and clarity of this passage. The grandeur comes through in the sweeping vision of so much of human life; you can feel the balance as the poet works with pairs of opposites (birth/death, planting/harvesting, killing/healing, and so on). And the clarity comes through in the simple, straightforward language. That's why so many readers have felt this passage resonates with truthfulness.

The Greats: Great philosophic poetry (in Ecclesiastes), religious tales (the Book of Job), prophetic books (Isaiah, Amos, Micah, and others), and beautiful erotic poetry (known as the Song of Songs or the Song of Solomon) are excellent examples of biblical poetry. The authorized King James Bible is the traditional source for the poetry of the Old Testament.

Homeric poetry

The word *Homeric* refers to Homer, traditionally supposed to be the author of *The Iliad* and *The Odyssey*. These two epic poems have been translated extremely well several times — never better than in the last 20 years — and they're works you should definitely add to your must-read list.

The Iliad is the story of the Trojan War. The Trojans and Greeks fight for nine years, until the episode of the Trojan horse, through which Troy is invaded and destroyed. *The Odyssey* (which has been called the best story of all time) tells of the postwar wanderings of Odysseus. He has a series of adventures with an unforgettable gallery of gods and magical beings. Meanwhile, his faithful wife, Penelope, waits for him at home on the island of Ithaca. You may prefer reading these works in school with the help of an instructor; or you may just want to look for a good translation and start reading yourself.

The Iliad is not just a war story. Each battle scene, each death is singular, with a pathos all its own — as in this one, in which an unlucky young soldier is felled by Agamemnon:

> Then wide-ruling Agamemnon ripped the spear
> From his hands, wrenched it away, wild as a lion,
> Struck the boy on the neck with his sword,
> Relaxed his limbs. So he fell there, slept a bronze sleep,
> Unlucky boy, far from his wedded wife
> Who helped the townspeople so, far from her
> Of whom he'd had no joy yet. Yet
> For her sake he had given up much.

In a few lines, you get a young man's life in the moment of his death.

The beginnings of Chinese poetry

Chinese history has been dominated by a series of dynasties, in which a single family has provided a line of rulers. The Zhou Dynasty (1066–256 B.C.) saw the first emergence of literature and culture in China. The first important anthologies of Chinese verse were in circulation around 500 B.C. China's first great poet, Ch'ü Yüan, emerged at this time. Tradition has it that he wrote *Nine Classic Songs* and the lovely lament *Li Sao (Falling into Trouble)*.

During what's known as the Eastern Zhou (770–256 B.C.), two great religious leaders/philosophers/poets emerged. The first was Lao Tzu (his name means "Old Master"), reputed founder of Taoism. The book known as the *Tao Te Ching* or *The Way of the Tao* is associated with him, although it may well be an anthology. Many of its compressed, poetic sayings resonate in the mind:

> Rule a large nation
> As you'd cook a small fish

You have to guess what he means. One good guess: Rulers should rule gently, with care, and not overdo it.

Confucius (Chinese name: K'ung Fu-tse) lived from 551 to 479 B.C. and became an important teacher, administrator, and jurist. He was also crucial for the history of Chinese poetry, because he collected and edited much of the ancient Chinese writings.

The Classical Period (750 B.C.– A.D. 476)

The term *classical* usually refers to the highpoints of Greek and Latin poetry. The story of these two great languages and cultures makes up a golden millennium in recorded history.

Check out the following books to read more from this period:

- *7 Greeks,* translated by Guy Davenport
- *The Aeneid,* by Virgil, translated by Robert Fitzgerald
- *Archaic Greek Poetry: An Anthology,* translated by Barbara Hughes Fowler
- *The Erotic Poems,* by Ovid, translated by Peter Green
- *The Essential Horace: Odes, Epodes, Satires, and Epistles,* translated by Burton Raffel
- *Metamorphoses,* by Ovid, translated by Rolfe Humphries
- *The Nature of Things,* by Lucretius, translated by Frank O. Copley
- *The Poems of Catullus,* translated by Peter Whigham
- *Sappho: A New Version,* translated and with an introduction by Willis Barnstone.
- *Seven Famous Greek Plays,* edited by Whitney J. Oates and Eugene O'Neill, Jr.

Greek poetry

Classical Greek poetry is a treasure-trove of good things. Many readers feel that the Greek poets, among the first poets in Western European history, set a standard for creativity and excellence that has yet to be equaled.

Lyric poets

The Greek lyric poets flourished for eight centuries. One of the earliest and best is Sappho, who lived around 600 B.C. Almost all that remains to us are fragments — bits of her poems quoted by later writers. In those fragments, we hear a fresh, direct, and almost contemporary voice.

Here, Sappho tells a woman she's in love with that she envies the man sitting next to her:

He is more than a hero

He is a god in my eyes —
the man who is allowed
to sit beside you — he

who listens intimately
to the sweet murmur of
your voice, the enticing

laughter that makes my own
heart beat fast. If I meet
you suddenly, I can't

speak — my tongue is broken;
a thin flame runs under
my skin; seeing nothing,

hearing only my own ears
drumming, I drip with sweat;
trembling shakes my body

and I turn paler than
dry grass. At such times
death isn't far from me

Magic, isn't it, to hear such a strong voice from 2,600 years ago?

The Greats: In addition to Sappho, other luminous lyric poets of this period include Anacreon, Pindar, Theocritus, Callimachus, and many others.

Dramatists

The Greek dramatists wrote their plays in verse so powerful that the plays of Sophocles *(Oedipus Rex; Antigone; The Trojan Women)*, Aeschylus *(The Oresteia Trilogy)*, Euripides *(The Bacchae; Medea)*, and Aristophanes *(Lysistrata; The Frogs)* are still being produced today. If you ever have the opportunity to see any of these plays performed, take advantage of it.

Latin poetry

One of the towering presences in classical Latin poetry is Virgil, who wrote *The Aeneid* (very much a Roman version of *The Odyssey*), as well as philosophical poems about farming (the *Georgics*) and herding sheep (the *Eclogues*). Many fine translations of *The Aeneid* exist.

Another great epic poet is Lucretius, who wrote *On the Nature of Things*, a wild and wildly beautiful philosophical poem that seeks to explain everything from the gods to vision to human history.

Latin, unlike Greek, was not a language naturally given to beauty or delicacy. It was given to sentences like "the farmer and his wife have bought the horses" or "the walls of the city soon were destroyed by Caesar's brave men."

Yet Latin lyric poetry is a wonderful thing. Three poets in particular are worth your attention:

- ✔ **Catullus:** He wrote poetry to his beloved Lesbia.

- ✔ **Horace:** Horace was perhaps the greatest of all Latin lyricists and wrote a wide range of philosophical, erotic, and descriptive poetry.

- ✔ **Ovid:** His *Metamorphoses* tries to explain the universe as a place of endless transformations. Ovid's erotic poetry (the *Amores,* the *Book of Love,* and others) is some of the best out there, in our humble opinion.

The poetry of India

The Gupta Empire (A.D. 322–550) is sometimes called the "Golden Age of India." It spread across northern India and involved a revival of Hinduism and the establishment of standards for literature and art. Among the most famous poets of this era is Kalidasa, who wrote plays and poems still performed today.

Dark and Golden Ages (A.D. 476–1000)

The Roman Empire began to crumble a few centuries into the Christian era, and the Goths, Visigoths, Ostrogoths, Lombards, and everyone else except the Green Bay Packers overran the Romans, leading to a period known as the *Dark Ages* in Europe. Much good poetry was written in this era; in Europe, most of that poetry was in Latin. The era was anything but dark, however, for poetry in the Middle East and Asia. This period witnessed golden ages in Japanese and Chinese verse, as well as a poetic Renaissance in Arabic verse.

If you're interested in reading more poetry from the Dark Ages and Golden Ages, check out any of the following:

- ✔ *Beowulf,* translated by Seamus Heaney

- ✔ *Beowulf and Other Old English Poems,* translated by Constance B. Hieatt

- ✔ *Ten Thousand Leaves: Love Poems from the Manyoshu,* translated by Harold Wright

- ✔ *Three Chinese Poets: Translations of Poems by Wang Wei, Li Bai, and Du Fu,* translated by Vikram Seth
- ✔ *Classical Arabic Poetry,* translated by Charles Greville Tuetey

The Manyoshu and Japanese poetry

Japan saw two great ages of poetry and two great anthologies: the *Manyoshu,* which includes the work of Kakinomoto Hitomaro and Yamanoe Okura, and the *Kokinshu,* which includes the work of Ono no Komachi — one of the best female poets in history — and Ariwara Narihira.

The *Manyoshu* contains some of the finest love poetry in history. It's also a wonderful document of a thriving poetic culture. Schools of verse arose. Poetic competitions, something like the contemporary slams (see Chapter 12 for more information), were established, complete with prizes and revered poets as judges. Groups of poets wrote cycles of poetry together, including the playful tanka chain, an intricate braid of poems in which poets responded to one another's work. In this era, the long Japanese tradition of poetry by women reached the first of many high points.

This anonymous poem from the *Manyoshu,* written in the voice of a mother whose son is going on a journey, gives some idea of the delicate depth of Japanese poetry of this period:

> If snow falls on the far field
> where travelers
> spend the night,
> I ask you, cranes,
> to warm my child in your wings.

The *Manyoshu* is still widely considered to be the apex of classical Japanese verse.

Arabic poetry

Arabic poetry was vital even before the advent of Islam. Around A.D. 550, Imr El-Qais, "The Wandering King," wrote his influential odes in the anthology *Mu'allaqah (Necklace-Beads).* Here are a few lines of his, from "The Great Ode," one of the earliest and most famous of all Arabic poems. The speaker, torn with love for a woman, watches her pack up to leave and realizes it's hopeless:

Here was the place I watched her
Load her camels for going. Here, by thorn trees
Was I stung, tears as bitter as colocynth.

Two friends waited, already swaying on camelback.
Man — they called to me — don't let this grief kill you.
Better to bear with patience what pain may come.

Colocynth is a bitter fruit with an appearance somewhat like watermelon. It's used as a purgative.

With the establishment of Islam, Arabic became a transnational language of poetry, law, religion, and culture from the Middle East to Asia. Muhammad (A.D. 570–632) was the prophet and founder of Islam. The holy book of Islam, the Koran, is filled with sacred poetry. It is the basis for much Islamic law and life.

The golden age for classical Arabic poetry spanned 600 years (A.D. 600 to 1200). At its height, it was being written from Spain to India. The great poets' verses have become sayings and idioms far and wide. The written poem is often considered an artwork in and of itself. Many are the verses of intense desire, the desert landscapes, the laments for great kings and fallen warriors.

Two great poets of the early Islamic era are Umar Ibn Abi Rabiah and Al-Khansa, the major female poet in classical Arabic. During the dynasty of the Ummayad caliphs in Damascus, Syria (A.D. 661–750), Arabic poetry reached new heights; during this period, the *ghazal* (pronounced *guzzle*) was introduced. This playful, sensuous verse form, excellent for love poetry and mystical poetry, spread throughout the Middle East and Asia, and today it is practiced all over the world.

During the dynasty of the Abbasids, centered in Baghdad (A.D. 750–1055), Arab poets encountered the influences of Greek, Roman, and Persian poetry. Great poets included Al-Mutanabbi and the Syrian poet Abū-l-`Alā' al-Ma'arrī. One of the great poets of the "golden age" of Arabic verse was Muhammad ibn Ghalib al-Rusafi (who died in 1177), still one of the most popular of all poets in the Arab world. Ghalib was a master of the *ghazal.*

Po' Li Po

The famous Chinese T'ang poet Li Po (A.D. 701–762) lived a life of carefree wandering and spontaneity. He was said to embody the Taoist and Zen ideal of *wu-wei* (literally, "doing nothing"). A self-proclaimed kinsman of imperial princes, he was at one time appointed as a court poet to the emperor, but he lost his position because of his wild, drunken behavior. Yet he wrote surprisingly insightful, highly imaginative poems during his drunken bouts. He wrote often of longing and nature: The moon appears in over a third of his poems. As irony and (some might say) poetic justice would have it, Li Po drowned one evening when he fell out of a boat. He was trying to embrace the moon.

China: The T'ang Dynasty

The T'ang Dynasty (A.D. 618–907) was the setting for what's known as the "golden age" of Chinese poetry. Tu Fu is one the best-known poets in the world, as are Li Po, Wang Wei, Po Chü-i, and Li Ho. The emperor Xuan Zong was a great patron of poets.

Other fine poetry was written in the Han, Sung, and Ming dynasties.

Old English

What people now refer to as *Old English* (also known as *Anglo-Saxon*) first appeared in anonymous stone inscriptions from around the 600s. Most of this poetry is anonymous.

Beowulf, an epic, is one of the finest poems you can find. It tells the tale of a warrior, Beowulf, and his showdowns with a series of monsters. The most famous of these is Grendel, who has the bad luck to get into Beowulf's clutches. Old English verse was *alliterative,* that is, it was based on repetition of initial consonant sounds. Here, the first two half-lines repeat the initial *s* sound, the second line has two *m* sounds in it, and so forth.

Soon he saw   — that shepherd of sorrows —
that he'd never met   in all middle-earth,
all ways of the world,   a warrior who wielded
a grip this grievous,   so strong he groaned
in frenzy, fear,   no breaking free.
He hurt to be home   flee to his hideout,
lair of devils —   but no such doings
as he'd done before   in olden days!

The period also produced shorter poems, such as "Caedmon's Hymn," "The Battle of Maldon," "The Wife's Lament," "The Wanderer," and "The Dream of the Rood." The riddle was another favorite form for Old English poets.

The Middle Ages (1000–1450)

The Middle Ages was dominated, in Europe, by the Catholic Church and its official language, Latin. Yet it was during this period that European poets began to write extensively in their native languages. The modern European languages all had their beginning (as literary languages, anyway) during this time.

French got up and running with the epic battle poem *The Song of Roland.* German produced both courtly love poetry and chivalric romances such as *Parzifal* and *Tristan und Isolde.*

Courtly love poetry concerned personal love and was written by and for people belonging to the courts of kings and nobles. Some scholars believe that the love poetry of the 12th century — especially that of the Provençal poets, such as Bertran de Born and Arnaut Daniel — may have helped create our very concept of love as it is now known and practiced.

The chivalric romances were tales of knights and their kings and damsels. They spread throughout all the languages of Europe, and they gave us the tales of King Arthur and the Round Table.

Italian had a true golden age, with the lyric poetry of Petrarch. And perhaps the finest poet of the age, Dante, wrote *The Divine Comedy.* In this epic religious poem, the speaker finds his way into a guided tour through Hell, Purgatory, and Paradise:

> In the midst of the road of our lives,
> I found myself on a darkened path
>> With the right way lost.
> Ah! It is so hard to say how savage
> And bitter and rough that road was
>> That as I think of it, the fear returns.

In English, Geoffrey Chaucer wrote *The Canterbury Tales* and *Troilus and Criseyde.*

In the Middle East, this era was the highpoint of Arabic and Persian poetry, including the work of Omar Khayyam, Rumi, and Hafez in Persian, and Ghalib in Arabic verse.

A special word on the *The Rubaiyat* of Omar Khayyam. Its English translation by the Victorian writer Edward FitzGerald contains four lines that are among the most famous in English:

> A Book of Verses underneath the Bough,
> A Jug of Wine, a Loaf of Bread — and Thou
>> Beside me singing in the Wilderness —
> O, Wilderness were Paradise enow!

FitzGerald's translation started a wave of new interest in Persian verse — a wave still flowing today.

In China, the Sung Dynasty (960–1280) ushered in a great era of innovation in forms and styles. One of the finest of Sung poets is Hsin Ch'i-chi.

In Japan, one of the masterpieces of world literature, *Monogatari* or *Tales of Genji,* was written by Lady Murasaki Shikibu. Not only is *Tales of Genji* one of the earliest novels in history — but also it included a great deal of influential poetry. *Genji* inspired the long tradition of occasional journals — in both prose and poetry — kept by women. As a craze, it lasted for 200 years, but the poetic journal is still practiced today.

Another great anthology of Japanese verse, the *Shin Kokinshu,* appeared in 1265. In the 1300s, the great dramatic tradition of the Noh play began.

The Greats: *The Song of Roland; The Poem of the Cid;* the Nibelung cycle; *Tristan und Isolde; Parzifal;* Bertran de Born, Arnaut Daniel, Walther von der Vogelweide, Giovanni Boccaccio; Francesco Petrarca; Dante; Geoffrey Chaucer, Omar Khayyam, Rumi, Hafez, and Ghalib.

If you want to read more from this era, turn to any of the following:

- ✔ *The Canterbury Tales,* by Geoffrey Chaucer, translated by Nevill Coghill
- ✔ *The Inferno of Dante: A New Verse Translation,* translated by Robert Pinsky
- ✔ *Lyrics of the Troubadours and Trouvères: An Anthology and a History,* translated by Frederick Goldin
- ✔ *The Nibelungenlied,* translated by A.T. Hatto
- ✔ *The Rubaiyat,* by Omar Khayyam, translated by Edward FitzGerald
- ✔ *Selections from the Canzoniere and Other Works,* by Francesco Petrarca, translated by Mark Musa
- ✔ *The Song of Roland,* translated by Patricia Terry
- ✔ *The Tale of Genji,* by Lady Murasaki Shikibu, translated by Arthur Waley
- ✔ *Tristan,* by Gottfried von Strassburg, translated by A.T. Hatto

The Renaissance (1450–1674)

The *Renaissance* (French for "rebirth") was a period of rebirth of interest in the Greek and Latin writers, and an explosion of knowledge in the arts and sciences. The Renaissance started in Italy, moved to France, and worked its way northward. In Italy, great epic poems emerged, as well as many fine lyric poets, including Michelangelo himself. In Spain, an incredible period of dramatic poetry, or plays in verse, started up in the 16th century. Lope de Vega is probably the best known poet from that period. The great French dramatic poems were written in the 17th century by Racine, Corneille, and Molière.

Here are some books worth consulting for a taste of the Renaissance:

- *Edmund Spenser's Poetry,* 3rd Edition, edited by Hugh Maclean and Ann Lake Prescott

- *Elizabethan Drama: Eight Plays,* edited by John Gassner and William Green

- *English Renaissance Poetry: A Collection of Shorter Poems from Skelton to Jonson,* edited by John Williams

- *Le Cid,* by Pierre Corneille, translated by Vincent Cheng

- *Life Is a Dream and Other Spanish Classics,* edited by Eric Bentley, translated by Roy Campbell

- *Phaedra: Tragedy in Five Acts, 1677,* by Jean Racine, translated by Richard Wilbur

- *The Portable Milton,* edited by Douglas Bush

- *The Riverside Shakespeare,* 2nd Edition, edited by G. Blakemore Evans

- *The Sonnets,* by William Shakespeare

- *Tartuffe: Comedy in Five Acts, 1669,* by Molière, translated by Richard Wilbur

The English Renaissance

The English Renaissance brought the world such writers as Shakespeare and Sir Walter Raleigh, but at least 30 or 40 other first-rank poets were working in England as well, many of whom were very good playwrights, too. Dramatic, lyric, epic, and historical poetry all flourished. Many of the poetic forms we find most familiar today became firmly established among English poets. *Blank verse* (unrhymed iambic pentameter) was the form in which Shakespeare and many of his fellow dramatists wrote their plays. Ballad forms were used both in folk poetry and in the songs and madrigals so popular at the time. And the sonnet was an international craze; poets wrote tens of thousands of them in most of the major European languages.

The Greats: The Renaissance produced so many great poets that we can't possibly list them all here. If you want to get a true feel for the Renaissance, read Shakespeare, as well as the poetry of Sir Philip Sidney, Edmund Spenser, John Donne, Ben Jonson, and George Herbert. The highpoint and end of the English Renaissance was John Milton's *Paradise Lost,* a vast religious epic. You could fill a good-sized bookstore with the great dramatic poetry of the period. Try Christopher Marlowe's *Faust;* Shakespeare's *Romeo and Juliet, Hamlet,* or *The Tempest;* Ben Jonson's *Volpone;* Pedro Calderón de la Barca's *Life Is a Dream;* Pierre Corneille's *Le Cid;* Jean Racine's *Phèdre;* and Molière's *The Misanthrope.* And even with all that, you've only just gotten started.

Renaissance poetry around the world

Across the Atlantic, people were writing poetry in the English colonies of North America, including Mistress Anne Bradstreet (1612–1672), who published her first book of forthright, charming poems in 1650. She thus became the first published "American poet." In "A Letter to her Husband, absent upon Publick Employment," she compares their union to that of turtle-doves or the fish called mullets:

> Together at one Tree, oh let us brouze,
> And like two Turtles roost within one house,
> And like the Mullets in one River glide,
> Let's still remain but one, till death divide.

Bradstreet's fresh directness — a way of turning the ordinary experience of household, family, and self into poetry — foretold the future of American verse. She began a line of American women poets that would include, among many others, Emily Dickinson and Sylvia Plath.

As for South America, before the Spanish and Portuguese conquerors overran the continent, immemorial poetic cultures already were in full flower. In what is now Guatemala, the Quiche Mayans compiled the *Popul Vuh,* an account of the history of the Mayans from the creation of the world to the year 1550. Defeat and genocide inspired some beautiful poems, including those of the 16th-century Mayan text known as *Chilam Balam:*

> Before the conquerors came
> there was no sin,
> no sickness, no aches,
> no fevers, no pox.
> The foreigners stood
> the world on its head,
> made day become night.
> There were no longer
> any lucky days
> after they came into our lands.

A great deal of Spanish American poetry meditates on the pre-Columbian, the mysteries and wisdoms of indigenous peoples. From Mexico to Brazil, the facts of a violent colonial past, along with the rainforest and the jungle, are still realities in poetry today.

This period was a crucial one for poetry in India. The Mughal Empire (1526–1857) not only spread Islam throughout the subcontinent but also introduced Arabic and Persian poetry, which had a huge impact on poetry in several languages.

Japanese poetry saw the birth of one of its greatest practitioners during this period. Matsuo Basho (1644–1694) became a recognized master of the form known as the haiku. He became a celebrated teacher and judge of poetry, and his poetic journals, interspersing prose commentary with wonderful haiku, remains a favorite throughout the world.

The 18th Century

The Renaissance's span of 200 years encompassed rapid changes in the way poets in Europe thought and wrote. The 18th century was dominated by an intellectual movement known as the *Enlightenment* — so named because people were placing greater and greater confidence in the power of human reason to improve life and discover the truths of nature. As of 1700, the age of science and technology had just begun. The Industrial Revolution was ahead, as was the American Revolution, the world wars, the Internet age, and much else. Poetry benefited from all these developments, and poets developed new ways to express life in their changing circumstances.

Some readers think that, coming between the vastness of the Renaissance and the brilliance of the Romantic era, Enlightenment poetry is a disappointment. Not so! We like the stateliness and balance of the poetry of the Enlightenment.

Listen to these lovely couplets from Alexander Pope's *Essay on Criticism,* a long poem on how to form judgments about poetry. He's recommending that the first thing any poet (or critic of poets) should do is be awake to Nature:

> First follow Nature, and your judgment frame
> By her just standard, which is still the same;
> Unerring Nature, still divinely bright,
> One clear, unchanged, and universal light,
> Life, force, and beauty must to all impart,
> At once the source, and end, and test of art.

You can feel the Enlightenment's quest for clarity and perfection in verse. The form here is rhymed couplets, very stately, very regular. Enlightenment poets shared the Englightenment faith that clear-sightedness and reason could lead to a new era of understanding. That's the "universal light" provided here by Nature — it's the truth itself. Both poets and scientists alike strove toward that light in this era.

In Japan, the haiku tradition was upheld by two of the very greatest of poets, Yosa Buson and Issa Kobayashi.

The Greats: In addition to the poets and poems already mentioned, the poetry of the Irishman Jonathan Swift (the same man who wrote *Gulliver's Travels*), the poetry of Samuel Johnson, John Dryden, and Alexander Pope, and the satires of France's Voltaire are all standouts of the Enlightenment.

For more poems from the Enlightenment, check out the following books:

- ✔ *The Norton Anthology of English Literature, Volume 1,* edited by M.H. Abrams

- ✔ *The Essential Haiku: Versions of Basho, Buson, and Issa,* translated by Robert Hass

Chapter 7

An Intelligent Hustle through Poetic History: The 19th Century to the Present

- -

In This Chapter

▶ Identifying the different periods of poetry from 1800 to the present

▶ Knowing the great poets from each period

▶ Figuring out where to find great poetry from every era

- -

*I*n this chapter, we follow the amazing story of poetry through Romanticism, Symbolism, Modernism, and Postmodernism, and touch down lightly at the present moment. We define each period and recommend some of the finest poets of each era. With all the excitement packed into three centuries, the most recent 300 years of poetic history is just about a match for the preceding 4,700!

The 19th Century

This century saw the Industrial Revolution reach full throttle, bringing great strides in technology, creating great wealth and great poverty, and introducing many social and political changes across the world. Poetry, too, was changing rapidly. Three developments especially marked this eventful poetic century: Romanticism, Symbolism, and the beginning of modern American poetry.

The Romantic Period

Some readers get confused by the term *Romantic*. People in the Romantic period weren't any more inclined to love than those who lived in other periods. The word *Romantic* came to mean a new, often revolutionary outlook, emphasizing the importance of personal emotions, the inspiration of the artist, innovation in ideas and the arts, the feeling of new beginnings, and unity with nature (which in some writers almost became a religion). Some of these developments came about as a reaction to the industrial revolution.

The Romantic era is one of the three or four greatest periods in the history of poetry. In Europe especially, poetry was the most-read literary form. Several novels in verse, including *Don Juan* (by English poet George Gordon, Lord Byron) and *Eugene Onegin* (by the Russian poet Alexander Pushkin) were international bestsellers. But the real poetry of the era was lyric poetry, personal, intense, titanic. When many people think of the image of The Poet, they're thinking of Romantic poets and poetry.

One of the great geniuses of this age, or any age, was Johann Wolfgang von Goethe. As a poet, playwright, novelist, philosopher, and politician, he helped create and sustain the notion of Romanticism and of the Romantic poet. His ideas about nature, the emotions, the soul, and the importance of poetry found their way into poetry all across Europe. Goethe was very prolific, and his lyric poetry fills volumes. Perhaps his best-known work is his monumental verse drama *Faust* (1808).

As with Shakespeare in English, so with Pushkin in Russian. Almost every Russian can recite some Pushkin. He was a true innovator of the Romantic school, a fiery Byronic figure just as good at love poems as he was at vast epic tapestries. And he had a great ear for the music of the Russian language.

Pushkin's *Eugene Onegin* is one of the most successful of all tales told in poetry; it was and is an international success. The tale is unforgettable yet puzzling: Eugene, the main character, is by turns admirable and frustrating. Tatyana, the girl who loves him, is the type of romantic heroine doomed by love. Pushkin wrote several verse tales, as well as important verse drama, including the historic *Boris Godunov,* a sort of ethnic creation myth for the Russian people.

In the British isles, Romanticism brought in a rush of fresh, visionary poetry. Some of the names of this poetic explosion include Scotland's Robert Burns and England's William Blake, Samuel Taylor Coleridge, William Wordsworth, John Keats, George Gordon, Lord Byron, and Percy Bysshe Shelley. Each of these poets had his own voice, but there was an energy in common, a new vision of the universe and humanity's place in it, a revolutionary fervor, a feeling of new beginnings.

Here's "Love's Philosophy" by Shelley. Watch how he moves from a joyful vision of all creation as one — and focuses down to his own interests:

> The fountains mingle with the river
>   And the rivers with the Ocean,
> The winds of Heaven mix for ever
>   With a sweet emotion;
> Nothing in the world is single;
>   All things by a law divine
> In one spirit meet and mingle.
>   Why not I with thine? —

The gusty pleasure of this verse, the way the poet connects the joy in nature with his own desires — that's a Romantic moment.

The Romantic period brought about a revolution in the kind of language poets used. England's Wordsworth and Germany's Friedrich Schiller, among many others, sought simpler, more direct language. The ode — passionate, serious, elaborate, meditating on nature as a way to explore the soul of the poet — was perhaps the era's most characteristic verse form. Because of the emphasis on sincerity and emotion, *lyric poems* — shorter, often songlike poems usually of a personal nature (what most people today think of when they think of poetry) — became the dominant genre and have remained that way. Sonnets were widely written for the first time since the Elizabethan period (the time of Shakespeare); epics, when written at all, tended toward personal subjects rather than public events.

The Greats: The Romantic standouts include lyric poetry by the German poet Johann Wolfgang von Goethe and other German Romantics, including Friedrich Hölderlin, Friedrich Schiller, and Heinrich Heine; the plays, verse novels, and lyric poetry of Russia's Alexander Pushkin; Victor Hugo, the huge presence in French Romantic poetry; Giacomo Leopardi of Italy; Robert Burns of Scotland; the English Romantic poets, including William Blake *(Songs of Innocence and Experience),* William Wordsworth, Samuel Taylor Coleridge ("Kubla Khan," "Rime of the Ancient Mariner"), John Keats ("Eve of St. Agnes," "Ode on a Grecian Urn"), Percy Bysshe Shelley, and Byron.

To read more Romantic poetry, check out the following:

- ✔ *Don Juan,* by George Gordon, Lord Byron, edited by Leslie A. Marchand

- ✔ *Eugene Onegin: A Novel in Verse,* by Aleksandr Pushkin, translated by Vladimir Nabokov

- ✔ *Faust: A Tragedy,* by Johann Wolfgang von Goethe, translated by Walter Arndt, edited by Cyrus Hamlin

- ✔ *Poets of the English Language, Volume 3: Romantic Poets,* edited by W.H. Auden and Norman Holmes Pearson

✔ *The Prelude, 1979, 1805, 1850,* by William Wordsworth, edited by Jonathan Wordsworth

✔ *Selected Poems,* by William Wordsworth

✔ *Women Romantic Poets: 1785–1832: An Anthology,* edited by Jennifer Breen

The Victorian Period

The Victorian Period was a time of big changes in society. The industrial revolution — and the intense ambivalence it caused among people of the world — was in full swing. The United States was growing up. Science and technology had started transforming human life at an astonishing rate. And many poets wrote about those changes. A heightened interest in human psychology, in the interior life of human beings, led to the popularity of the *dramatic monologue,* in which a speaker delivers what appears to be a speech about his or her personal situation. England's Robert Browning; Alfred, Lord Tennyson; and Matthew Arnold all wrote masterful dramatic monologues.

The Greats: English Victorian poets, including Alfred, Lord Tennyson (*In Memoriam* and much very accomplished poetry); Robert Browning and Elizabeth Barrett Browning; Christina Rossetti; Matthew Arnold; Gerard Manley Hopkins; the French Symbolists, including Charles Baudelaire *(Fleurs du Mal),* Jules Laforgue, Tristan Corbière, Arthur Rimbaud, Paul Valéry, Paul Verlaine, and Stéphane Mallarmé; Americans Walt Whitman and Emily Dickinson (well-represented in many fine anthologies); and Japanese poet Masaoka Shiki.

Here are some great books to check out if you're interested in exploring poetry of this period:

✔ *The Essential Browning,* by Robert Browning, edited by Douglas Dunn

✔ *French Symbolist Poetry,* translated by Carlyle Ferren MacIntyre

✔ *In Memoriam,* by Alfred, Lord Tennyson, edited by Robert H. Ross

✔ *Leaves of Grass,* by Walt Whitman, edited by Harold W. Blodgett and E. Sculley Bradley

✔ *The Norton Anthology of Literature by Women: The Tradition in English,* edited by Sandra M. Gilbert and Susan Gubar (for an excellent representation of Emily Dickinson)

✔ *Selected Poems,* by Alfred, Lord Tennyson

✔ *Selected Poems of Baudelaire,* translated by Joanna Richardson

The Symbolist movement

In France, a poetic movement called *Symbolism* got under way. Symbolist poets sought to evoke states of feeling through their poetry, rather than spelling out exactly what their poems meant. They were interested in the intense, almost magical spell language could cast on the beholder, and they explored new uses of metaphors and images in an effort to get language to mean new things.

Symbolist poets build entire poetic worlds out of intensely private symbols. Some people consider the English poet Blake to be one of the first symbolists. Romantic poets such as Hölderlin of Germany and Shelley of England used symbols in a strong, new way, too.

But the Symbolist movement began in 1857 with the publication of *Fleurs du Mal (Flowers of Evil)* by Charles Baudelaire. It culminated with the Big Four of French Symbolism: Arthur Rimbaud, Stéphane Mallarmé, Paul Verlaine, and Paul Valéry. These poets come close to creating a completely symbolic world, evoking states of feeling or awareness, often without locatable, concrete meanings. Their poetry *suggests* things, in other words, without *stating* those things directly. That's difficult to do.

Read this stanza from "Memory" by Arthur Rimbaud:

> Longing for thick, young arms of pure grass!
> Gold of April moons in the heart of the holy bed! Joy
> Of abandoned woodyards by the river, prey
> To August nights that made the rotten things sprout!

Each of the pictures in this passage is full of emotions — crowded, conflicting emotions. You can't really tell what the images *mean,* but still you can feel some of the longing and joy. This stanza is really just a group of symbols, but you're not told exactly what the symbols are connected to. Because the poem is titled "Memory," you can assume these are pictures from the speaker's memory, with which the speaker associates various states of feeling. The idea is to feel your own way along these surprising bursts of images — to feel the implications, the suggestions that arise, without trying to impose too much of a sense on it all.

The layering of these symbols, one on top of the other, was key to the 20th-century movement known as *Modernism,* in which the *meaning* of a poem sometimes bounced among images rather than being stated straight-forwardly. This required a more agile reader capable of following a series of complex associations. It also helped create the public image of modern poetry's difficulty.

As a movement in France, Symbolism reached a peak in the 1870s and 1880s, but it never really went away. It was a bridge into 20th-century poetry. Two of the finest Symbolist poets, Valéry and Paul Claudel, wrote poetry well into the 20th century. Among the 20th-century poets in whom Symbolism is a strong influence are France's Marguerite Burnat-Provins; Austria's Rainer Maria Rilke; Nicaragua's Rubén Darío; Russia's Marina Tsvetaeva; Ireland's William Butler Yeats; U.S. poets Wallace Stevens, T.S. Eliot, Hart Crane, and Adrienne Rich; Mexico's Octavio Paz; and Chile's Pablo Neruda.

American poetry: Whitman and Dickinson

Leaves of Grass, written by U.S. poet Walt Whitman (shown in Figure 7-1), was a book mostly of long-lined, open-form poems Whitman kept editing and re-editing his entire life. Although lengthy, *Leaves of Grass* is inviting and comfortable to read. Its expansive free verse cast a vibrant, personable shadow over world poetry for the next 150 years.

Figure 7-1:
Walt
Whitman.

Dip anywhere into Whitman's poetry, and a celebratory gust of wide-openness hits you in the soul, as in these lines from "Spontaneous Me" in *Leaves of Grass:*

Spontaneous me, Nature,
The loving day, the mounting sun, the friend I am happy with,
The arm of my friend hanging idly over my shoulder,
The hillside whiten'd with blossoms of the mountain ash,
The same late in autumn, the hues of red, yellow, drab, purple, and
   light and dark green,
The rich coverlet of the grass, animals and birds, the private, untrimm'd
   bank, the primitive apples, the pebble-stones,
Beautiful dripping fragments, the negligent list of one after another as I
   happen to call them to me or think of them

You don't see traditional end-rhyme or regular meter in this passage. (It has a great deal of rhythm but no strict meter repeated from line to line.) Just as traditional meters and stanza forms had characterized poetry of the previous 1,300 years, Whitman's expansiveness, his open and free manner, his boundary-busting, led the way into modern poetry.

Meanwhile, living in her parents' house in Amherst, Massachusetts, Emily Dickinson was writing short, intense poems that experimented with rhyme and form, fearlessly exploring death, immortality, pain, and paradox, as in Poem 1732:

> My life closed twice before its close;
>   It yet remains to see
> If immortality unveil
>   A third event to me,
>
> So huge, so hopeless to conceive
>   As these that twice befell.
> Parting is all we know of heaven,
>   And all we need of hell.

In her personal life, Dickinson was as inward as Whitman was outward, but her tight, short, concentrated poems are just as original as his. She seldom sought publication, and the first collection of her works appeared in 1890, four years after her death. She blended the compression of the metaphysical poets with ballad forms and rhymed stanzas related to the hymns she heard in church. Whitman and Dickinson are, for many people, the beginning of American poetry.

Shiki and the New Style in Japan

Japan had always been an isolated country and culture. But in the latter half of the 19th century, that began to change. In 1868, the emperor Meiji was restored to the throne after a long period of Shogun rule. Leaders began to reorganize and modernize Japanese society and customs. One result was an opening of culture to Western influences, especially to French Symbolism. A movement known as the *New Style,* an attempt to forge a new, contemporary Japanese poetry, arose in the 1880s.

One of the most important figures in Japanese poetry of this period was Masaoka Shiki. He was a scholar of both Japanese poetry and Western poetry. Shiki undertook to purify the rules of the haiku, and it is his understanding of that tradition that is best known in the West today. When Western poets write haiku, they are practicing the ways Shiki taught. Shiki was at the forefront of the movement to modernize Japanese literary art, and he wrote some of the century's best Japanese verse.

The 20th Century

The 20th century was the Century of Poetry. The world had never seen such an explosion of styles, such a diversity of audiences, such a widening of the poetic horizon.

What made the 20th century so poetic? The first half of the 20th century endured an economic depression preceded and followed by the trauma of two world wars. These three events called into question almost everything people knew about the world. So did the global triumph of technology: the automobile and airplane, the atom bomb, and the coming of the computer and the Internet. Several of these innovations — radio, telephone, and television, in particular — helped spread information and learning. That started to change society, very rapidly so, especially after World War II, when the world saw the rise and expansion of middle-class society in many countries. Poets were able to be in touch with one another's work more quickly and easily, which led to new influences and new combinations of tradition, style, and even subject matter.

The Modern Era (1901–1945)

We know: It's weird to think that the modern period is *over*. But *modern*, used as the name of a period, means a particular combination of things:

- Experimentation and innovation in poetry; the notion that the old ways of writing couldn't address the novelty and chaos of modern life.
- A radical break with the past.
- A new interest in psychology and the forces of history.
- The rising dominance of free (or open-form) verse as opposed to traditional forms.
- A new interest in writing about the forbidden side of life. The poetry of Whitman and Hart Crane, for example, contains homoerotic themes.

Many people think of Modernism as starting a little bit before World War I and ending with Hiroshima and Nagasaki in World War II.

The Greats: Ezra Pound, T.S. Eliot, William Butler Yeats, Hilda Doolittle ("H.D."), Robert Frost, William Carlos Williams, Langston Hughes, Gertrude Stein, Wallace Stevens, Marianne Moore, André Breton, Jacques Prévert, Eugenio Montale, Rainer Maria Rilke, Georg Trakl, Marina Tsvetayeva, Anna Akhmatova, Federico García Lorca, Leopold Sédar Sénghor, Pablo Neruda, and Octavio Paz. And they are just the beginning.

Try the following anthologies of Modern poetry for more excellent examples:

- *The Norton Anthology of Modern Poetry,* 2nd Edition, edited by Richard Ellmann and Robert O'Clair

- *Poems for the Millennium,* Volume 1, edited by Jerome Rothenberg and Pierre Joris

We cover ten important Modernist poets in the following sections.

Rabindranath Tagore

The poetic career of Bengali poet Rabindranath Tagore (shown in Figure 7-2) bridged the 19th and 20th centuries. A prolific writer of fiction, essays, travel diaries, as well as other works of non-fiction, Tagore wrote 100 books of poems. Tagore was a mystical, philosophical poet, deeply influenced by the Bengali and Sanskrit traditions. For his visionary, sensuous poems, Tagore won the Nobel Prize for Literature in 1913. He was knighted in 1915 but resigned his knighthood in 1919 in protest over the British massacre in Amritsar. His well-known books include *Gitanjali, Songs of Kabir,* and *The Gardener.*

Figure 7-2:
Rabin-
dranath
Tagore.

William Butler Yeats

The Irish poet William Butler Yeats transformed himself from a late Romantic poet to a Modern poet with a wild, vivid voice. One of the most often-quoted of all Modernist poems is Yeats's "The Second Coming." In this poem, the speaker seems to think the present is a mess and the future about to be born is worse:

> Turning and turning in the widening gyre
> The falcon cannot hear the falconer;
> Things fall apart; the centre cannot hold;
> Mere anarchy is loosed upon the world,
> The blood-dimmed tide is loosed, and everywhere
> The ceremony of innocence is drowned;
> The best lack all conviction, while the worst
> Are full of passionate intensity.
>
> Surely some revelation is at hand;
> Surely the Second Coming is at hand.
> The Second Coming! Hardly are those words out
> When a vast image out of *Spiritus Mundi*
> Troubles my sight: somewhere in the sands of the desert
> A shape with lion body and the head of a man,
> A gaze blank and pitiless as the sun,
> Is moving its slow thighs, while all about it
> Reel shadows of the indignant desert birds.
> The darkness drops again; but now I know
> That twenty centuries of stony sleep
> Were vexed to nightmare by a rocking cradle,
> And what rough beast, its hour come round at last,
> Slouches towards Bethlehem to be born?

Published in 1923, this poem had much to say both about the chaotic state of Yeats's Ireland and about the state of the world. It is a horror movie of the soul. The music, as in all Yeats, is unearthly and gorgeous.

Ezra Pound

The American poet Ezra Pound helped the rest of the century's poets "make it new" (a favorite saying of his). Influenced by Chinese and Japanese poetry, Pound wrote poetry focused on the *image* (a concentrated moment of revelation, epiphany, or complex emotion), showing the occasion for emotion but not talking about it. Perhaps the best example is his poem "In a Station of the Metro":

> The apparition of these faces in the crowd;
> Petals on a wet, black bough.

There it is: A single moment of vision and revelation. You see faces in the crowd and immediately are confronted with an image from nature — unexpected, with an unexplained connection with the faces. You are supposed to forge that connection yourself — think, perhaps, of how both the faces and the petals may be beautiful. That's a Modern moment.

Hilda Doolittle

The American poet Hilda Doolittle ("H.D.") was a protégé of Ezra Pound and part of the movement Pound called *Imagism*. Sick of the "blurriness," "messiness," and decadence of late-19th-century verse, the Imagists started the movement to make poetry tougher and more precise. Their main inspirations were Greek classical poetry, Japanese haiku, and French Symbolism.

One of the most memorable of the Imagist poems is "Oread," by H.D.:

> Whirl up, sea —
> whirl your pointed pines,
> splash your great pines
> on our rocks,
> hurl your green over us,
> cover us with your pools of fir.

An *oread* is a nymph of the mountains or woodland.

Imagist poems, at their best, were short, direct, and, like this one, breathtaking. H.D.'s main inspiration here is Greek poetry. A nymph appears to be addressing the sea. Notice that exhilarating metaphor, the notion of "pines," green and pointed, as waves. This poem is saying something about perception — that a wood nymph can understand an ocean wave only in terms of the forest. By the end, you're really feeling the stinging reality. It's both a visual and tactile image *and* a metaphor for being overwhelmed by experience. And *that's* an image.

Marianne Moore

Famously eccentric, the American poet Marianne Moore carved out her own unmistakable niche in Modernism. Humor can be seen throughout Modernism, but Moore is perhaps the most consistently delightful of the era's poets. She keeps the reader off-balance, starting with her selection of topics.

She also is famous for her original stanza forms. The following stanza, from "The Monkeys," has six lines. Each line contains a set number of syllables: 15-16-10-10-10-11. And there is a rhyme scheme on top of that — the first two lines rhyme with one another, the third line is unrhymed, the fourth and sixth lines rhyme with one another, and the fifth line is unrhymed:

The Monkeys

winked too much and were afraid of snakes. The zebras, supreme in
their abnormality; the elephants with their fog-colored skin
   and strictly practical appendages
      were there, the small cats; and the parakeet —
         trivial and humdrum on examination, destroying
      bark and portions of the food it could not eat.

Notice how much fun Moore seems to be having: the title that also begins the
poem, the "fog-colored" skin of the elephants, the behavior of the parakeet.
Moore was a Modernist in her sheer originality.

T.S. Eliot

The American poet T.S. Eliot (shown in Figure 7-3) combined French
Symbolism, a wide reading in the classics, English literature (especially the
metaphysical poets of the Elizabethan and Jacobean eras), and a frightening
sensitivity to the modern world to create a new kind of poetry. "The Love
Song of J. Alfred Prufrock," *The Waste Land,* and Eliot's religious poetry,
including *The Four Quartets,* are among the monuments of the first half of the
20th century.

To many, Eliot's *The Waste Land* expresses the spiritual decay and moral
paralysis of the 20th century. It's also a repository of the Modernist
influences discussed in the previous sections of this chapter, including
Symbolism and Imagism.

The Waste Land is a nightmare, like Yeats's "The Second Coming," yet with its
own ineffable music:

Who are those hooded hordes swarming
Over endless plains, stumbling in cracked earth
Ringed by the flat horizon only
What is the city over the mountains
Cracks and reforms and bursts in the violet air
Falling towers
Jerusalem Athens Alexandria
Vienna London
Unreal

Take a tour of *The Waste Land* with a good teacher, who can help you breast the
tide of its images and references (the poem comes complete with footnotes).

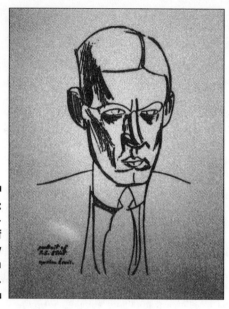

Figure 7-3:
A pen-and-ink sketch of T.S. Eliot by Wyndham Lewis.

Marina Tsvetayeva

The Russian poet Marina Tsvetayeva's passionate, often tortured verse recorded love, suffering, and the sweep of history in jagged yet songlike poems.

In "The Poem of the End," she writes about a bridge, one of the most familiar of all symbols:

> Last   bridge   I won't
> give up or take out my hand
> this is the last bridge
> The last bridging between
> water   and firm land

Bridges symbolize all sorts of passages — from youth to age, from ignorance to understanding, and (as here) from life to death.

André Breton

The French poet André Breton helped create _Surrealism,_ a movement in the arts, literature, and film that explored the unconscious and its role in producing art.

New voices, new audiences

Throughout the 20th century, poets from various cultural groups, often long repressed or discriminated against — ethnic and sexual minorities, women, the poor, the young — began to forge their own poetic identities. An aboriginal poetry scene emerged in Australia. In South America, indigenous peoples contributed some of the century's best verse, as in the agonized Surrealism of Peru's César Vallejo, a poet of mixed Inca and Spanish heritage. In India, a country of great poetic traditions, a dizzying number of poets began to publish in many languages. African poetry prospered on two tracks: an ancient oral tradition, and a newer written verse, including the work of Ghana's Kofi Awoonor, Mozambique's Noémia de Sousa, Nigeria's Christopher Okigbo, and Uganda's Okot p'Bitek.

Modernism deeply affected Chinese poets, but writers were prevented from participating fully in this world revolution by the political convulsions that shook China all century. Mao Tse-tung, leader of Communist China, was also an accomplished poet. Suspicious of the free-thinking, questioning experiments of modernism, he imposed standards that stressed realism, folk poetry, and patriotism. That forced China's best poets to find a way to please the censors while writing exquisite verse. (Much the same thing happened in the European Communist countries.) An ironic, resigned, symbolic kind of verse emerged. Some of the poets of this period include Lu Hsun, Hu Shih, Feng Chih, and Yen Chen.

In "Since Akkad, Since Elam, Since Sumer," by Aimé Césaire of the island nation of Martinique, the speaker reflects on the way people of African descent have been made to carry the weight of oppressors' history:

> I have borne the body of the commandant. I have borne the railroad of the
>   commandant. I have borne the locomotive of
> the commandant, the cotton of the commandant. I have borne on my
>   woolly head (which does so well without a pad) God, the machine, the route —
>   the God of the commandant.
> Master of three roads I have borne under the sun, I have borne in the mist I have borne
>   over smoldering shards managing ants
> I have borne the parasol I have borne the explosive I have borne the iron collar.

In the Arabic-speaking world, the Tammuzi poets looked for a way to break away from tradition and explore modern experience in Arabic poetry. Two of the most famous Tammuzi poets are Lebanon's Yusuf al-Khal and the astonishing Syrian poet Ali Ahmad Sa'id, known as Adonis, author of the following passage:

> thus I no longer hesitate to say:
> "the I and the other
> are me,"
> and time is but a basket
> to collect poetry

In the United States of the 1920s, the Harlem district of Manhattan saw the rise of a distinctive African American culture expressed in all the arts. This decade of activity came to be called the *Harlem Renaissance*. Poets such as Claude McKay, Countee Cullen, and Langston Hughes (shown in the figure in this sidebar) first came to widespread notice. As the century closed, African American voices were among the most prominent of American poets, including, Robert Hayden, Gwendolyn Brooks, Maya Angelou, Amiri Imamu Baraka, Lucille Clifton, Al Young, Yusef Komunyakaa, Rita Dove, June Jordan, and Audre Lorde.

For a brief taste of Surrealism, read this passage from Breton's "A Man and Woman Absolutely White":

> In the depths of the parasol I see the marvelous prostitutes
> On the side near the streetlamps their gowns are the color of polished
> wood
> They are walking a great piece of wallpaper
> At which one cannot look without that choking feeling about the heart of
> ancient floors in buildings being demolished
> Where a slab of marble lies fallen from the fireplace
> And a skein of chains is tangled in the mirrors

Even though the images and phrases in a Surrealist poem don't work together in conventional, conscious ways, their novel combinations nevertheless do produce associations in your mind. You look into a parasol and somehow see prostitutes. Depending on your associations regarding that world, you already may feel an element of the degraded and the forbidden. They are carrying wallpaper — and suddenly you're in the midst of a demolished building. You may feel sadness in reading these lines somehow: Demolition involves endings, abandonment, and violence. And demolished buildings are usually forbidden places.

Notice how the poem challenges you to analyze *yourself* as you analyze *it*. Surrealism is, thus, not just about the workings of a single poem; it's also about the workings of the mind — and that is part of its fascination.

Pablo Neruda

The Chilean poet Pablo Neruda led a whole generation of South American writers to renovate poetry in Spanish. Neruda (shown in Figure 7-4) created a poetry based on "the things of this world," as he put it. See and feel the concreteness of the images in his famous poem "Walking Around." The speaker is a man "tired of being a man." He is restless and sad, ready to burst out:

> The smell of barber shops makes me sob out loud.
> I want nothing but the repose either of stones or of wool

At the end, the speaker walks among the surprising, mundane things of the world:

> I stride along with calm, with eyes, with shoes,
> with fury, with forgetfulness,
> I pass, I cross offices and stores full of orthopedic appliances,
> and courtyards hung with clothes on wires,
> underpants, towels and shirts which weep
> slow dirty tears.

Léopold Sédar Senghor

Senegal's Léopold Sédar Senghor combined French Symbolism with Surrealism and an awareness of African origins and traditions. With the poets Aimé Césaire and Léon Gontion Damas, Senghor helped found a movement called *Négritude,* whose adherents were aware and proud of their African heritages. Senghor eventually was elected prime minister of Senegal and served from 1960 to 1980, becoming the first black member of the Académie Française in 1984.

The Postmodern Era (1945–1989)

If the Modernist period was marked by anxiety, the Postmodern period was marked by irony. There was much to be ironic about. Big business dominated much of the politics of the world, prompting poets to point out the many ways in which making money doesn't guarantee a good life. Many lines of poets — including the Hiroshima poets of Japan, the Beat poets of 1950s America (some of whom appear in Figure 7-5), and folk, pop, rap, and performance poets — insistently parodied and questioned the assumptions of the political establishment and the company man.

Figure 7-4:
Pablo
Neruda.

Figure 7-5:
Bob Donlin,
Neal
Cassady,
Allen
Ginsberg,
painter
Robert
LaVigne, and
Lawrence
Ferlinghetti
in front of
City Lights
Bookstore in
North
Beach, San
Francisco,
1955.

The Cold War and the threat of global annihilation were seldom far from artists' minds. To many writers, this threat sapped life of all meaning, and despair was not far away. In poetry, a sense of the breaking up of the old and an uncertain future emerged in the poetry of many languages.

A Stein is a Stein is a Stein. . . .

Gertrude Stein is one of the 20th century's best-known and most influential poets. She played a double role: as cultural hostess and as poet. In 1907, Stein moved to Paris, where, with her companion, Alice B. Toklas, she held a long-running salon, a meeting place for poets, artists, and thinkers, one of the central nodes of the Modern and Experimental eras. People as diverse as Picasso, Hemingway, and James Joyce were her visitors. Many Americans became expatriate artists in the first half of the century, and the Stein/Toklas salon was a favorite resort. Stein encouraged and helped many standouts in 20th-century literature and art.

Stein also was and is a very influential Experimental poet. She constantly and boldly tested the distinctions between poetry and prose, writing stories, books of poems, opera librettos, and memoirs in a rhythmic ("a rose is a rose is a rose"), humorous ("I am because my little dog knows me"), and surprisingly philosophical and profound style. Her reknown and reputation have never been higher than they are right now.

The Postmodern era was also an age of political contention. Protests against the United States' involvement in the Vietnam War spread worldwide. And local movements for human rights — which, in the United States, spawned the civil rights movement and feminism — produced a new generation of poets. In China, the failed revolution at Tiananmen Square in 1989 sent several poets into exile. Perhaps the best-known of these (and maybe the best-known

Chinese poet of the late 20th century) is Bei Dao. He is one of a group known as the *misty poets*. They were more introspective than "official" poetry was supposed to be, more likely to examine their subjective lives.

Bei Dao's poetry is full of protest. These four lines were dangerous ones for a poet to write in Mao's China:

> Listen. *I don't believe!*
> OK. You've trampled
> a thousand enemies underfoot. Call me
> a thousand and one.

If this poetry seems "Western," it's because Western poetry has absorbed so much from the Chinese tradition. That tradition is as large and various as the country from which it comes. As China changes, so does its poetry. Following those changes will be one of the great pleasures of the 21st century.

The Greats: Postmodern greats include Amiri Imamu Baraka, Robert Lowell, Elizabeth Bishop, Charles Olson, Allen Ginsberg, Frank O'Hara, John Ashbery, Basil Bunting, Ed Dorn, Gary Snyder, A.R. Ammons, Sylvia Plath, Anne Sexton, Robert Creeley, Adrienne Rich, Sharon Olds, Bob Dylan, John Lennon, Paul McCartney, Nicanor Parra, and Violetta Parra.

Check out the following for a sampling of Postmodern poetry:

- ✔ *The Harvard Book of Contemporary American Poetry,* edited by Helen Vendler
- ✔ *The New American Poetry: 1945–1960,* edited by Donald M. Allen
- ✔ *The Norton Anthology of Modern Poetry,* edited by Richard Ellmann and Robert O'Clair
- ✔ *The Pittsburgh Book of Contemporary American Poetry,* edited by Ed Ochester and Peter Oresick
- ✔ *Postmodern American Poetry: A Norton Anthology,* edited by Paul Hoover
- ✔ *The Postmoderns: The New American Poetry Revised,* edited by Donald M. Allen
- ✔ *The Vintage Book of Contemporary World Poetry,* edited by J.D. McClatchy

Women's voices

The 20th century also saw important women emerge in poetry everywhere. Americans H.D., Marianne Moore, and Gertrude Stein were three great pioneers. Among the many extraordinary North American female poets of mid-century, we may include the work of Muriel Rukeyser, Lorine Niedecker, and Elizabeth Bishop. Other fine women poets are Russia's Anna Akhmatova,

Howling about *Howl*

In the summer of 1955, ringleader Beat poet Allen Ginsberg wanted to write a fearless poem that would sum up his life. He intended this highly personal work to be read by himself and a few others, and it wasn't originally intended for publication. But a few months later, he recited the first part of his now-famous poem *Howl* to a packed crowd at the Six Gallery in San Francisco. City Lights book publisher and poet Lawrence Ferlinghetti published *Howl and Other Poems* the following year, and controversy soon followed. Copies of the book were seized and banned by U.S. Customs and the San Francisco police. Ferlinghetti was arrested and accused of distributing indecent writings, and a long obscenity trial ensued.

With a host of prominent literary figues and the ACLU backing Ginsberg, Judge Clayton W. Horn ruled that the book was not obscene. The *Howl* trial was thus a landmark case for the freedom of speech and for the press. The national publicity surrounding the trial put Ginsberg and Ferlinghetti in the national spotlight, and *Howl and Other Poems* became a bestseller.

Poland's Wislawa Szymborska, Canada's Margaret Atwood and Nicole Brossard, France's Anne-Marie Albiach, China's Shu Ting, and Japan's Shiraishi Kazuko. South American poetry can boast of the work of Uruguay's Delmira Agustini, Mexico's Rosario Castellanos, and Chile's Gabriela Mistral. And that's just a start.

As of about 1970, poets began to write what became known as *feminist poetry.* Feminist poetry explores the lives of women and often tries to make the reader conscious of how the social or political realities of our society affect women. Some of the poets most influential for feminists include Sylvia Plath, Anne Sexton, Adrienne Rich, Carolyn Kizer, Marge Piercy, Alicia Suskin Ostriker, Sharon Olds, and Judy Grahn.

A strain of feminist experimental verse evolved, in which poets explored the notion that there may be a characteristically feminist way of pushing the boundaries. Some of the most interesting women experimental poets include Kathleen Fraser, Beverly Dahlen, Maureen Owen, Joan Retallack, Lyn Hejinian, the sisters Fanny Howe and Susan Howe, Marie Howe (who was unrelated to Fanny and Susan), Norma Cole, Carla Harryman, Rae Armantrout, Mei-mei Berssenbrugge, Leslie Scalapino, Haryette Mullen, Erin Mouré, Cole Swensen, Myung Mi Kim, and Maxine Chernoff.

Experimental poetry

As the 20th century progressed, poets experimented more and more with new ways to make artworks out of language. Here's a Cubist poem, "Departure," written in France in 1919 by the French poet Pierre Reverdy, a forerunner to the Postmodern experimental poets. It's a good example of the ways poets experiment with the fragment.

The woman's voice and protest poetry

Three of the most interesting writers of political protest poetry in this century are women, and all three have suffered heroically under persecution, imprisonment, and exile. Noémia de Sousa of Mozambique was very active in her country's struggle to free itself of colonial rule by Portugal. Her outspoken public statements, and her poetry critical of the ruling regime, brought official denunciation and persecution, and she was forced to live in exile in France and Portugal.

Cuba's Maria Elena de Varela, self-taught and idiosyncratic, won her country's National Award for Poetry in 1989. Two years later, she published poems and essays critical of the Castro regime.

She was thrown into prison, beaten, and starved. Since 1994, she has lived in Puerto Rico, where she continues to write poetry calling for freedom and justice in Cuba.

Naslima Tasrin is a Bangladeshi poet. Her poems are feminist, often secular, and often critical of Islamic fundamentalism. (In fact, some of the mullahs, Islamic religious leaders of her country, have offered to pay anyone who will kill her.) In 1994, she was driven into hiding, surfacing in Sweden, where she continues to write some of the best feminist protest verse in the Islamic world.

> The horizon slips down
> > Days are longer
> > Journey
> A heart leaps in a cage
> > A bird sings
> > It will die
> Another door will open
> > At the end of the hall
> > Where a star
> > Flares up
> A dark woman
> > Lantern of the departing train

Reverdy condenses the feelings of taking a journey into a few shards of language like a Cubist collage. First, an awareness of horizon. The long days mean spring, summer, time to travel. The heart becomes a bird that leaps up and sings. Its death is predicted flatly; it's a shock. The poem turns there, as if from the knowledge of death. You are already looking out on the platform: There is a dark woman (more foreboding? or just waiting for a train?), and the train's lantern comes into view, "flares up." Or perhaps the lantern is the dark woman, who has become a star to lead the traveler.

If you want to read about the poetic theories behind such poetry, you may want to consult publications such as *Poetic Journal, L=A=N=G=U=A=G=E* (available through *The L=A=N=G=U=A=G=E Book,* edited by Charles Bernstein and Bruce Andrews), and *How(ever)*.

Prose poetry (another form of experimentation) has enjoyed a major surge in popularity since the 1970s. Think of *prose* as part of the ceaseless flow of language itself. Here is a passage from *a.k.a.* by Bob Perelman. Watch how different kinds of language intrude on each other, how the passage starts to portray the way these languages relate to one another.

> The speakers vibrate through the entire house. Brahms' lust scans the swept garden. Number streams down onto the trees. Born witness to his own fragmentation, a child breaks into speech. Hear against it a matter of course.
>
> The reward you were tacitly promised when you began reading this sentence is now yours. You are that smoke. Black wisps of leaf tended by an orange flame, iced antennas against a starry sky. I dressed as a tiger and knocked at the varnished doors.

Here you have not one voice talking but a mosaic of voices. You're tossed among images, statements that seem to make sense and others that fall apart. The "you" in the second paragraph *seems* to be an address to the reader — but you can't really be sure. Perhaps it is some other "you," some person known to or created by the poet alone. Again and again, your attention is brought back to how words and their relations bring out meanings as your mind considers them.

This form, poetry in prose, or mixed with prose, has inspired some of the most ambitious work of the last 20 years. Perelman's *a.k.a.;* Lyn Hejinian's *My Life;* Ron Silliman's *Age of Huts;* Barrett Watten's *Bad History;* Beverly Dahlen's *A Reading;* Monique Wittig's *Lesbian Body;* Fanny Howe's *Lives of a Spirit;* Carla Harryman's *The Words;* Aaron Shurin's *The Paradise of Forms;* Bernadette Mayer's *Proper Name;* Leslie Scalapino's *The Return of Painting, The Pearl,* and *Orion;* and many, many more.

New York, Paris, Vancouver, and London have writing scenes where innovative poetry flourishes, but the San Francisco Bay Area is the world's hotbed of experimental poetry, with many presses, reading series, and a faithful audience. Here's a poem, "The Mouth," by San Francisco Bay Area poet Laura Moriarty (shown in Figure 7-6) that moves between fragment and prose.

> We have words
> Over definition
> Terror
> Something to lose
> Loose
> In us
> Harshness
> Oracularity
>
> A stone bath or wood room vivid and liquid ritual means
> the wished for repetition against the sense of what is said
> at the same time taking in the heart the belly the groin the
> mouth and legs the ass the chest and eyes.

Figure 7-6:
Laura
Moriarty.

This poem is strung between two concepts about meaning, linear meaning ("over definition") and meaning that includes the supernatural, the body, and the sublime. It is very much a lyric: Notice how the heavy syllables of the word *oracularity* almost separate in your mouth. Are you in the stone room of a Greek oracle or a hot tub? The parts of the body are opposed to the "sense of what is said." The "wished for repetition" may be a chant, a prayer "loose in us" or simply the refrain of a song. Could the words of that prayer or refrain be "Over definition" in the sense of "beyond definition"? Would those words include this poem? Certainly the open form of this poem is not going to allow a single resolution; it will continue to be available to alternate inter-pretations. For example, the "wished for repetition" could be the list of body parts, so perhaps the body itself is the refrain, or the spell. The meanings of the poem hold together, but not inside one interpretation.

Performance poetry

The 1980s saw a surge of interest in poets reciting their work in public. It was a world movement: For Ghana's Ama Ata Aidoo, Peru's Eduardo Calderón, and the Zuni storyteller Andrew Peynetsa, poetry is primarily to be spoken and heard.

Up sprang an immediate, often impromptu poetry, often harsh or crass, designed to be delivered in a dramatic or histrionic way before an audience.

This kind of poetry made use of everything poets could get their hands on: music, television, movies, humor, slang, confession. Its main gods were poets such as Whitman, Neruda, Ginsberg, and Bob Dylan — poets interested in a poetry close to the pace and impact of speech.

African American poetry has always had a strong element of performance, from the earliest days of slavery through the poetry of the Harlem Renaissance to the 1970s work of Gil Scott-Herron to the cultures of rap and hip-hop at century's end. One of the birthing moments of the performance poetry movement was the "choreopoem" *For Colored Girls Who Have Considered Suicide When the Rainbow Was Enuf* by Ntozake Shange, a major contributor to the Nuyorican Poets' Café (founded in 1974), a venue on the Lower East Side of New York for multicultural performance art. Shange, an African American poet, combines popular culture, jazz, African and American history, feminist politics, urban legend, and dance.

Events called *poetry slams* became widely popular in the 1980s and 1990s. The slam was founded in Chicago in the 1970s by Marc Smith, at the Green Mill Lounge on Broadway Avenue. Prominent slams were held annually in Chicago, San Francisco, New York, and Boston. Very often, slams are competitive poetry readings in which audience reaction is used to determine the "winning" poet. Several venues throughout the world put on annual slams to determine the champion poet of the year.

The Global Era (1989–Present)

We hereby declare a new period in literary history: the *Global Era*. Poetry now participates in the Internet age, the connected era, in which worldwide influences join together in poetry to mix traditions, ethnicities, and even genders. Mixtures — that's what global poetry explores. Television, radio, and movies have taught people how to think in rapidly shifting images; they mix almost anything with almost anything else. It can be confusing and exhilarating at the same time. Global poets try to tap into both the confusion and the exhilaration.

In the Global Era, you can find poetry that rhymes and poetry that doesn't. Forms are joining with other forms, new with old, to make all sorts of hybrids. Prose poetry (which has been around since at least 1842) is a hallmark of the Global period; you could take it as poetry written as prose, or prose with the concentration and rhythm of poetry. And performance poetry is challenging written poetry as the premier poetic form of the age.

Anne Waldman, who began her career in the Postmodern era, is a bridge to the Global era. Her poetry, as in this passage from "Iovis XIX," often shifts back and forth in history, tone, and mood, and it's usually well worth the ride:

my friend dark night a result
friend a light of me combine
to find alas no woman at the table
of Israel, of Lebanon, Palestine
how do they sleep? of Syria
& shine or shrink the tale as of void
& radio it says hands-on broadcast
a hundred deejays wait, not one a woman
the scholar & savage equal points of light
rub dry sticks together
a sham, a delusion, kind of affectation
never felt lonesome in it

At first, you may find this poem hard to read. But if you read it aloud — or hear Waldman, a remarkable performance poet, read it — the poem becomes clearer. The question isn't, "What is this *about?*" but rather "What's *happening* here?" Notice how all sorts of ideas and images interrupt one another and rub together. There is even rhyme in the *combine / Palestine / shine* passage.

In Waldman's poem, you get images from politics (the absence of women), personal life, popular culture. You can even catch glimpses of *statements,* as when the speaker tells of a world in which "the scholar and savage" may be "equal points of light." (Both may have important things to tell us these days — both rub "dry sticks" together, the savage to make fire, the scholar to enlarge human knowledge.) And in a whirling, infinitely active, always interesting world such as ours, the speaker says he or she "never felt lonesome." It would be difficult to feel lonely, with all these different voices around.

The Greats: Global greats include Miguel Algarín, Victor Hernández Cruz, Charles Bernstein, Ron Silliman, Lyn Hejinian, Arkadii Dragomoshchenko, L.L. Kool J, Dr. Dre, Patricia Smith, Ntozake Shange, Barrett Watten, Fanny Howe, Norma Cole, Francisco Alarcón, Kathleen Fraser, Erica Hunt, Michael Palmer, Tom Raworth, Emmanuel Hocquard, Rosmarie Waldrop, Ammiel Alcalay, and Anne Waldman.

Check out any of the following to get an idea of the kind of poetry being written in the Global Period of the here and now:

✔ *Aloud! Voices from the Nuyorican Poets Café,* edited by Bob Holman and Miguel Algarín

✔ *An Anthology of New (American) Poets,* edited by Chris Stroffolino, Lisa Garnat, and Leonard Schwartz

- *Moving Borders: Three Decades of Innovative Writing by Women,* edited by Mary Margaret Sloan
- *Poems for the Millennium,* Volume 2, edited by Jerome Rothenberg and Pierre Joris

Poetry: Over 5,000 years old and still youthful, still growing. An amazing story. The great thing about this story is that it's far from over. New chapters are being written all over the world at this very moment.

Part III

Writing Poetry: A Guide for Aspiring Poets

The 5th Wave By Rich Tennant

"Yes, I think I can consider myself a published poet. I submitted all of my Personal Ads in the form of a Haiku."

In this part . . .

*I*n these chapters, we give guidance, advice, and encouragement to anyone interested in writing poetry. Here you'll find discussions of the attitude, discipline, and habits you need to become a practicing poet. We show you how writers get from first thoughts to actual poetry.

You'll find out how to write in free verse (which we call *open-form poetry*) as well as how to write in five popular traditional forms. Then, generous sorts that we are, we offer a range of exercises to stoke the creative fires and help you find the kind of poetry you'd like to write. We follow that with chapters on how to read your poetry at public readings, open mikes, and poetry slams, as well as the best way to seek publication for your poetry.

Whether you're already a poet or on your way to becoming one, you'll find the tips, advice, and suggestions you need in the chapters in this part.

Chapter 8

Calling the Muse

· ·

In This Chapter

▶ Developing good habits as an aspiring poet

▶ Organizing your writing time

▶ Recognizing inspiration when you feel it

▶ Turning raw material into poetry

▶ Staying in touch with what's happening in the poetry world

▶ Meeting other poets

· ·

So who gets to be a poet? Anyone who wants to be. Anyone willing to read, write, work, and live with poetry. There is no entrance fee, no initiation ritual, and, last we looked, you can't get kicked out of the club.

So how do you go about doing this poetry thing? Should you jot down thoughts as they come, on old receipts, napkins, scraps of newspaper? (Some fine poets, such as Frank O'Hara of the New York School, did it that way.) Or will you lose all those scraps of paper? Should you be more methodical? Write every day. Keep a journal. Revise and revise. Stay current with the latest in the poetry world. Become part of a community of poets. Find a mentor who will read your poetry and give you good criticism.

Something more along the lines of the methodical route will likely serve you best. So in this chapter, we suggest ways to corral inspiration and turn it into poetry.

Ignore any advice in this chapter if it doesn't work for you. These aren't rules; they're guidelines. Pick and choose! Build a *modus operandi* (a "way of working") all your own.

How to Live If You Want to Be a Poet

No *one* way of life works for every poet. But poets do tend to share a few traits:

✔ **They have passion.** Poets care about something very much, and this passion drives their work. Passion for what? It could be passion for making words, or passion for a way of seeing. Or it could be a commitment to a public theme of some kind — or just a passionate attachment to life itself. So find a reason to care and something — many things — to care about.

✔ **They think like poets.** What kind of thinking is that?

- They like to play with words. They pay attention to the beauty, quality, and specificity of words. They love the pleasure of using the "right" word and the equal pleasure of using the surprising word.

- They think in images, metaphors, and music.

- They find ways "behind the scenes" of their conscious minds; that is, they seek divergent ways of thinking, forms of writing that shake them loose from habits and ruts.

✔ **They read a lot and write a lot.**

✔ **They are sensitive people and do many things to enhance their awareness and sensitivity.** What kind of things? They read, they write, and they practice paying attention. Some poets explore alternative consciousness, which leads them into meditation, religion, drugs, and so forth. We don't necessarily recommend any of these directions; we only want to point out where poets have gone in search of inspiration.

✔ **They are open to experience.** Curiosity makes the poet. It means that whatever you encounter, you do so with your eyes open.

✔ **They work hard to improve.** This work involves two major disciplines: revision and learning from criticism.

✔ **They associate with other poets whose work they admire.**

Reading Like a Poet

A poet who doesn't read is like a composer who doesn't listen to music. To quote the marvelous poet and teacher Gerald Stern, "The great writer who doesn't read — *il n'existe pas!*" (meaning, "He doesn't exist"). So read a lot, and then read some more. Here are some things to read, along with the reasons why:

✔ **Classics in poetry and fiction,** to learn the traditions of literature.

✔ **Journals of art and culture,** to learn what's happening in the arts.

✔ **The latest in fiction and nonfiction,** to find out what writers are creating right now.

✔ **The newspaper and major current-events journals and magazines,** so you know what's happening in the world.

 ✔ **Poetry,** lots of poetry, different kinds of poetry, poetry from all over. Reading a variety of verse — in different styles, from different periods and countries, by different kinds of people, about a variety of subjects — will show you the huge range of possibilities for poetry, help keep your mind wide open (essential for a poet), and also help you train your ear and eye, understanding how poetry works and building your personal tastes.

 ✔ **Junk, grocery-store paperback novels, relaxation reading,** because it doesn't hurt.

Some aspiring poets are afraid to read — especially poetry. They're afraid of being influenced too much by other minds and voices. But we say you should risk it. You *have* to hear those other voices, get a taste for those other minds, to know what's happening in the world of poetry, so you can speak to the present. Don't be afraid that other people are better than you are. Remember what the jazz guitarist John Scofield says regularly to his students: "If you want to improve, get out and play with people who are better than you are." Makes sense, doesn't it?

Writing Like a Poet

Have you ever heard someone describe himself as an athlete, only to add that he hasn't touched the basketball court (or football field or swimming pool) in 30 years? Well, we have news for that guy: He's no athlete. He's just a person who likes to *talk* about being an athlete.

Similarly, there's no way you're a poet unless you find the time to write poetry and work at it — and not just *making* poems but also *revising* them. If you're serious about being a poet, you can't just write poetry in bits and pieces — you have to schedule time to write.

Finding the right time and place to write

Carry around a tape recorder or a notebook. Use these tools as storage space for the stuff that rains down on your brain during the day — all the little ideas and phrases and words that occur to you, but that you would forget if you didn't jot them down. Then transfer that material from your notebook into a journal during your writing time.

How long do you need to set aside? At least an hour. And if you care about poetry, you won't cheat yourself out of the time you need to write it. Decide the following:

✔ **When you're at your best.** Are you a morning, noon, or night person? Many poets get up *very* early — early morning is a poetic time (birds are singing, garbage collectors are banging, and so on). Others wait until the depths of night. Know what works best for you.

✔ **What setting is best.** A quiet library? A park bench? A crowded café? Most folks need the following:

- **A quiet place,** somewhere free of distractions and interruptions.

- **Good lighting,** which can help your vision and your mood.

- **Writing tools,** such as a computer, pens, pencils, paper, a dictionary, poetry books, and so on.

- **Comfort foods and comfort sounds.** Some people need music; others can't work with it on. Some folks find that a snack nearby aids inspiration. Pay attention to what *you* require, and make sure you have it.

The way poets write

Each poet has his or her own way of composing poetry. Here are six interesting poetic m.o.'s:

✔ The Roman poet **Virgil** was said to walk through his gardens all day long, and by sunset, if he'd had a good day at work, he had produced . . . a single line.

✔ Elizabethan and Jacobean poet **Ben Jonson** said he would write out a prose paragraph stating the poem's content, and *then* sit down and write the poem. Now that's discipline!

✔ Renaissance English poet **John Milton** went blind in 1651, yet he didn't start creating *Paradise Lost* in earnest until 1663. How did he do it? He *dictated* it to a secretary. So if someone says, "Milton wrote *Paradise Lost*," you can be irritating and reply, "No, he *composed* it."

✔ Modern American poet **Theodore Roethke** had an interesting use for his bed. Whenever he got stuck while writing a poem, he would hop into bed, and when he felt he had solved his poetic problem, he would get up and start to write again.

✔ **Frank O'Hara,** a poet of the New York School, wrote a whole book of poems titled *Lunch Poems.* O'Hara, seldom known to turn down a party, would have lunch with his New York pals, then return to his job at the Museum of Modern Art, put a piece of paper in his typewriter, type out a poem, and then get back to his "real job."

✔ African American poet **Maya Angelou** has a very idiosyncratic way of setting up her "office." She rents a hotel room, then leaves her house at 6:00 a.m. and tries to get to "work" (in her hotel room) at 6:30. She lies across the bed to write, so she has a permanent callus on one elbow. She insists that everything is taken off the walls. "I go into the room," she writes, "and I feel as if all my beliefs are suspended. Nothing holds me to anything. No milkmaids, no flowers, nothing. I just want to feel and when I start to work I'll remember."

Recognizing inspiration

For 5,000-plus years, poets have described an agitated, exalted state, a peak experience, white-hot, out of which they created poetry. No doubt about it, this happens. Shakespeare appears to have written the first draft of *Hamlet* in about six weeks. (Doesn't it make you *sick?*) Rainer Maria Rilke, after working on his incomparable *Duino Elegies* for more than 20 years, finished them in an attic study in two of the most famous weeks of poetic inspiration. Sylvia Plath's last six months alive, during which she wrote the poems in the collection *Ariel,* were of that white-hot variety, all original, tortured, supremely inspired verse.

Some think inspiration is the voice of the Divine whispering directly into our souls. Others believe it's the individual's mind (yours!), working subconsciously, stitching experience, memory, desire, and language into a crazy quilt that the poet somehow discovers and turns into poetry. Many creative people talk about access to the subconscious, even access to childhood — you eventually trust your subconscious to come up with what you're looking for, to solve problems. One good reason to have regular working habits, then, is to visit your subconscious regularly, give it a chance to read itself, so to speak, crystallize what's welling up in there. Regular work habits make *you* better at reading what your subconscious is up to. Yet the subconscious doesn't keep office hours: It can also be dreamlike and elusive, so carry a pen and notebook with you wherever you go.

Sometimes you *know* you're inspired: You taste that elevated, breathless excitement. At other times, however, inspiration sneaks up on you. Unless you're very sharp, you may not even realize it's happening. Many of us, after all, just *think,* not especially paying attention to ourselves, just watching our mental movies. Then, maybe, we snap out of it: "Hey! Wait a minute! What was that again?"

Be awake to your own processes. Just as an athlete gets to know her body and its ways, get to know when your mind is most open to the muse.

When is inspiration likely to happen? Almost *any* time. But poets have often written about the following situations, which seem to lead to moments of intense creativity:

- ✔ **Whenever you're alive.** From overpowering elation to quite modest events (say, a wheelbarrow wet with rain, something the American poet William Carlos Williams created a famous poem about), connections and realizations could happen anytime. Sometimes the words and impressions come at the very moment of experience; some poets say they need to write them down before the ideas fade. Others find having the experience and recollecting it later works best for them.

- ✔ **Between waking and sleeping.** Some folks keep notebooks by the bed-side, to capture their thoughts when they're in transition from conscious to subconscious states and vice versa. Many people jot down dream material (and daydreams as well), scrawling in notebooks in the middle of the night.

- ✔ **While listening to music.** Because music involves your emotions and experience in extremely complicated ways, taste in music (like taste in poetry or any art) is intensely personal. Many people feel that listening to music allows them to access their memories, dreams, and mental associations.

- ✔ **During diversions.** When you're really concentrating hard on something (a math quiz, or a tangled bike chain, or sawing at a tree limb 40 feet above the ground, or watching an exciting hockey game), your subconscious mind may try to slip in an image, a phrase, or an idea while you're not looking.

The subconscious often tries more than once. You may miss its suggestions the first time. But it may try again, like a distant phone ringing. If the same image or word or notion keeps surfacing now and then, pay attention to it. If you *know* that's how inspiration happens, you're one step closer to using it in your verse.

Empty page, full imagination: Getting started

Some people can just turn to a clean page and start writing. If you're like that, fine. Get going. God bless.

Other people are stymied by the empty page. If you're part of this group, waiting for inspiration can keep you from writing. Sometimes, sitting down and writing anyway, even when you can't think of anything to write about, is important — think of it as exercising muscles you'll need later. Besides, some of your best writing can come to you when you feel like you're plodding along in a rut, without anything to say.

Some poets need warm-up exercises for their minds and bodies. If you need a warm-up, give one or more of the following a try:

- ✔ **Free-write.** Free-writing is a technique pioneered by Peter Elbow, a well-known teacher of writing. It's simple to do: Just put pen to paper and write. What you write doesn't matter. If you can't think of anything to say, write, "I don't have anything to say, I don't have anything to say." Ten to fifteen minutes of free-writing often loosens people up, and you may discover you've written something interesting — in spite of yourself.

- ✔ **Rewrite a famous poem.** Go to your favorite anthology, select a poem, and put it in different words. Poet, teacher, and anthologist J.D. McClatchy recommends writing out the poem you've chosen — triple-spacing the poem on the page — and writing a response in between the lines. Then erase the original and work on your response to it as a separate poem — one *you've* created.

- ✔ **Try one of the Surrealist games.** Cut words out of a newspaper, draw them out of a hat, and arrange them in any way you want. Then write a poem reversing the words.

If you're itching to start, start. Write what you're on fire to write. That's what this time and place are for. If you want to be *extremely* methodical, you could establish a pattern and do it the same way every time, like this:

1. **Begin with some exercises *or* copy material from your daily notebook into your journal.**

   Feel free to expand or work on anything as you do so.

2. **Read the previous day's work aloud.**

3. **Revise your previous work.**

4. **Generate new writing.**

Keeping a journal

A journal is a single, locatable repository for your writing, a stockpile of raw material for future poetry. What can you put into a journal? Here are some examples:

- ✔ **Drafts and revisions of poems.** A journal can be your "workshop," where you go through the process of going from first thoughts to more finished versions of poems. Keep track of your versions (some poets number them; some use different colored pens or pencils; some simply start a new page when they start a new version). Watching your poems grow and develop will, in itself, reveal to you how your poetry takes shape.

- ✔ **Pasted-in newspaper articles, magazine art, drawings, and "found" objects.** Maybe you've come upon someone's family photograph in the street, and that photograph suggests a poem to you.

- ✔ **Poems you've read and loved.** Why not build your own personal anthology? That in itself could yield inspiration.

- ✔ **Exercises in traditional forms.** Write sonnets, ballads, haiku, ghazals, and other tightly formal poems. Pay your dues! Master these forms even if you'll never use them. They teach you the foundations of your craft. (Turn to Chapter 10 for information on how to write these traditional forms of poetry.)

- ✔ **Lists of subjects to write about.** Just list them. Someday you could return to this list, select an item, and write a poem around it.

- ✔ **Sentences and phrases.** Phrases ("smooth as sippin' whiskey") or sentences ("The only reason I have this job is to have this job") you overhear during the day, or fragments, thoughts, and ideas that just occur to you all make great candidates for entry into your journal.

- ✔ **Words you never heard of before.** Expand your understanding of your chosen material: words. Write down words you'd like to use someday in a poem (like *frangible*) or sentences made up of unfamiliar words, just for their sound ("The frangible zerk mewled at the eumoirous thyristor"). Journals can be where you become more familiar with the possibilities of language.

- ✔ **Metaphors.** When nice metaphors occur to you with no poem around them ("the sea is the eyelid of the shore"), put them in your journal. They may come in handy later.

Moving from journal entry to poem

Some journal entries are complete poems the moment you write them. They just drop down out of nowhere, right into your brain. But most journal entries aren't poems just yet — they're the *raw material* for poetry, the stuff poetry is made of.

So how do you know when your journal entry has become poetry? You *never* know for sure, actually. Many poets keep working and reworking their poems forever. But distinguishing between a journal entry (in which you just say something) and a poem (in which you use language and thought to make something new happen) is important.

Here's a passage from a journal:

> I'm feeling mad today because I love this guy and he isn't really being that responsive. I mean, he gives me signals like he's interested, but then he acts as if he hasn't got a clue.

Sure, you may be able to imagine *situations* in which this could be poetry. (A couple of examples: What if this were your *dog* talking? What if this prose passage came smack in the middle of a Shakespearean sonnet?) But most of the time, entries like this are only the *beginning* of something poetic. Arranging them in lines can't hide that fact:

> I'm feeling
> mad today because I
> love
> this guy and he isn't
> really being that
> responsive. I mean, he
> gives me signals like he's
> interested, but then he
> acts as if he
> hasn't
> got a clue.

Even though we've arranged this into interesting lines, it's still prose — just chopped up prose. In this new form, the words are more fun to read — a few of the lines even rhyme — but it's still not poetry yet. You're looking at the ore, not the processed gold (ore is good, gold is better).

In poetry, some event takes place. Something happens to the reader. What that something is (a revelation, an epiphany, a redirection, a surprise, a paradox, an outrage, a jest) and how it happens is up to the poet. So as you read poems (and write ones of your own), allow room for both discovery and rediscovery of these events. Robert Frost wrote, "For me, the initial delight is in the surprise of remembering something I didn't know I knew." Emily Dickinson famously said she knew she was reading poetry "if I feel physically as if the top of my head were taken off." Poetry is *that* startling, that surprising; it can change the way you see things.

In the journal entry, you know the writer is feeling "mad" because she says so. But do you really *feel* it? On a scale of one to ten, with ten being a poem in which you can really feel the poet's anger, her passage is maybe a three. You can guess she really wants this guy to open up to her. But you're *guessing* at her emotions, not *knowing* them.

Using her journal as a jumping-off point, the writer later came up with these lines:

> I am a car bomb triggered to
> your front door come
> out come out

Now she's a *lot* closer to poetry. Why? Because she has found a metaphor for her emotional state. Her love is a *car bomb*. Think that metaphor through:

- ✔ **Car bombs are a form of attack often aimed at one person.** So is this woman's love, evidently. And this is more explosive than saying, "I'm feeling mad."

- ✔ **The writer is triggered to his front door.** How is she "triggered"? Our guess: Perhaps because she is so attuned to his movements, so sensitive that any move he makes is meaningful.

✔ **The last words, "come / out come out," reveal that she really does want the guy to "come out," by showing his feelings to her.** But if he does come out — blam! — she explodes. So there is some nice *ambivalence* (the coexistence of opposing or very different emotions) going on: The speaker seems to be feeling frustration and even anger (that she cannot connect somehow with this man), but the explosion suggests there may be some relief (in the release of the pent-up emotions?) as well.

The poet went from a straightforward journal entry to a few lines in which an *event* took place. Her progress suggests a few things about getting from journal entry to poem:

✔ **Think in images and metaphors.** This poet's first good move was to find a metaphor for her emotional state: the car bomb. The metaphor says a lot more, and a lot more powerfully, than three lines of prose did.

✔ **Concentrate on *showing* rather than *telling*.** This poet's second good move was to realize that simply declaring "I'm feeling mad today" didn't bring her emotional state alive. She had to find a way to bring the reader into her anger and frustration. Often, this means you won't *name* the feeling or meaning you're getting at. As songwriters have known for years, many of the most effective love songs never mention the word *love*. Instead, they find other ways to involve the reader. Poetry often works by *indirection*. (As Emily Dickinson puts it, "Tell all the Truth but tell it slant.") In our example, the poem never mentions the word *love*, yet you get more of her passions than you would have if the word *love* had come bopping in.

✔ **Think with music, rhythm, and form.** Another interesting move the poet made was to drop all punctuation. That approach makes you, the reader, work a little to group the words into understandable units — and maybe become a little more conscious of each word. She *could* have written:

> Come out,
> Come out!

But instead she wrote:

> come
> out come out

which slows you down a little and forces you to punctuate the phrase in your mind (and give it the tone carried by an absent exclamation point). It maybe even leads to a smile when you realize who's talking, to whom, and why. She has involved you more. And that's what most poets want to do.

Choosing subjects

As you forge a personality as a poet, you'll find that *what* you write about and the *form* you write in are almost as important as *how* you write.

If you're struggling for things to write about, check out the following lists of subjects from two separate journals.

List #1	*List #2*
Friendship	Friendships based on making sure nothing goes wrong
Clothes	Why men wear clothes until they're just about falling off their bodies
Kittens	The first time I pulled back the blankets to get in bed and discovered that my cat had chosen that place to have her 13 kittens
Words	How odd it is to say the word *plentiful*
Butterflies	Seeing a real butterfly land on a plastic flower
Death	Having a cancerous blip scraped off my face, knowing it won't spread but still realizing that cancer has come visiting

Compare the two lists. The prize goes to List #2, of course. Why? Because it's more specific. *Friendship* is fine, but what *about* friendship? What *kind* of friendship? When you come up with *abstractions* as subjects or titles for poems, stop and think about whether you're dwelling on generalities or saying things people have said before. You may have a lot of new things to say about friendships based on making sure nothing goes wrong, however, so that topic is a stronger one.

Write about anything you want, but when considering subjects for your poems — and when stockpiling subjects in your journal — follow these suggestions:

- ✔ **Choose limited subjects over broad ones.** Not *clothes* (broad) but *how men wear clothes until they're almost falling off* (amusingly limited).

- ✔ **Choose concrete and specific subjects over abstract and general ones.** Not *death* (abstract) but a *cancerous blip* (chillingly concrete). Not *words* (general) but the word *plentiful* (specific).

- ✔ **Choose original subjects over those you've seen before.** There are, we're guessing, about 12,571,813 poems about cats, give or take a few. Many of them are *identical*. But how many are there about cats giving birth in *your bed?*

Making these choices can help you write better poems — and discover better subjects.

Rewriting until it hurts a lot better

Some poets want their poetry to be the red-hot, first burst from their minds. In the words of Allen Ginsberg, "First thought, best thought." They're wary of tampering too much with the material they've produced in the initial heat of creation. But we've rarely met poets, no matter how devoted to inspiration and the authentic, who didn't revise like obsessed demons. The superb poet James McMichaels once read a six-line poem to his class, after which he said, "I've revised this thing 300 times, and it *still* isn't ready."

Inspiration is usually just the *beginning* of a poem. Ezra Pound compared the making of poems to sculpture: You start out with something promising and keep refining, chiseling away, getting rid of anything you don't need. Dorothy Parker called it "killing your babies." (Sweet metaphor, huh?)

Be ready to cross out anything if it doesn't work — *anything,* no matter how reluctant you may be to part with it. And follow these three guidelines for revision:

> ✔ **Treat everything you write as provisional.** Nothing is set in stone; everything is subject to change at any time.
>
> ✔ **Be tough with yourself.** Cut out anything that:
>
> > • You've seen in print before (the "George Orwell rule").
> >
> > • Seems trite or obvious.
> >
> > • Doesn't need saying or has been said or *implied* elsewhere in the poem.
>
> ✔ **Never keep something in your poem just because it helps you make a rhyme or fills out a meter.** Find a different solution instead of retaining anything second-rate.

Your subconscious is very useful in revision. For example, if you're writing a poem and it's time to go to bed, you may close your journal, yawn, and turn in. But your subconscious is still working on that poem all the time, even while you're sleeping. If your subconscious feels something in the poem isn't working, that realization will occur to you here and there, sometimes consciously (as when you read it and immediately think, "That isn't working") and sometimes subconsciously (as when the offending word or phrase just keeps coming to your attention). Pay attention when such things happen; the subconscious is very often right.

Make revision a large part of your daily writing routine. Revision is hard work, and it brings with it some disheartening moments. Sometimes, when you've revised, hardly any poem is left. But you learn a great deal as you revise — about the poem in front of you, about yourself, and about poetry in general. You don't necessarily figure out how to write as you write the first time, but you may figure out how to write as you *rewrite*. So be open to revision — it's how you and your poems get better.

From "Bed" to "The Bed": A case study in revision

The poet Linda Jarkesy kept track of her revision history with a poem originally titled "Bed" and later retitled "The Bed." Here is her first draft:

I dream myself
a cool white bed. It is nothing
like the bed I sleep in now,
(which is hardly a bed,
being a futon),
but a huge bed, with
a smooth wood frame.
The headboard
and footboard curve back, away
from each other.

The bed sits in the middle of a room,
a big room,
with sun-streaked wood floors, and
bare white walls, and open windows.
There is nothing else in the room,
but through the window you can hear
a sound, which could be
waves breaking on the shore, could be
winds whistling through the pines.

The dream
isn't about the bed. It's
not about sleeping, either, nor
about having sex in the bed (although
that could be imagined) — it's really about
simplicity, about a lack of clutter, about
perfection.

Now here is the poem in its fourth and final draft. Read the two drafts together and compare them to note the changes Jarkesy made.

I dream myself
a cool white bed. Its frame
is made of smooth,
light wood. Pale
silk sheets stretch taut
against the mattress.

The headboard and footboard
arch back, sweeping
away from each other.

The bed
rests on a sun-streaked floor.
Through a window,
you can hear a sound,
which could be
waves breaking
over rocks.

Or wind,
or the low rush of traffic
on a city street.

There is nothing else.

It is just the room,
the bed,
the sound,
and the air — a tinge
of cold — and all of it
shimmering, shimmering.

Jarkesy says that she wrote "Bed" in "one quick spurt," but after deciding she wasn't thrilled with it, she put it aside. She came upon the poem about a year later. "I realized," she writes, "that there was still something in the image of the bed that was holding my interest." So she set about to revise the poem and improve it.

So what exactly did Jarkesy change about the poem? Here are a few of the improvements:

- ✔ **She cut out every detail and word she didn't absolutely need.** Whatever was attracting Jarkesy, it was, as she writes, "largely hidden by the many extraneous details that the first draft included. The poem needed a lot of pruning if it was ever going to be successful, so I set to work. . . . The first step was to cut lines: in particular those that felt like authorial intrusions ('which is hardly a bed, being a futon'), as well as those that felt repetitious or merely boring ('a big room')."

- ✔ **Jarkesy says she also "thought about line breaks and the shape of the poem."** Note how she shortened and rebroke lines. Jarkesy writes, "The central image of the poem — that of the white bed — was quite sparse. I wanted the poem to reflect that sparseness, both in its short lines and in the cleanness of its language."

- ✔ **She listened to her subconscious.** Jarkesy was on the track of whatever was attracting her. At first, she wasn't sure what that something was, but as she worked, it became clearer: That sparse feeling was what was attracting her. At one point, she realized she had gone *too* far, so she added in a few details (such as "the low rush of traffic / on a city street" and the "silk sheets").

✔ **She changed the title.** The title went from "Bed" to "The Bed." Ask yourself what difference this subtle change makes to you as the reader, and how it changes your feelings about the poem.

✔ **She decided to show rather than tell.** Jarkesy took the poem to a writing workshop to get other writers' reactions, and one writer pointed out that the last seven lines were "doing far too much explanatory work in giving the reader an analysis of the image" presented in the rest of the poem. "What the poem needed," Jarkesy tells us, "was to stay with the image, to allow the reader to do her own imaginative work with the language." So Jarkesy crafted a new last stanza, with the lovely final line.

The resulting poem is a *lot* better. It invites you in and presents a spare but intriguing image. Instead of telling you what it means, the poem allows you to use your own imagination. It's mysterious but full of sensual images and details. And Jarkesy's good work paid off. The final version was printed in the Spring 2000 issue of the *Denver Quarterly*.

Getting Connected to the World of Poetry

Poets stay in touch with what's going on in the poetry world. And it definitely is its own world, with news, announcements, stars, breakthroughs, controversies, and a history as old as civilization. Being part of this world — meeting people who like to write, read, and listen to poetry, and who are, in fact, passionately committed to these things — is an excellent way to learn more, make friends in the art, and meet *mentors* (experienced poets and teachers who act as guides or counselors). Poetry need not be isolating — in fact, it can lead you to a fascinating community of like-minded artists.

How do poets stay connected to the world of poetry? Here are some ways:

✔ **They read.** Just as car mechanics read the latest *Auto Mechanic*, many poets read the latest *American Poetry Review, Conjunctions, New American Writing, Poetry Flash, Poets & Writers, The Poetry Project's Newsletter*, or other journals related to the poetry scene. See what other people are writing and how they're writing it. Some poems you'll like, some you won't — but all will be instructive. Also, read the reviews in journals, such as those in *Poetry, The Hudson Review*, or *The New Criterion*. These reviews are influential, much-read discussions of recent books of poems, and they're a great way to discover how poetry is getting talked about.

✔ **They get Web-smart.** The Internet is a poetry asylum; become an inmate. Consult Appendix C for poetry-oriented Web sites.

✔ **They attend poetry readings.** Readings happen at colleges and universities, museums, bookstores, bars, coffeehouses, and writing centers. Go. Better yet, go and read your own poetry at open-mike readings.

✔ **They take courses.** Many colleges and universities offer creative writing courses. So do some community centers, such as your local YWCA. Find out what's available in your community and take advantage of it.

✔ **They go to workshops.** A *workshop* is a small group session given by an experienced poet, who discusses the work of the group and invites discussion of that work. Usually, you have to send in a set of poems as an application and pay a fee to attend. Workshops are offered by colleges, universities, some bookstores and coffeehouses, and community arts centers. Some are even offered by writers in their homes. Workshops offer an intensive critique of your own poetry and that of other people. They are a good way to learn a lot at one time — and they bring you into contact with an experienced teacher and other writers.

✔ **They meet other poets.** Perhaps you know some guitarists. When they get together, *all* they want to do is look at one another's guitars. Poets are into *their* art, too. When they congregate, they like to talk about what they've liked and disliked recently, who's publishing, what they're working on, what problems they're working out. Many writers like to be part of such a scene, because they can learn a lot from their peers.

Don't fear your fellow writers. They're fascinating folks, with an interest in common. So where can you go to find other poets? College, university, or nonprofit writing centers; bookstores or coffeehouses; the Internet. Knowing that a lot of other people share your interests and your dilemmas is a good feeling, so make the effort to get to know other poets.

Chapter 9

Writing Open-Form Poetry

● ●

● ●

Y ou're probably familiar with the words *free verse*. They conjure up long, flowing lines across the page, ebbing and flowing like emotions themselves. That certainly seems to be the case with English poet D.H. Lawrence's "Bavarian Gentians," an almost hallucinatory poem about a deep blue flower:

> Bavarian gentians, big and dark, only dark
> darkening the day-time, torch-like with the smoking blueness of Pluto's
>   gloom,
> ribbed and torch-like, with their blaze of darkness spread blue
> down flattening into points, flattened under the sweep of white day

Pluto was the god of the underworld in Roman mythology; a *gentian* is a kind of flower, usually with deep blue leaves; and *Bavarian* means coming from Bavaria, a region in the south of Germany.

Most people believe that free verse doesn't have to have rhyme or rhythm. You can just write — no more of those tightly constricting forms. But take another look at Lawrence's poem: It has plenty of echoing sounds ("the smoking blueness of Pluto's gloom"), plenty of rhythm ("Bavarian gentians, big and dark" or "darkening the day-time, torch-like with the smoking blueness"). Lawrence's poem doesn't have meter, but it has plenty of rhythms. And plenty of *patterns,* too: repetitions ("dark, only dark / darkening the day time"), consonant sounds, choirs of vowels ("down flattening into points, flattened under the sweep of white day"). What a feast — and how *worked* it is: You can tell that, for all the spontaneous, *incantatory* (chant-like) quality of these lines, a poet with a remarkable ear slaved over this passage.

So *free verse* isn't that free and easy after all.

To cut through all this misunderstanding surrounding the term *free verse*, maybe not calling it *free verse* would be best. In this book, we refer to it as *open-form* poetry, a name deriving from the theories of Black Mountain poet Charles Olson, who spoke of "open verse." The term *open-form poetry* makes two points that the term *free verse* doesn't:

- ✔ As soon as you start writing a poem, you've chosen a *form*. You can't help it.
- ✔ As soon as you start writing open-form poetry, you discover rules you're imposing on yourself.

In this chapter, we put together some guidelines for writing open-form poetry. We discuss why your attitude and approach are principal parts of writing open-form poetry, as well as point out some of the pitfalls awaiting the open-form poet. Even though open-form poetry allows for a great degree of independence and self-expression, poets who choose the open-form have to earn every ounce of freedom by showing the greatest attention to detail in their poems.

Understanding Open-Form Poetry

The word *open* in the term *open form* has a positive meaning (what it *is*) and a negative meaning (what it's *not*) — and we cover both in the following sections.

What open-form poetry is

Open form allows poets to do nearly anything that can be done with language — the poet has more options with this kind of poetry. Open forms have rhythm, music, and even some rhyme, but the poet keeps those aspects changing and changeable throughout the poem.

When writing open-form poetry, you're trying to be open to how your mind works — your individual set of memories, associations, and subconscious cerebral murmurs. You're trying to pay attention, through the poem, to something you can't actually *see* directly (according to famed poetic theorist Sigmund Freud): the backstairs workings of the subconscious mind.

Poets today speak of *zigs* and *zags* — sudden swings in tone, feeling, and subject. Here are a few, courtesy of U.S. poet Charles North in his poem "Shooting for Line":

In short, we hold certain truths to be self-evident but the
     answers in code in the glove compartment,
and they eat up the presumed distance and the leftovers
like an unenacted crime bill or Sophocles' *Oedipus at Colonus.*
It seems likely no one leaves *all* hope behind, a calling card
fringed in tears and a raised border
but the wounds are bathed in salt, also the cocker spaniel.

What do you see in this poem? The Declaration of Independence, Greek
tragedy, automobile interiors, a dog. This is what people mean when they use
the words *zig* and *zag* to refer to poetry — North's poem changes subject in
virtually every line.

Some poets say it's not *them* doing the zigging and zagging; it's the poem, or
the subconscious mind working in the poem. So pay attention when zigs
and zags beg to happen in your own poetry. If a word, image, or zig occurs
to you — no matter how seemingly mundane, irrelevant, inappropriate,
frightening, or contradictory it may be — consider using it. It popped up for
a reason — or maybe no reason at all — but that's what makes it interesting.

Many poets speak of "trusting the poem" — being faithful to the way the
poem "opens up" as you write it, not editing out things you don't like, are
afraid of, or find irritating, rude, or distressing. If new pathways come up,
explore them. Be not afraid.

What open-form poetry isn't

Open forms allow you to do nearly anything you can do with language. The
operative word there is *nearly.*There are, in fact, things you *don't* do if you're
writing in open forms. Open forms are not *closed* — meaning you don't
restrict the lines to only one shape, length, or musical rule. No traditional
sonnets, ballads, or rhyme schemes can be found in open-form poetry. Sure,
you can have a line or two of iambic verse — as long as they're there for a
reason. Think about why those lines should be iambic. Ask yourself whether
the iambic verse contributes anything. If the answer is "no," consider a different form.

Knowing the Rules of the Open Form

The open form *is* a form. When you use the open form, you start to impose on
your poem — and yourself — all sorts of rules. You won't know what they are
until you get there, however, because each poem is its own form.

Think of open-form poetry as a way of thinking — an especially intense
awareness of every single aspect of the poem, from subject and tone to music

and rhythm, from the physical shape of the poem to the length (in space and in time) of the lines, from the grammar you use to the parts of speech. As the poet Charles Olson wrote, the poet "has to behave, and be, instant by instant, aware."

When you write an open-form poem, try to be very conscious. Everything in the poem, every feature, every aspect, must have a reason for being there. Be conscious of the following:

- ✔ **Economy.** Cram as much energy as possible into each word. Cut everything that doesn't absolutely need to be there.

- ✔ **Grammar and syntax.** Are you always using complete sentences? Well, that's fine — but you could also do it another way. Decide whether you have a *reason* to write in complete sentences for this poem. If you can come up with a reason, fine. If not, consider alternatives — bursts of words, single words, word fragments. And who says you have to use "proper" grammar? Or punctuation? Try breaking a few rules, if that improves the poem.

- ✔ **Parts of speech.** Some teachers say you shouldn't use adjectives or adverbs; they prefer nouns and verbs instead. That's an excellent starting point: Use only the words you need. If all you're doing is prettifying something, forget it. Use adjectives only when they're surprising ("your green voice"), contradictory ("aggressive modesty"), or give information the reader simply can't get elsewhere ("It was a Welsh ferret" — how else would we know a ferret was Welsh?).

- ✔ **Rhythms.** Look at the rhythms in your lines. Does the rhythm of the line contribute to its meaning? Anything sing-songy? If so, is it good that it's sing-songy? Often, open-form verse falls into *iambs* (a group of syllables consisting of an unstressed syllable followed by a stressed syllable, as in "alas!") and dactyls (one stressed syllable followed by two unstressed, as in "penetrate"). Don't let this happen unless there is a reason for it.

- ✔ **The physical lengths (the number syllables and the actual length) of the lines you use.** Avoid falling into exactly the same lengths. Every length should have a reason behind it.

- ✔ **The length (in time) it takes to read each line aloud.** If each line takes about the same number of seconds, figure out whether there's a reason for it. If there isn't, consider other shapes and lengths.

- ✔ **Line endings.** Poets realize that line endings carry a certain emphasis or pressure. Your lines should end where they end for some reason. The way a line ends — where, and after what word or punctuation mark — should be the best way to end. Do you want a pause there? What's going to happen when your readers go to the next line? Something unexpected? Some surprise? Read a lot of open-form verse, and you'll notice that poets use a great deal of *enjambment,* winding the words around the ends of lines in gorgeous and meaningful ways.

As an example of a successful open-form poem, one in which each aspect of the poem is meaningful, each word bristling with released energy, we offer these lines by Lorine Niedecker:

> Now in one year
>   a book published
>   and plumbing —
> took a lifetime
>   to weep
>   a deep
>   trickle

You could read this poem literally: The main events of the year were the book I published and a plumbing job I had to get done. But you probably can feel more in there. For example, notice the following:

- ✔ **The odd echo between *published* and *plumbing*.** The words share four sounds (*p, l,* short *u,* short *i*) and the same rhythm, a trochee (DUH-duh). With so much in common, the two get associated somehow in your brain. How are publishing and plumbing related? It may be just literal: They were the two big events of the year. Then again, what sort of plumbing is the poet talking about? Does she mean pipes and water? Or could the word *plumbing* be a metaphor for what you do when you write poetry — *plumb* (search deeply) your emotions and experience? What if the book was what took a lifetime, and the deep trickle was what became the poems? (You can come up with other possible readings as well. *Plumbing,* some may say, has overtones of sex or bodily functions.)

- ✔ **Rhyme and rhythm!** You see rhyme and rhythm both in the intriguing juxtaposition between *published* and *plumbing* and between *weep* and *deep.* And hear the rhythms, especially the last three lines:

>   to weep
>   a deep
>   trickle

  The first two are iambs (duh-DUH), and the last one is a trochee (DUH-duh), with a very short last syllable. There's a reversal, a dwindle at the end. It even *looks* like a trickle.

- ✔ **The shape of the poem in space and time.** The poem gets smaller, both in terms of the number of syllables and the length of the lines (in both time and space — it takes less time to say *trickle* than it does to say *a deep*). The last three lines are two syllables, so you could say the poem trickles to its ending. Also, the poem tapers to an end, like a *plumb* (a lead weight attached to a line to show the vertical). Plumbs are used by architects, surveyors, construction workers, and, yes, plumbers.

If you come away with an impression of pain or perhaps sorrow, the summary of a year and also a lifetime, of long, hard work to write and to "plumb" — well, then, you have to say that this is a superb little poem.

Niedecker appears *very* conscious of every element of her poem, down to the dash in the middle, which seems as though she's about to explain what she means by plumbing — but doesn't really. That's open-form poetry as a *way of thinking*.

Using the Open Form in Your Own Writing

Poets have described open-form verse in various ways. In the following sections, we suggest ways to use those ideas as a basis for your own poetry.

What *kind* of open-form verse you write depends on you. Practice with these different approaches. They may seem difficult or nutty at first, but after a while you'll start thinking in one of them, or in an open form all your own. And you'll find that you may work harder with your open-form poems than you ever anticipated. In the end, open form is both a challenge and a pleasure.

Going for the breath: Framing individual lines

As you read poetry, you become sensitive to the way you breathe. You read a group of words and then pause before reading another group of words — it's just natural. Pay attention to that when you write poetry as well. Let those natural pauses determine where lines end. The *breath*, as it's called in the poetry world, is a natural way to frame individual lines. It will be different from poem to poem, from line to line, but it can help guide both your writing and your reading.

Our guess is that Lorine Niedecker (in the poem earlier in this chapter) is using the breath as the measure of her open-form lines. How do we know? We don't. But read the poem aloud. There seems (to us) to be a very strong pause — almost as you may have with an intake of breath — between the lines. Reading straight through seems very *un*natural — each line is roughly "equal to a breath," as some poets say.

Not all poets have the same length of breath. Some poets use a long, rolling breath, rather like a song or incantation. Beat poet Allen Ginsberg once wrote of himself, "My breath is long — that's the Measure, one physical-mental inspiration of thought contained in the elastic of a breath." One of Ginsberg's great inspirations was fellow poet Walt Whitman. You can hear the length of the long, rolling breath in the lines of Whitman's poem, "O You Whom I Often and Silently Come":

O you whom I often and silently come where you are that I may be with you,
As I walk by your side or sit near, or remain in the same room with you,
Little you know the subtle electric fire that for your sake is playing within me.

Like Ginsberg, you can regard your breath as your personal measure. Listen
to your breath as a source of rhythm, pace, tone, and *inspiration* — a word
based on the Latin word *inspirare,* meaning "to breathe in." Whitman's breath
is different from Niedecker's, which is different from Lawrence's (earlier in
this chapter).

How can you use the breath in writing open-form poetry? In revision, do the
following:

- ✔ **Read aloud an open-form poem you've been working on, paying close
  attention to the breath as you read.** If you pause naturally in mid-line,
  break the line there. If you can't get a line to fit with a breath, something
  may be wrong with the way it's written. Think about it, and try some
  revisions that may help the line "find" a breath-length that fits naturally.

- ✔ **Vary the breath rhythms throughout the poem.** Don't keep them all the
  same length.

- ✔ **Check to be sure the breath contributes to the sense of the lines.** Does
  it? If not, determine why not. Rework the length of the lines until you feel
  the breath and the lines work together.

- ✔ **As in all open-form poetry, take special care with line endings!** Line
  endings generate much of the tension, much of the specialness that
  makes open-form verse *verse.* Slave over your line endings!

Treating the page as a field

Poets speak of the page as a *field,* a place in which each part of the poem
starts to have a meaningful relation to each other part. The fun part is that
you get to decide what the different aspects of the field will mean. In the following sections, we cover three ways you can use the page as a field in your
own open-form poetry.

Make the form of each stanza meaningful

One way you can use the page as a field is to make the form of your stanza,
and the movements of the lines in that form (left, right, up, down), meaningful in and of themselves. A good example of this kind of field-writing is the
three-line stanza of William Carlos Williams. He made up an open-form stanza
that he called the *variable foot.* It plays by some interesting rules:

✔ Each stanza contains three lines.

✔ Each line is indented from the previous one, moving left to right.

✔ Each indentation is *meaningful*. It signals a shift in thought, as the mind builds on what was just said or goes in a new direction.

✔ Each line is a *unit of sense*. That is, each line makes a statement or an important part of a statement.

✔ Each line has one *beat* (one major rhythmic stress, related to the unit of sense).

✔ Each third line propels the reader into the next stanza somehow.

Here is the beginning of Williams's famous poem "The Descent":

The descent beckons
        as the ascent beckoned.
                Memory is a kind
   of accomplishment,
       a sort of renewal
           even
   an initiation, since the spaces it opens are new places
       inhabited by hordes
              heretofore unrealized,
   of new kinds —

Williams is saying some beautiful things here. As a reader, you don't know yet what he means by "ascent" and "descent," although they may mean something simple like "success" and "failure," or "happiness" and "sorrow."

Do you feel the beats in his lines? Each line is one unit of sense and gets one beat. So the sixth line, *even,* gets one beat, and so does the much longer, prosy seventh line. Can you feel why? Perhaps out of sheer excitement, out of discovery. The speaker just said that memory is a "sort of renewal," which is easy enough to see — but then a new thought occurs — memory is *even* an initiation! Why is it an initiation? Maybe because memory opens up new spaces for you, filled with "hordes" of new things you never knew. No memory is ever alike; as you change, memory changes and teaches you new things. So "even" deserves its beat, for sheer excitement, and the next line, which is what "even" introduces, is all one beat as well.

Each third line propels you into the next stanza. The poem has both a left-to-right movement and a downward movement — a descent! It's like a stairway. You can see how Williams planned his stanza out — not according to rhyme or meter, but according to the way he wanted his argument to move.

Manage the relationships of the words and syllables

A second way to treat the page as a field is defined by Charles Olson, who spoke of the field as "the place where all the syllables and all the lines must be managed in their relations to each other." Olson imagined that all the words in a poem created a tension with one another, like the particles in an atom or the parts of a suspension bridge. The poet manages the relationships of the words and syllables, feels the tension, and orchestrates it.

Kathleen Fraser's "Vanishing Point: Third Black Quartet" is the tenth section of a beautiful poem titled "Wing." In "Vanishing Point," Fraser uses the page as a field in this way. You can almost feel the words vibrating in their tense interrelations:

```
forward edge itself to be volume by necessity as if partial          erase
edge itself to be volume by necessity as if partial erase            other
itself to be volume by necessity as if partial erase               corners
to be volume by necessity as if partial erase                       planes
be volume by necessity as if partial erase                      accumulate
volume by necessity as if partial erase                              depth
by necessity as if partial erase                                 condensed
necessity as if partial erase                                           in
as if partial erase                                            preparation
if partial erase                                                 stagework
partial erase                                                     historic
erase                                                              tendons
of                                                               elaborate
pearly                                                             ribcage
lucent                                                              marked
decision                                                           midway
and                                                                  with
little                                                             grains
tasks                                                                  of
of                                                                  light
pain                                                             talking
had                                                                softly
tried                                                              among
to                                                          disintegrating
lift                                                                cubes
to lift                                                               the
tried to lift                                                     falling
had tried to lift                                                    wing
pain had tried to lift                                               will
of pain had tried to lift                                           draw
tasks of pain had tried to lift                                      the
little tasks of pain had tried to lift                              mind
and little tasks of pain had tried to lift                            as
decision and little tasks of pain had tried to lift                    a
lucent decision and little tasks of pain had tried to lift           bow
```

itself   the   wing   not   static   but   frayed,   layered,   fettered,   furling

Fraser, clearly conscious of all the elements in this poem, has created a shape that's brand-new. You can read this poem in many ways — it's impossible to read this poem in one "correct" order. You can start almost anywhere and get different strings of words (the exquisite "little tasks of pain" or the "falling wing will draw the mind as a bow"). The left edge appears to melt away as you read down ("as if partial erase"). You can read down from the upper right corner, or across the space ("tendons of elaborate pearly ribcage"). You remember the title and think of the many physical "vanishing points" in the poem. And notice the shape of the white space in the center of the poem: It resembles a wing, which recalls that this is part of a work with the title "Wing."

Fraser has thought it all through, has created all the relations — without using a single complete sentence and only two commas! Surprising meanings erupt from the unexpected combinations of words — such is the energy she has created in this field.

Fraser's poem shows you how very *formal* an open-form poem can be.

Plan the meanings of different parts of the page

You can also write with the page as a field by planning the meanings of different parts of the page. You can draw lines, boxes, or circles to separate different parts of the page and say what will happen in each part. Treating the page as a field immediately makes space meaningful. It's like marking out the field for a new kind of sport. When play starts, you're bound by the rules you've made up and the lines you've drawn. Within those lines, however, almost anything can happen. Open form, indeed.

Treating white space as time

You may have seen poems that were groups of words scattered all over the page. One way to approach a reading of such a poem is to treat white space as time — by *pausing* before continuing to the next word you encounter. The larger the space between words, the longer the pause.

Try this principle with the following, the ninth poem in a series titled "29 Songs" by Objectivist poet Louis Zukofsky:

In Arizona
      (how many years in the mountains)
The small stumped bark of a tree
Looks up
      in the shape of an adored pup

The indians do not approach it
The round indian tents
      remain where they are

> The tanned whites
> > are never seen by it
> And one can imagine its imploring eyes

You pause longer between the first and second lines than you would between the second and third lines, and even longer between the two stanzas. If you treat white space as time, you'll begin to sense a rhythm to the poem closely tied to the way the lines are laid out.

Treating white space as time is one of the best ways to write open-form poetry. Take special care with line endings: On which word will the line end? To what word will it lead? How much space or time is there before the next word?

When writing your own open-form poetry, you can treat white space as time by doing the following:

- ✔ Vary the spatial relationships of the lines. The pauses should be a variety of lengths — all having to do with the sense and impact of the verse.

- ✔ Use enjambment to wrap the sentences around the ends of lines.

- ✔ Read your verse aloud constantly as it develops. Rearrange lines and line breaks if the reading doesn't feel right.

- ✔ Cut everything you don't absolutely need. Because pauses will be directing the reading, you may decide (as many poets do) that you don't really need punctuation (which usually directs your pauses). Let it go!

Chapter 10

Working with Traditional Forms of Verse

In This Chapter

▶ Exploring traditional forms of poetry

▶ Respecting the tradition of formal poetry

▶ Making sense of the rules for the ballad, the psalm, the sonnet, the ghazal, and the tanka

*W*hen you think of poetry, you may think of ballads, sonnets, rhyming couplets, iambic pentameter, A-B-A-B, verses, stanzas, and refrains. And what you're thinking of are *traditional* forms of verse — forms that have come down through the centuries, each form with its own rules and challenges. Open-form verse (covered in Chapter 9) is different every time you use it — in essence, you *create* a form each time you write an open-form poem. But with traditional verse forms, you accept measures, restrictions, and laws others have made, or ones that have accrued through the years.

No matter what kind of poetry you end up writing, knowing how to write in traditional forms can be a great benefit. Almost all of these forms remain vibrant today — poets are still singing loud and strong through them, making them do modern tricks. Practicing traditional forms is an excellent way to:

✔ Work on the craft of poetry.

✔ Begin a writing session.

✔ Break writer's block.

✔ Write good poems.

You're never done working with the traditional forms — you can always beginning afresh. *Remember:* Writing poetry is a lifelong apprenticeship, one to be savored.

Respecting the tradition

As a poet, you'll write the way you want to write — and that's great. But when you're starting out, and when you're trying traditional forms, take the forms seriously and (at least at first) follow the rules strictly. Start by trying to find the perfect rhyme (instead of something that comes close), and try not to vary many feet in your chosen meters.

Later, you can vary the rules — write a sonnet that doesn't rhyme or one that doesn't use meter, mess with the rhyme schemes, or use *slant rhyme,* daring to rhyme *shoe* with *snow,* for example (slant rhyme is an excellent way to tune your ear). But first experience the way traditions help you organize your poems and reach for language you rarely use. Let the old forms stretch you in new directions.

Ballads

Traditional *ballads* are stories told in verse — often stories of a romantic or lurid sort. Ballads still are being written today, especially in the form of popular songs.

Ballads take many forms. A popular one is the four-line stanza in which the first and third lines are written in iambic tetrameter (four iambs) and the second and fourth are written in iambic trimeter (three iambs), with a rhyme scheme of ABXB (the third line, X, need not rhyme or may rhyme with A).

Here's what two such stanzas may sound like:

> The winter moon had tipped and spilled
>   Its shadows on the lawn
> When Farmer Owen woke to find
>   His only daughter gone;
>
> She'd taken all the clothes she had
>   Against the biting cold,
> And in a note to him she wrote,
>   "I've taken all your gold."

Stick to this stanza type and write a ghost story, mystery, suspense tale, news event, or heroic story (stories of the Knights of the Round Table and Robin Hood were written in this form). Make the story and the language as modern as you can. You'll see that this sturdy little form is excellent for carrying a tale.

Psalms

The Hebrew poets who compiled the Psalms worked with a very interesting verse form. It consisted of *distichs,* verses of two lines. The lines could be of almost any length. The first line was a statement, and the second built on that statement, usually in one of three ways:

- **Sameness:** The poet can amplify the first half by restating all or part of it in some way, as in Psalm 102:

    > I am like a pelican in the wilderness;
    >> I have become like an owl among the ruins

- **Antithesis:** The poet can state something in the second half that opposes the statement in the first half, as in Ecclesiastes 3:4:

    > A time to weep
    >> and a time to laugh

- **Complement:** A complement balances two halves of a statement, as in Proverbs 19:21:

    > A man may have many plans in his mind
    >> but the counsel of the Lord — that will stand

You, too, can write a psalm. The rules are few. Pick a very mundane event in your life and write it down straightforwardly in all the *first* (left-hand) lines of the distichs, leaving the *second* (right-hand) lines blank, like this:

> Today I came down to breakfast
> And I was hungry
> So my mother brought me some cornflakes
> She poured them in a bowl
> And gave the bowl to me

Now fill in the second lines. Use sameness, antithesis, and complement. Amplify, illustrate, question, comment, contradict the first halves in as many ways as you can think of:

> Today I came down to breakfast
>> Or breakfast came to me   [antithesis]
> And I was hungry
>> eating rose by rose the wallpaper   [sameness, amplification]
> So my mother brought me some cornflakes
>> Morning Mom, bringer of breakfast   [amplification]
> She poured them in a bowl
>> Pouring them in the garden would be strange   [antithesis]
> And gave the bowl to me
>> I accepted it, humble as cornflakes   [complement]

The fun (and hard) part is to create second lines that echo material in the first lines but also *transform* that material. You may find your second lines becoming surreal or humorous or divergent. The right-hand lines don't have to make sense or be logically related to the left-hand ones.

Psalm-writing is a good way to get invention juices flowing, and it can yield interesting poems. Have fun with it. Break your own rules now and then. The idea is to think divergently.

Sonnets

Time to pay your dues. Try writing a sonnet.

Here are the rules:

- ✔ It must consist of 14 lines.
- ✔ It must be written in iambic pentameter (duh-DUH-duh-DUH-duh-DUH-duh-DUH-duh-DUH).
- ✔ It must be written in one of various standard rhyme schemes.

If you're writing the most familiar kind of sonnet, the *Shakespearean,* the rhyme scheme is this:

A
B
A
B
C
D
C
D
E
F
E
F
G
G

Every A rhymes with every A, every B rhymes with every B, and so forth. You'll notice this type of sonnet consists of three *quatrains* (that is, four consecutive lines of verse that make up a *stanza* or division of lines in a poem) and one *couplet* (two consecutive rhyming lines of verse).

Ah, but there's more to a sonnet than just the structure of it. A sonnet is also an *argument* — it builds up a certain way. And *how* it builds up is related to its metaphors and how it moves from one metaphor to the next. In a Shakespearean sonnet, the argument builds up like this:

- ✔ **First quatrain:** An exposition of the main theme and main metaphor.

- ✔ **Second quatrain:** Theme and metaphor extended or complicated; often, some imaginative example is given.

- ✔ **Third quatrain:** *Peripeteia* (a twist or conflict), often introduced by a *but* (very often leading off the ninth line).

- ✔ **Couplet:** Summarizes and leaves the reader with a new, concluding image.

One of Shakespeare's best-known sonnets, Sonnet 18, follows this pattern:

> Shall I compare thee to a summer's day?
> Thou art more lovely and more temperate.
> Rough winds do shake the darling buds of May,
> And summer's lease hath all too short a date.
> Sometime too hot the eye of heaven shines,
> And often is his gold complexion dimmed;
> And every fair from fair sometime declines,
> By chance, or nature's changing course, untrimmed;
> But thy eternal summer shall not fade,
> Nor lose possession of that fair thou owest,
> Nor shall death brag thou wanderest in his shade,
> When in eternal lines to time thou growest.
> > So long as men can breathe or eyes can see,
> > So long lives this, and this gives life to thee.

The argument of Sonnet 18 goes like this:

- ✔ **First quatrain:** Shakespeare establishes the theme of comparing "thou" (or "you") to a summer's day, and why to do so is a bad idea. The metaphor is made by comparing his beloved to summer itself.

- ✔ **Second quatrain:** Shakespeare extends the theme, explaining why even the sun, supposed to be so great, gets obscured sometimes, and why everything that's beautiful decays from beauty sooner or later. He has shifted the metaphor: In the first quatrain, it was "summer" in general, and now he's comparing the sun and "every fair," every beautiful thing, to his beloved.

- ✔ **Third quatrain:** Here the argument takes a big left turn with the familiar "But." Shakespeare says that the main reason he won't compare his beloved to summer is that summer dies — but she won't. He refers to the first two quatrains — her "eternal summer" won't fade, and she won't "lose possession" of the "fair" (the beauty) she possesses. So he keeps the metaphors going, but in a different direction. And for good measure, he throws in a negative version of all the sunshine in this poem — the "shade" of death, which, evidently, his beloved won't have to worry about.

✔ **Couplet:** How is his beloved going to escape death? In Shakespeare's poetry, which will keep her alive as long as people breathe or see. This bold statement gives closure to the whole argument — it's a surprise.

And so far, Shakespeare's sonnet has done what he promised it would! See how tightly this sonnet is written, how complex yet well-organized it is? Try writing a sonnet of your own.

Poets are attracted by the grace, concentration, and, yes, the sheer difficulty of sonnets. You may never write another sonnet in your life, but this exercise is more than just busywork. It does all the following:

✔ Shows you how much you can pack into a short form.

✔ Gives you practice with rhyme, meter, structure, metaphor, and argument.

✔ Connects you with one of the oldest traditions in English poetry — one still vital today.

Writing experimental sonnets

Poets have begun to take the sonnet in some new places. David Trinidad's "Monster Mash" is a Shakespearean sonnet (it rhymes and maintains recognizable iambic pentameter) — while creating a poem with nothing but the names of old horror movies:

Frankenstein, Godzilla, The Blob, Phantom
of the Opera, The Wolf Man, The Hunchback
of Notre Dame, Children of the Damned, Them,
Queen of Outer Space, Creature from the Black

Lagoon, Curse of the Cat People, The Mum-
my, The Green Slime, The Brain that Wouldn't Die,
Invaders from Mars, It! The Terror from
Beyond Space, Dr. Cyclops, Freaks, The Fly,

Bride of Frankenstein, The Invisible
Man, The Mole People, Dr. Jekyll and
Mr. Hyde, Mothra, The Incredible
Shrinking Man, Dracula, The Crawling Hand,

Attack of the Fifty-Foot Woman, King
Kong, Tarantula, 13 Ghosts, The Thing.

Today, poets are using traditional forms in nontraditional ways. When you feel comfortable in a form, explore new avenues with it yourself.

Ghazals

The *ghazal* (pronounce it "guzzle" with a slight gargle on the *g*) is one of the few Arabic verse forms to have a big impact in the West. It came into European poetry through 19th-century German poets and got into English-language poetry in the late 1960s. Here are the rules:

- **Every line must have the same number of syllables.** American and English writers usually settle on iambic pentameter or something close, but you can choose any number of syllables you like.

- **The ghazal is a series of couplets (at least five, but there's no upper limit).**

- **The first couplet rhymes.** For example:

    October: the horizon, grey and wide,
    Is staggering — you're dancing in the tide.

- **The closing words of the second half of the second line are repeated in the second line of each succeeding couplet.** It could be the last word, or a several-word phrase — it's up to you. This is called the *radif.* Here, our radif is "dancing in the tide," which has to appear at the end of the second line of each succeeding couplet.

- **The remaining couplets don't have to rhyme, and they can shift around in subject and tone.** Make them as independent as you want, but always, come back to that radif ("dancing in the tide").

- **The *makhta,* or the poet's signature (first name, last name, or both) appears somewhere in the last couplet.**

Here's an example of a ghazal we wrote ourselves, following all of these rules:

October: the horizon, grey and wide,
Is staggering — you're dancing in the tide.

My uncle died and left me twenty sheep
Stacked in my basement. Dancing in the tide

Of debts, divorce announcements, and debris,
I chuck it all, go dancing. In the Tide

There was a lottery coupon, and I won.
Now all my friends come dancing in the tide.

As ocarina orchestras obfusc,
Maureen Watts goes dancing in the tide.

Poets love the ghazal because it's both free and patterned. It's halfway between a traditional, rhymed form and a free, associative one. Closed, yet wide open. Get in and drive it anywhere!

Tankas

The Japanese *tanka* is a verse form from classical Japanese poetry. Even older than its better-known cousin, the *haiku,* the tanka is a quiet, meditative form focused on the natural world and the poet's emotions. A tanka is essentially a haiku (three lines consisting of 5, 7, and 5 syllables each), except with two more lines of 7 syllables each. Traditionally, the tanka begins with an observation of a natural scene:

> Invisible hands
> caress my face; have I walked
> through a spider's web
>
> woven this morning to catch
> flies writhing with my surprise

Many poets find that the tanka falls naturally into a haiku followed by a couplet. The haiku tends to focus more on observation, the couplet on reflection. But you don't have to observe this movement in your own writing. The tanka is a *syllabic* form, so just follow these simple rules:

- ✔ Avoid end-rhyming the lines.
- ✔ Vary the rhythms from line to line.
- ✔ Use enjambment to keep sentences and clauses twisting around the ends of the lines.
- ✔ Avoid ending too many lines in a row with a one-syllable word.

Chapter 11

Putting Pen to Paper: Writing Exercises for Poets

● ●

In This Chapter

▶ Practicing your poetry

▶ Breaking logjams in your writing

▶ Thinking divergently, with a poet's mind

● ●

*I*n this chapter, we give you a series of writing exercises geared toward poets. They come from experienced teachers of creative writing — Charles Bernstein, Maxine Chernoff, Kelly Holt, Daniel J. Langton, Bernadette Mayer, Brighde Mullins, and Eileen Myles — who throughout their careers have designed these exercises for their students to help them:

✔ Get started and get their invention flowing.

✔ Practice writing.

✔ Rid themselves of habits and ruts.

✔ Start thinking with a poet's mind.

You'll find many ideas here, but you don't need to try them all. Simply read through them, start anywhere, and try one that appeals to you.

Writing in a Journal to Improve Your Poetry

You can write in a journal, like Walida Imarisha in Figure 11-1, to help improve your poetry. Here are some subjects to use as journal topics:

✔ Food

✔ Finances

- ✔ Writing ideas
- ✔ Love
- ✔ Beautiful and/or ugly things you've seen
- ✔ A daily history of your own writing life
- ✔ Reading/music/art you encounter each day
- ✔ Weather
- ✔ Descriptions of people you see
- ✔ Subway, bus, car, or other trips (for example, writing about the same bus trip you take every day)
- ✔ Pleasures and/or pains you've experienced
- ✔ Mail (sent, received, snail-mail, e-mail, imaginary mail, other people's mail)
- ✔ Answering machine messages/telephone calls
- ✔ The body
- ✔ Dangers

[Exercise contributed by Bernadette Mayer]

Figure 11-1:
Walidah
Imarisha
writes in her
journal.

© David Huang

Dedicate a journal to one subject alone (for example, many poets keep *dream journals,* recording images and events in their dreams), or mix it up.

Discovering Your Own Poetry

Poets need to be objective, to see their poems from outside of themselves. To find out more about what *you* do in your poems, make some analytical lists. Look for patterns and habits, and think about ways to break out of them or vary them. Try sitting down with your poems and listing the following:

- ✔ **The colors that appear directly or in hints.** Compare this list to the colors you never use, and look for patterns.

- ✔ **The body parts mentioned in your poems.** See if you put an emphasis on one part of the body (if you do, it is usually the face or the head).

- ✔ **Plants or flowers (which can be tied to the colors you use).** Again, look for patterns.

- ✔ **Animals.** Are the animals you discuss in your poems rare in your life (such as tigers) or common (such as dogs)? Are they usually alive or usually dead? Are there preferences you hadn't noticed before (insects over mammals, for instance)?

[Exercise contributed by Daniel J. Langton]

Underline every noun in your poems. Then underline every adjective. Is there a pattern in the nouns or adjectives you use? Many beginning poets have an adjective describing every noun. Is this the case in your poems? Does the last word of each line turn out to be a monosyllable? Beginning poets attempting rhyme tend to have this pattern as well. Find ways to avoid or vary any pattern or habit that resembles a "rut" or has no poetic reason for existing.

Using Description in Your Poetry

This exercise helps you focus on description. Select an object outside — a building, statue, street sign, or billboard, for example — that you pass frequently. Then describe it in the following different ways:

- ✔ Describe it in such a way that others hearing your brief account are able to draw it (an exact visual take).

- ✔ Describe it using point of view, first from far away, then from up close.

 ✔ Describe its relation to the landscape.

 ✔ Describe how it changes over time, with shifts in the weather, and at different times of day.

[Exercise contributed by Brighde Mullins]

You can also try looking in a mirror and describing what you see, without using the word *I* or any adjectives. Concentrate on nouns, verbs, and comparisons.

Generating Material with Divergent Thinking

Poets find new words for new ideas and new attitudes toward their experiences — and that takes divergent thinking. Here are some exercises that encourage you to think in unaccustomed ways and create new material for poetry.

Finding your own way of writing

Reading aloud from a text that is full of rich description can be a great help to your own writing. The best texts for this purpose are often travel or nature writings. Take five to seven minutes to write down words, phrases, and sentences that really strike you. Steal freely. You're gathering material to write with.

Now write a poem out of those words. Repeat, delete, or change the order of the words you've harvested as you please — but don't add anything that was not in your original list. Invent a title for the poem in your own words.

This exercise helps you see that your way of writing is exactly that — a *way* of your own. You don't even need a subject matter to write. When you have words, you can have your way with them. Your *way* is how you move through language and manipulate it — it's your signature. Understanding that can open a lot of doors.

[Exercise contributed by Eileen Myles]

Experimenting with different forms

Get out your trusty book of poetic forms. Now write a poem in a different form each day for 30 days, following the order as they're covered in the book, moving from A to Z. Think of this exercise as your very own short course in poetic technique!

Working with various topics

Choose a topic, and write an essay in which you get your ideas about that topic as clear as possible. Keep the essay to one paragraph. Then turn that block of prose into a poem.

Rewriting well-known texts

Try selecting a well-known text, such as "The Pledge of Allegiance," and substituting each word in it with the word seven entries down in your dictionary. So the line

> I pledge allegiance to the flag

might become

> Iamb Pleiades allegretto toady theater of war flagellate

With exercises like these, which produce chance poetry, the idea is to get your invention flowing and create new resources. Nothing obliges you to use any of what's generated. But if something intrigues you, build on it, explore, see where it leads.

[Exercise contributed by Bernadette Mayer]

Pulling from a grab-bag of ideas

Here's a grab-bag of poem ideas to try. Write a poem:

- ✔ Made up entirely of the first or last lines of famous poems.

- ✔ Of 26 words, in which each word begins with a letter of the alphabet. (You can also scramble the order.)

- ✔ In which all the words in each line start with the same letter. This can be combined with the preceding idea.

✔ Consisting entirely of overheard conversation.

✔ That does not mention any objects.

✔ That contains everything you hear or that happens to you over the course of a limited amount of time (for example, 15 minutes, 1 hour, 1 day).

✔ Composed of everything on your answering machine or voice mail over the past week.

✔ Composed entirely of excuses. Make the excuses relate to things you wouldn't make excuses for: "I'm sorry my nose is in the front of my head, but you see, I _____."

[Exercise contributed by Charles Bernstein and Bernadette Mayer]

Using techniques of chance and collage to compose poetry

This exercise is called variously "Tzara's Hat" (named after the Dada poet Tristan Tzara, who invented it) or "Exquisite Corpse." Cut words out of newspapers or magazines and throw them into a hat. Fish out the first 20 and arrange them — in the order in which you fished them out — into a poem:

> Health bullets vulnerable next covering for statistics
> On hockey licensed victims' LaBella proportion stops
> Cuba hits dead
> Propelled family anything

Write a response in the same number of lines, words, or syllables. One possibility is to *reverse* the words and phrases, either verbally or in some conceptual way:

> Malaria wounds are invincible, the last opening; five myths
> Off the unauthorized criminals of baseball. ElFeo promotes lopsided
> Florida, gets smacked by the inhibited corpses
> Of vacuum orphans.

The point of collage exercises (like the preceding one) is to create combinations of words, phrases, and sentences that may generate new material for your poetry. Use some of what you generate, all of it, or none of it. Or, if something gives you an idea, start writing.

Mistranslating from other languages

Mistranslation is a technique pioneered by, among other groups, the Teacher's and Writer's Collective in New York. A similar exercise also appears in *The Oulipo Compendium,* edited by Harry Mathews.

Select a poem in a foreign language, one you can pronounce but not necessarily understand, and approximate the *sound* of the poem in English words (so, for example, the French word *blanc* becomes *blank* in English, and *toute* becomes *toot*). Here's an example of a poem to start with (Alfred De Vigny's "Les Destinées"):

> Le moule de la vie étair creusé par nous.
> Toutes les passions y répandaient leur lave,
> Et les événements venaient s'y fondre tous.

You could use this poem to create a new one:

> Lame-mule day. Larva eat air. Cruise, ape. Our new
> Toot lay passion? Sí. Hear a panda on Lou. Laugh!
> Hey! Lazy venom! Aunt Vinny! Aunt Ziff! Auntie Ray, too.

Rewrite it to suit your own style.

Try picking a book at random and using its title as the key phrase for an *acrostic,* going letter-by-letter down the left edge of the page. For each letter in this key phrase, go to the corresponding page number in the book. (A = page 1, B = page 2, and so on), and copy the first line or sentence on that page as the first line of the poem. Continue through all the letters in the key, leaving stanza breaks to mark each new key word. Variations include

- Using the author's name rather than the book title.

- Using a friend's name — or your own.

- Using a different book for each letter or word in the acrostic key.

[Exercise contributed by Charles Bernstein]

Thinking about your life's transitions

Take 15 or 20 minutes to write about some transition time you've experienced today. That may include

- Your commute from work to school.

- Getting from your house to the bus stop.

✔ Driving.

✔ Waiting in a train station.

Choose a particular moment in your chosen transit — it can be as short as the time it takes a traffic light to change. Reflect on it. Warp the speed at which it took place. Then elongate that moment into the length of a poem or paragraph.

[Exercise contributed by Kelly Holt]

Getting ideas by taking a walk

Take a walk and make a poem out of it. Walk 14 blocks and write a line for each block — a walking sonnet. Or write one poem per mile. Take notes and create a poem. Write down all the text you observe on a walk (street signs, shop names, billboards, advertisements on buses, and so on), and write a poem using *only* that material.

[Exercise contributed by Charles Bernstein and Bernadette Mayer]

Using language from one subject to write about another

Try using language from one subject area to write about another subject that is very much unrelated to it. For example, use science terms to write about childhood, or philosophic language to describe a shirt.

[Exercise contributed by Bernadette Mayer]

Revising Your Poetry

You may wonder why we include exercises for revision in a chapter on writing, but revision is one of the most important aspects of creation. So getting some practice with it — and seeing revision from several possibly unexpected angles — is a good idea.

Hiding half of your poem from sight

Take one of your poems and fold it in half horizontally, so you can see the top half of the poem but not the bottom half. Rewrite the half you *can't* see — without looking at the original. Compare the original to your revision. Which one is shorter, more compressed? If the new half is better, keep it. You can also pick and choose between the virtues of the two versions. As a variation, fold the poem *vertically,* and rewrite the left or right half.

[Exercise contributed by Maxine Chernoff]

Reworking poems you don't like

Select one of your poems that you're dissatisfied with. Read it through. Now put it away. Try to write the same poem again without referring to the older version. You often get a new and better poem this way.

[Exercise contributed by Maxine Chernoff]

If you've written a poem, but you don't know what to do with it to revise it and make it better, take your first or second draft and put it into three or four different poetic forms:

- Turn it into a block of prose.
- If you've used short lines, reformat them into longer lines.
- If you've used long lines, reformat them into shorter lines.
- Reformat the piece into stanzas of two lines or three lines.
- Rewrite the poem in an extremely constricting form, such as a sonnet.

The point of this exercise is to look at the poem in another way. How does each reformation change the poem? What does it add or take away? Which of the forms works best, and why? What new ideas do you get from seeing the poem anew?

[Exercise contributed by Kelly Holt]

Collaborating with Other Writers

Experiment with collaborative writing with a group of other writers. (These exercises also make good party games when poets get together.) Here are some examples:

- **Keep a public journal, posted on either a common message board on the Web or a paper pinned up in a common room.** Everyone can write his own contributions daily. As a variation, each contributor makes an entry, but leaves it somehow incomplete (writing only half a phrase, leaving a word out, or asking a question). The next contributor must finish the incomplete entry and write a new incomplete entry. Or two writers can alternate days to write in the journal.

✓ **Have 14 poets each write one line of iambic pentameter (without consulting one another).** Collect the lines, throw them into a hat, and select the lines at random. Voila! A collaborative sonnet. Try different arrangements of the lines.

✓ **Write a verse novel together.** Make up an incomplete story with three characters with names and descriptions, plus a situation, such as a kidnapping or some other mystery — but don't establish complications or resolutions. Now, each writer writes a "chapter" of no more than 30 lines, employing all the characters, in whatever form she wishes. Collect and order the chapters, read the novel, then have each person write a "final chapter" of 30 lines. Collect, read, select, and combine.

✓ **Have everyone write on the same topic and then choose bits from everyone's poetry and combine them into one big poem.**

✓ **Have one poet write a poem, printing it out with extra space between each line. The other poets now write lines in the blank spaces.**

✓ **Have one poet write a poem.** Then the other poets reverse the poem (writing the opposite of the words and statements found in the poem) or rephrase the poem using different or outlandish language (get out that thesaurus!).

✓ **Have one person write an incomplete poem, leaving holes that other writers must fill in.** As a variation, have someone select a poem and write it out — leaving out three or four words per line. Indicate the part of speech of each missing word. The other poets in the group have to come up with words to fill the blanks. Read the new version aloud.

✓ **Have one poet bring in material from dreams and the others write poems in response.**

✓ **Take a long walk with a group of other poets.** Everyone takes notes and makes the notes into poems. Mix and match, toss into "Tzara's Hat," or play other collaborative games.

[Exercise contributed by Charles Bernstein and Bernadette Mayer]

These exercises are a tour of the many aspects of the poet's art. Moving through them will challenge various aspects of your talent, and perhaps help you identify your strengths and areas where you can improve. They're also enjoyable in and of themselves — writing poetry is one way you *can* mix work and pleasure.

Chapter 12

Going Public with Your Poetry

In This Chapter
▶ Starting a reading or writing group
▶ Performing at readings, open mikes, or poetry slams

*E*ventually, you may decide you're ready to take your poetry out into the world. That's an exciting decision — it can bring great changes for you and your poetry. And if you do it with the right attitude, you're bound to see the poetry you read and write from a new perspective — that of your readers — which is something every poet needs to do. Some writers claim they don't write to be read by an audience. Fair enough. But very few writers who have taken their verse public have failed to learn something from the experience.

In this chapter, we consider two ways to join a community of readers and writers: starting a poetry group and reading in public.

Starting a Reading or Writing Group

No one has counted, but there are possibly thousands of poetry groups in existence. From the U.S. 1 group in Northern New Jersey, to the lovers of Indian poetry who meet in a garage each month in a small town in Illinois, to teenagers who gather to rap, poetry is everywhere.

Getting started: Questions to think about before you begin

If you want to start a group that reads or writes poetry together, you have a few things to decide:

✔ **How big of a group do you want?** Try a group of three to five people. Some reading groups are larger, but anything larger than ten can require a lot of work. Plus, the more people you have in your group, the less time each person has to discuss poetry or have his poetry discussed.

✔ **How often do you want to meet?** Try meeting monthly. A once-a-month meeting gives members something to look forward to, is easier to schedule, and allows folks to get their reading done. But you can find weekly groups, as well as groups who meet once a season.

✔ **Where do you want to meet?** Some poetry circles meet at the same place every time; some rotate among the homes of the various members; some meet at bars, coffee shops, or bookstores that agree to host them.

✔ **How ambitious do you want your group to be?** In her book *How to Read a Poem . . . and Start a Poetry Circle,* Molly Peacock warns against trying to do too much. The main thing is to keep the circle from being a burden on anyone, especially yourself. Poetry groups should be a pleasure — a time to enjoy and contemplate poetry in the presence of like-minded people. It's a nutty, high-pressure world, so why create one more pressure point in your poetry group?

✔ **How do you plan to get people to join?** Chances are, you already know the folks you'd like to invite. So invite them! Or you can always advertise at your local bookstore, coffee shop, community arts center, or college or university. Try running an ad in your local newspaper or events calendar. Your local library may also have a Web site that lists local poetry groups. Or you may be able to get such a list by calling the library.

The Poetry Society of America can send you a starter kit for a poetry circle or put you in touch with local poets or poetry groups. Contact them by calling 888-872-7636 (toll-free) or 212-254-9628. Or visit them online at www. poetrysociety.org.

Discovering ways to spend your meetings

The nice thing about poetry circles is that they don't have to have a particular agenda — the idea is to meet to discuss poetry. Most meetings will end with a discussion of "Who should we read next?" and people will have different suggestions and agree on the next poet. The Poetry Society of America's starter kit (see the preceding section) has suggestions for poetry books to read every month as well.

Poetry circles should be friendly, humane gatherings. So what if you cover only two poems? Or one? Or one phrase? You're doing what you like to do, which is its own reward. Relax and enjoy it.

If you're looking for ways to spend your meetings, try one of the following activities:

✔ **Attend a poetry reading together.** Dinner and a reading — not a bad group activity.

✔ **Invite a local poet to address the group.**

✔ **Watch poetry-related movies on video.** Some good ones include *Stevie, Il Postino (The Postman), Barfly, Dead Poets' Society, Shakespeare in Love,* and *Poetry Nation.* Or watch television shows about poetry, such as Bill Moyers's *The Language of Life,* which you can order on the Web at sites such as `www.moviesunlimited.com`.

✔ **Do some collaborative writing.** See Chapter 12 for some suggestions for ways to create poetry together in a group.

✔ **Play a Surrealist game.** "Tzara's Hat," in which members all write a line and pitch it into a hat, after which the emcee fishes out lines or phrases and creates the poem, is a great game to play.

✔ **Have a group Web site at which members can post poems or write poems collaboratively.**

✔ **Give a group reading at either your normal meeting place or a local venue (such as a bookstore or coffee shop).**

✔ **Arrange for a local teacher of poetry to give the group a writing workshop.**

Reading Your Poetry in Public

Performance poetry is a vigorous part of the worldwide entertainment culture. No, it's not as big as movies, sports, or popular music, but most major cities in the world have venues at which poets read their work in public. Many are the countries in which you can list *itinerant poet* as your occupation. In Iran, poets wander from place to place, reciting epic poetry about the exploits of, among other heroes, Alexander the Great. In India, poets read classic ghazals to appreciative audiences who recite the refrains. The tradition of oral poetry is still strong throughout Africa as well. So if you're considering reading your verse in public, you're in good company.

We consider three types of reading in the following sections. Each type is a world unto itself, and each brings with it an etiquette and a style. None should be embarked on without a little preparation.

Readings

The phrase *poetry reading* can mean almost anything. What it *usually* means is that a limited number of poets — common numbers are one, two, or three — get up and read, usually one at a time. Each poet usually reads 3 to 5 poems and usually reads for a total of 20 to 25 minutes. The entire reading typically lasts about an hour, more or less. Then the reading breaks up and becomes an onsite party or adjourns to a local coffee shop or bar to talk poetry.

A word on how to read your verse

Poetry is meant to be read aloud. All the rules of good public speaking — don't rush; use a positive conversational tone; project — hold true when reading poetry.

You want to come across as a humane, interesting person who writes interesting poetry. Don't whisper or appear cold and disdainful. And don't (unless you're at a slam) shout and gesticulate with wacky histrionics. (We've seen all three types, believe us.)

When it comes to reading your own poetry, read to a friend or practice in front of small groups before reading before large crowds.

Videotape or record yourself and watch the recording. Many people find doing this difficult, but that's what's good about it. The videotape shows you how you sound and look as you read. If you don't like something, you can work on it.

Most poets — even some experienced poets — could use some work as readers. They forget that poetry isn't just print, that a certain element of *performance* is involved when they read. So after you've selected the poems you're going to read, consider these things:

✔ **The volume, tone, and dynamics of your voice.** Poetry is one of the least monotonous things human beings do. Why read it in a monotone?

✔ **Your posture.** Don't slouch, and don't stand bolt-upright. Find a comfortable way to hold yourself.

✔ **The mood of your poems and how you will get that mood across.** If a poem is happy, don't make the audience sad. If it's intense, don't make the audience bored.

✔ **The difficult moments in your poems.** How will you bring these moments across to the audience? (Often, slowing down a little helps.)

✔ **How your poems come across as a group.** Are they all the same in length, subject, and tone? If so, mix them up.

✔ **Which poem you'll begin with and which you'll end with.** The typical audience needs a few minutes to begin to follow your reading well. You may want to warm them up with a shorter poem or two, or inject some humor or an anecdote into your opening remarks. Try for a certain rhythm that keeps the audience's attention throughout, and try to end with a highpoint of concentration, mood, or significance.

But readings can take other forms as well. After all, they involve a certain amount of spontaneity. We've attended affairs billed as readings that involved up to 20 poets and lasted for hours and hours.

So how do you go about getting the opportunity to participate in a reading? One way is to publish some poetry and get asked to read. Colleges, universities, and bookstores routinely invite experienced, known poets to read their work. In fact, the reputation of these places often rests partly on their ability to attract good readers. (Bookstore readings very often are by poets with a new book to sell — and that's as it should be.)

You can also set up a reading for yourself. We cover a few ways to do that in the following sections.

Holding a reading at your house

Having a reading in your home is a great way to start out slowly, before diving into the unfamiliar terrain of a more public place. The only disadvantage to holding a reading in your house is that your audience is made up of your friends, which means that they may be *too* nice about your poetry.

You can arrange this kind of reading as you'd arrange any party, with invitations and light refreshments. We have attended many readings in folks' living rooms and garages, and even a few in their kitchens.

Even if your friends are not the poetry type (whatever that means), they're your friends, and parties are an excuse for them to enjoy themselves — and they will. Imagine their pleasure when they discover they actually *like* hearing poetry. Also, after everyone has heard 45 to 60 minutes' worth of verse, they all have an experience in common that may furnish hours of post-reading chat.

Don't be the only poet. Invite a couple other poets to read, each for 15 to 20 minutes (and adhere to this limit).

There are many permutations to this kind of reading. Some (or all) of these may work for you:

- Ask friends to read your poetry for you.
- Invite them to bring their own poetry or their favorite poems to read.
- Create an open mike at home.

Reading at your local coffee shop or bookstore

Coffee shops and bookstores like it if you can bring people in who will buy coffee and books. So get chummy with the owners of the coffee shop or bookstore. One day, after the purchase of a year's worth of lattes or poetry books, broach the subject. If you set up a reading, do the public relations. The coffee shop or bookstore will do a certain amount in brochures and ads and on its Web site, but you have to get the word out and get folks to come. If you draw a good crowd, it'll be that much easier to get a second reading.

Reading at coffee shops or bookstores works best if people in your area put on readings anyway.

Giving a reading at your local community arts center

Some centers have community readings. Subscribe to their brochures and watch for announcements. If your center doesn't do readings, suggest it or volunteer to organize one.

Open mikes

Open mikes are just that: a chance for anyone to come up and read with a microphone. Some have admissions fees; others are free. At many open-mike readings, there's an old-fashioned pass-the-hat at intervals.

If you're at an open mike and they pass the hat, *please contribute*. It's probably how the open mike keeps going.

Finding an open mike that's right for you

You find open mikes at places such as coffee shops, bars, bookstores, colleges and universities, and community arts centers. Consult the Entertainment section of your local newspaper or your community Web site. Some local radio stations (especially public radio and college stations) also have community events announcements that may tell about open mikes in your area.

Some places have sign-up sheets for their open mikes. Some want you to sign up a few days in advance. For others, you can just walk in and sign up on the day of the event. Know the ground rules before you go.

Getting ready to read at an open mike

Visit your chosen venue before your performance — preferably at another open mike — to get a sense of the place and the poets who read there. Certain venues have their own atmosphere, and when people go there they act a certain way. Knowing such things before taking the mike for the first time is a good idea.

Introduce yourself to the person running the open mike. He may be connected with the sponsoring venue or may simply be someone who goes around putting on open mikes at different places. Either way, say hello and make friends.

Don't worry too much about the poets who read just before and after you. Audiences *do* compare readers; it comes with the territory. What you're here to do is perform and learn.

Surviving your first reading

When you're reading at an open mike, consider your audience. There may be five people in the place — or a hundred. Either way, you have a couple of things going for you:

- ✔ They're here, and you can show them a good time.
- ✔ A good number of them like poetry and enjoy hearing it.
- ✔ Most people like performers.

In this corner: Poetry contests through the ages

Poetry contests have been part of the poetry scene since the beginning of verse. The poetry of the Greeks and Romans featured many poetry contests among shepherds, evidently a great way to stay interested in governing sheep. By A.D. 885 in Japan, the first *uta-awase* (poetry-writing contests) were being held. The poets of Renaissance England conducted poetic duels in the press, where they tried to outdo one another in verse and bravado. Basho, the 17th-century Japanese master of haiku, often made money as a judge of poetry at poetry circles, where he would correct verses or act as a referee in haiku contests, which often offered prizes. Perhaps these qualify as the earliest known slams!

Nervous? Good. For most people, nervousness goes away once they get started. If you're *really* nervous, however, concentrate on your job: to give a good reading. That means connecting somehow with your audience. Concentrate on *being in the poem,* keeping a steady pace and making the poem accessible to the audience. Pay attention to your poetry. With experience, you'll find that at a certain point you forget you're up there. You're *into* the material, delivering it, feeling its rhythms and emotions — it's a peak experience.

For your first open-mike reading, start small, with a poem that takes just two or three minutes to read. Come prepared — practice ahead of time. Select a poem that moves your audience, something interesting. Avoid extremely personal poetry ("How I Broke Up with My Girlfriend," "Why I Never Have Any Money") unless you're feeling strong — you don't want to give the impression of being self-indulgent. When nerves come, welcome them and keep steady.

The main killer of poetry readings is rushing. The second killer is not knowing when to stop. Go up to the mike with a large-faced watch so that you can keep track of the time.

Read your poem, say, "Thank you," and leave the stage. We've seen some open mikes at which poets read for up to half an hour, which is obnoxious and could well get you uninvited for future open mikes.

Be ready for anything in terms of the audience's reaction — absolutely anything. They may do nothing at all. Or they may go crazy over your reading of the word *the.* This may be the kind of place at which it's cool to boo, or uncool to show *any* reaction, or where you're expected to offer vegetables if you like a poem. Try to learn from whatever happens. If someone approaches you after your reading and wants to talk about your work, talk. Never disparage other poets' work; instead, engage them in talk about the craft. (How did she put the poem together? What parts were especially challenging to write?)

Stick around. Don't come in, read, and bolt. If you leave immediately after you read, people may think that you don't care about the other readers. Besides, you can learn a great deal from watching and listening to other poets read.

If someone reads something you really like, find the person and tell him. It's a good way to meet other poets, and perhaps you'll learn what he thought of *your* stuff.

Poetry slams

Now we're into the roughest kind of public readings: the poetry slams (see Figure 12-1). Poetry slams are a lot of fun to attend, and participating in them can be entertaining and useful. But it's not a world for the faint of heart. *Slams* are, most commonly, competitive readings at which audience reaction, or the reaction of a panel of judges, decides who "wins." You may win nothing, or a cash prize, or a free drink.

You can find slams in all the ways you can find readings and open mikes. They take place in the same kinds of places as well. Poetry slams, just like readings and open mikes, have ground rules, and you need to be aware of them. Some require a mere sign-up; others require that you submit your poetry for consideration or read in an audition beforehand. Often, there is a time limit for readings — 3 minutes and 20 seconds is a popular limit. Know what the limit is and prepare accordingly.

A certain kind of poet, and a certain kind of poetry, goes over well at slams. Self-indulgence is expected. Performers will do just about anything in a poem (or a performance!) to win the audience.

What should you read at a slam? The kind of poetry that wins very often has:

✔ **Striking, often outrageous or violent stories with interesting characters.** We've heard poems about suicide, illness, drugs, crime, childhood abuse, discrimination, poverty, sex (there is a great deal of sex in slam poetry), and mental illness at poetry slams. But you'll find that different venues are associated with particular kinds of poetry — which is something to pay attention to as you shop for slams.

✔ **A strong, assertive first-person narrator (an *I*).**

✔ **Immediately striking language — often ribald, vulgar, hip, or slang.**

✔ **Lots of jokes and other humor.**

✔ **Constant allusions to contemporary popular culture (movies, TV, music), social history, politics, and poetry.**

✔ **An ending that leaves the audience with a concluding shock or joke.**

© David Huang

Figure 12-1:
San
Jose/Silicon
Valley Team
1999
competing
at the
National
Poetry Slam
in Chicago.

Slams are slams. If you're going to do them, you have to:

- ✔ **Like the rough-and-tumble of it, the theater, the zaniness.**

- ✔ **Embrace the need to be a real actor, a ham if necessary.**

- ✔ **Grow the triple-thick, titanium-coated rhinoceros skin you're going to need if response to your work is less than, shall we say, wonderful.**

- ✔ **Learn to be a good sport, to congratulate your conquerors, to be gracious and full of good humor if an audience or panel lets you have it.** Conversely, if you win, you should be just as gracious.

- ✔ **Promise yourself you won't go to only one slam.** Experience is everything, especially in this world halfway between fine arts and the World Wrestling Federation. Become part of the regular audience, get to know the poets and their entourages, and enjoy yourself.

Keep reading your poetry in public. Each chance to perform will teach you about yourself and your poetry. Many are the times that we've discovered — in mid-reading! — a flaw or problem we needed to fix in a poem. But that sort of discovery makes a reading worthwhile.

Recipe for fun: Slam across America

Ingredients: Assemble 100 of the best North American performance poets, 7 legs, 32 U.S. cities, a sizable amount of Grand Marnier, and a place in a large bus.

Directions: Drive the bus from Seattle, Washington, to Providence, Rhode Island, in one month. Stop at bookstores, cafés, bars, clubs, and concert halls. At each venue, have 15 to 25 poets get off the bus and duke it out slam-style (in which performance poets are pitted against one another for cash prizes and personal glory in audience-judged competitions). Promote new anthology: *Poetry Slam!: The Competitive Art of Performance Poetry*. Get back on the bus. Drive to the next city. Repeat for all 32 cities until you reach Providence. Get off the bus and take part in the National Poetry Slam, a 4-day poetry competition extravaganza involving 56 teams of poets from across the country. Laugh, cry, scream, and shout. Judge and be judged. Be part of a growing movement of performance poets who have delivered the spoken word to thousands of spectators and have breathed life into the notion of what a poetry event can be.

Go to freshpoetry.com/slamamerica/poets.htm or www.poetryslam.com to read more about the trip, the winners, the friendship, and to get information on how to get in on the fun. Call it the first-ever SlamAmerica Bus Tour.

It's the human connection that's most important when it comes to poetry readings. Folks get to hear your poetry. What could be better than that? What more direct way of sharing your poetry could there be than delivering your own words your own way? What's more, readings can be your introduction to a community of poets you may want to join. By organizing poetry circles or reading groups of your own, you can create your own community. However you go, keep your focus on poetry and on its power to touch people.

Participating in Your Local Poetry Community

Another way to go public with poetry is to be a part of your poetry scene. Here are a few ways:

- ✔ **Attend slams and open mikes.**
- ✔ **Take courses or attend workshops.**
- ✔ **Go to your favorite poets' readings.** And tell your friends about them.

✔ **Become a member of a local or national poetry organization.** Groups such as the American Academy of Poets or the Poetry Society of America offer very active Web sites, full calendars of events, and links to other groups and poetry sites.

✔ **Buy books of your favorite poets' work.** If your local bookstore doesn't have them in stock, order them. Hard-to-find poetry books are available at Web sites such as www.spdbooks.org.

✔ **Volunteer at poetry readings or festivals.**

✔ **Subscribe to poetry magazines or journals.** Locate a magazine that discusses your local poets and poetry events. Not only will you keep up with current events, but you also may well be supporting nonprofit literary organizations or publications.

All of these are good ways to sharpen and widen your listening skills, your knowledge of what's happening, and your circle of friends, acquaintances, and fellow poets.

Chapter 13

Getting Published

● ●

In This Chapter

▶ Getting ready to submit your work for publication

▶ Doing market research

▶ Sending out your poems in a methodical manner

▶ Publishing your poems on the Internet

▶ Self-publishing your work

● ●

*I*f you're an aspiring poet, you've probably looked at all the poetry you read in books, magazines, journals, and the Internet, and wondered, "How can *I* get in there?" Getting published *is* a mark of accomplishment, a building block in your career and a chance to learn something about your poetry through contact with editors and readers. And is it ever encouraging!

In this chapter, we offer some guidelines on publication, as well as the methods and attitudes to bring to your quest.

The advice here is a series of tips, not commandments. By all means, forge your own path in the way that suits you best.

Submitting Your Poetry to Journals, Literary Magazines, and Web-Based Publications

Most poets don't have literary agents who can land them a publishing contract with a magazine or book publisher, at least not until they've become quite established. This means you will need to personally undertake a serious effort to get in to print. While some very talented poets might have it easy getting published, that is not the norm. Most published poets have worked very hard before the day they saw their work in print. If you're ready to make the leap from showing your poems to your friends and mentors to showing the world your verse, this section provides step-by-step guidelines for putting your "getting published" plan into action.

Knowing whether you're ready

Getting published feels great: You see your poetry and your name in print, it gives you something to put on your résumé, and you can send copies to all your friends and family members. But don't try to get published until you're ready. (You don't want to look back years later on your published work and, after reading it again, want to change your name!)

How can you tell whether you're ready for publication? You can be relatively certain you're ready for publication if you:

- ✔ **Have not just started writing, but have written a fair amount and for some time.**

- ✔ **Have had your poetry read by knowledgeable friends or mentors who have given you frank, constructive criticism and some advice about the poetry market.**

- ✔ **Have done some market research.** You've done a great deal of reading in a variety of magazines and journals, and you know the journals to which a poet like you should send poetry like yours. You also know what journals to avoid (some welcome first-time writers, and others publish only well-known poets).

- ✔ **Are willing to commit yourself to being methodical about getting published.**

- ✔ **Have a realistic attitude.** You are aware that publication of poetry is extremely competitive (thousands of poets are trying to get published along with you); response is often slow or nonexistent (weeks or months later, you get your stuff back in the self-addressed stamped envelope you enclosed, and it may or may not be accompanied by a note); and you usually get paid only with a copy of the issue your poem appears in, if that.

- ✔ **Have a thick skin and are ready for rejection.** Rejection doesn't mean you're a bad poet — it can be a great opportunity to learn something about your poetry.

Where should you start? Many poets start locally, with regional journals and literary magazines — or *any* publication that prints poetry. So start looking around. Which colleges, universities, and writing groups are nearby? Do any publish literary magazines? If not, find the nearest ones — or cruise the Internet and check out Web sites that invite contributors.

Doing market research

As a poet, you need to be just as market-savvy as any other entrepreneur. You need to survey your territory and identify target publications to which you want to send your poetry. (If this suggestion sounds cynical, it's not meant to be; it's simply a piece of solid advice.)

Knowing what to look for

Your main guides as your read through magazines and journals should be your own tastes and interests. You want your poems to appear alongside other writing that you admire. So look at your poetry and imagine it in the pages of a specific journal. If you read a poem in a journal and like it, read more and decide whether this is the environment for your work, too.

Although there are over a thousand poetry journals in the world, these journals and their editors often have quite different ideas of what constitutes poetry. So before you start sending your stuff out, know your market.

Some journals may accept poetry

- ✔ **Only from people who live in a certain area.** For example, don't send to *ZYZZYVA* unless you live in the West.

- ✔ **Only about certain subjects.** If your poem is about plants, don't bother sending it to a journal that wants only poems about dogs. Don't send a poem on bowel surgery to *Cowboy Poets Today.*

- ✔ **Only in certain forms.** Don't send an epic poem to a journal named *Haiku;* the journal called *The New Formalist* is looking for poems in traditional forms, so a sprawling, Whitmanesque open-form poem isn't going to fly. *The Southern Review* has published leading poems in the great American tradition for generations — but its vision is very different from the hip, urban viewpoint you may encounter in *Painted Bride Quarterly.*

How can you find out which journal publishes which kind of poetry? Peruse the books that list journals and their self-described expectations. Go out and start reading literary journals. And talk to people who publish and edit.

Several publications list entries for literary journals in which the editors describe what they're looking for. The *International Directory of Little Magazines and Small Presses* lists hundreds of such entries. Another good resource is *Poet's Market.* Sometimes the information in these books furnishes good leads. Use these references as a good starting point. But get to know other important resource journals, such as *Writer, Writer's Market, Poets & Writers,* and the *Directory of Poetry Publishers.*

Finding places to start

Seldom will a mere ad or statement from a publication tell you all you need to know. You'll have to read a few issues of a journal to know its editorial finger-print. That you can do by writing or calling for copies, or by finding them at your local bookstore or library. Better yet, subscribe to a few magazines or journals. Share subscriptions with other poets and friends. Many poets — especially those just starting to get methodical about it — devote an hour or more a week to sampling different journals. If you're interested in poetry, you'll *want* to know the entire field.

You could start with the many fine, first-line publications put out by colleges in the United States, including the following:

- *The Antioch Review* (Antioch University)
- *The Beloit Poetry Journal* (Beloit College)
- *The Colorado Review* (University of Colorado)
- *The Georgia Review* (University of Georgia)
- *The Gettysburg Review* (Gettysburg College)
- *The Harvard Review* (Harvard University)
- *The Iowa Review* (University of Iowa)
- *The Kansas Review* (University of Kansas)
- *The Massachusetts Review* (University of Massachusetts)
- *The Michigan Review* (University of Michigan)
- *Ploughshares* (Emerson College)
- *Raritan* (Rutgers University)
- *Salmagundi* (Skidmore College)
- *The Southern Review* (Louisiana State University)
- *The Southwest Review* (Southern Methodist University)
- *TriQuarterly* (Northwestern University)
- *The Western Humanities Review* (University of Utah)
- *The Yale Review* (Yale University)

Colleges and universities aren't the only places that put out excellent poetry journals. Other journals are published independently by folks who love good writing. These include

- *Conjunctions*
- *The Greenfield Review*
- *Hambone*

- *The Hudson Review*
- *New American Writing*
- *The Paris Review*
- *The Partisan Review*
- *The Threepenny Review*
- *Tikkun*

American Poetry Review, a tabloid published in Philadelphia, is one of the most widely-read of all poetry journals. *Poetry Flash* out of Berkeley, California, is a true newspaper of poetry, oriented to one region of the country (in this case, the West) but quickly becoming national, as is *The Poetry Project's Newsletter* (published in New York City). *Poetry* is one of the longest continually-publishing poetry journals in the United States. And several leading magazines — including *Atlantic Monthly, The New Yorker, The New Criterion,* and *The Nation* — publish poems with each issue.

Establishing personal contacts

Personal contacts are *everything* in the world of poetry. People are the best source of information about the poetry market. If your circle of writing friends and mentors includes folks who have published poetry, ask them where they have sent stuff and what the editors like. Ask them whether you can use their names in a cover letter when you send your poems to editors they know.

Journals reflect the tastes of their editors, and what doesn't attract one may attract another. Knowing the editor, or knowing people who know the editor or have published in the journal, is a step toward knowing the journal. If you find that a journal's editor appears to share your tastes or interests, your chances of appearing in that journal someday may be greater. If not, don't waste your time or the editor's time by sending your material there.

Don't hesitate to make contacts. Networking is the nervous system of the poetry world. Take advantage of every opportunity to meet and speak with people who get published and people who publish. Become part of a community of poets.

Many poets begin by being published by their friends, colleagues, and fellow poets. Later, if they start a press or magazine, they may publish their friends in return. That's right: A number of publishing poets know or have met the editors who publish them. They meet them at readings, at poetry conferences, anywhere poets gather.

A poet by any other name?

Throughout history, poets have been known to take on pseudonyms or pen names. Take Enheduanna (born around 2350 B.C.), the earliest poet with a name we know: The word *Enheduanna* means "the high priestess of Nanna" in Sumerian. No one knows what her real name was.

Some poets take on shorter versions of their names, as did Dante (baptized Durante Alighieri) and Michelangelo (Michelangelo di Lodovico Buonarroti Simoni). Some Japanese poets of the classical era went by their nicknames. Basho's name means "banana plant" in Japanese (he took the name in honor of a plant near his house). The revered poet Issa's name means "bubble in a cup of tea."

Some women poets chose androgynous names for a variety of reasons. These include H.D. (short for Hilda Doolittle) and Ai. Some get their pen names by accident: The Irish poet George William Russell wanted to go by the name Aeon, but a typesetter got it wrong, and from then on Russell went as AE.

The modernist Portuguese poet Fernando Pessoa wrote under a number of names, which he devised as separate personas for himself. He even went as far as to have his different *personas* comment on one another's work! Other poets with more than one name include: Jack Kerouac (Jean-Louis Lebris de Kerouac), Pablo Neruda (Neftalí Ricardo Eliecer Reyes Basoalto), Claire Malroux (Claire Sara Roux), Doris Lessing (Doris May Taylor and Jane Somers), Maya Angelou (Marguerite Johnson), Anne Sexton (Anne Gray Harvey), and Sylvia Plath (Victoria Lucas).

Poets are still taking on different names today. In light of the Cultural Revolution and the Tiananmen Square massacre, several Chinese poets have taken on pen names as a form of political comment. World-famous poet Zhao Zhenkai adopted the pen name Bei Dao, which means "Northern Island." His pseudonym is a private symbol and a reminder of the kind of poetry the Communist government dislikes. Therefore, Bei Dao's name is a permanent protest against Communist oppression.

Self-renaming is especially popular in the world of performance or slam poets, who have taken names like Big Poppa E, Jennifer Blowdryer, Sapphire, and blackberry revolution. Why do poets take other names? Sometimes in imitation of others, other times to make a political statement, and, more often than not, to keep their identities as poets separate from the rest of their lives.

Sending out your poems

Many literary journals accept submissions by e-mail. Find out if that's a possibility for your target journal. Keep in mind that a brief cover-letter is still an important courtesy, even when e-mailing your submission.

But let's say you're ready to mail out your poems. How do you do it? Read on.

Typing and printing your poems

Your poems should appear, in type, *exactly as you want each poem to appear if it is published.* No page should have more than one poem on it. Don't double-space a poem unless you want it to be published double-spaced. Try not to break stanzas in mid-page. If you must do so, put a bracketed note — such as "[continued without stanza break]" — at the bottom of the page.

Put your name in the upper-right-hand corner of each page, so the editor can keep track of your submission if the pages become separated.

Proofread and spell-check everything. A typo in a poem is like a bad note in a symphony.

Getting organized

On your work desk, put a stack of 20 manila envelopes, size 9½-x-12 inches. Get a notebook that you can use as a log of your submissions. Next to that, put a neatly typed group of three to five poems — that's how many you're sending out at this first go. (Many poetry editors ask for three to five poems, but make sure you know your target journal's preference.)

Gather two of the manila envelopes and your group of poems. Then go to the post office and weigh the package. Find out how much first-class postage would be. Purchase that postage times 20. (The postage will be different, of course, if you're mailing abroad.)

Most editors expect that you are sending your poems only to their journal. Do not *multiple-submit* (send the same poem to more than one journal) unless the journals to which you are doing so explicitly allow it — and even then, make sure you explicitly tell all the journals involved you are multiple submitting these poems. Submitting the same poem to more than one journal at a time is messy, and it can lead to confusion and bad feelings if more than one journal accepts the same poem.

Writing a cover letter

Enclose a brief cover letter with your submission. The cover letter is a courtesy to your editor and will give him some important information, including the following:

- ✔ **Who you are (your name and contact information).**
- ✔ **The titles of the poems you're submitting.**
- ✔ **Whether and where you've been published before.** Providing this information is optional, but many editors like to know it. If you haven't been published before, you're not necessarily at a disadvantage (most

editors like discovering new talent), and if you have been published before, you're not necessarily any better off (it sets the bar higher, if anything — besides, your editor is dealing with large numbers of already-published poets, so join the club).

✔ **A sentence or two about the magazine.** This is where you can tell the editor what it was about his publication that inspired you to submit your work. Be concrete. Refer to something in the past that you especially liked. For example, "I admired the emphasis on experimental poetry in your Winter issue" or "I have enjoyed your journal's emphasis on working life and everyday experience — especially 'What Work Is' by Philip Levine." Such comments show the editor that you know something about the journal and are not picking it at random; they also engage the editor on a subject he cares about: choosing good poetry.

Cover letters can be as brief as the one shown in Figure 13-1.

Don't include the following in your cover letter:

✔ **Your assessment of your own work.** Offering your opinions (such as, "I believe these poems are timely and eloquent") serves no purpose and may only annoy the editor. Let the editor decide for herself whether she likes your work.

✔ **An explanation of the themes, meanings, or forms of the poems.** Saying something like, "'Your Second Dance' is about the fears and frustrations of doing something a second time when the first time wasn't so good" or "'Exploding Horses' is a triple dizaine in acephalic anapestic heptameter," is only stating the obvious. The editor can figure these things out for herself.

✔ **An explanation of your motives for seeking publication.** Throwing in a line like, "I've been writing a long time, and it's really time for me to get my poems out there," doesn't serve any purpose. The editor won't care what your motives are; she only cares whether your poetry will work for her publication.

Knowing what to include with your poem

When you submit poems to a journal, include the following in the envelope:

✔ **A cover letter.**

✔ **Your three to five poems.**

✔ **A self-addressed stamped envelope (SASE).** No editor will send your poetry back without one, and some won't even read your work.

February 14, 2001

Pat Smith
Editor
XYZ Poetry Journal
100 Main Street
Anytown, NY 10012

Dear Pat Smith:

Please consider the enclosed poems — "Your Second Dance," "November 1992," "Exploding Horses," "For Lena," and "Chortle" — for publication in *XYZ Poetry Journal*. My work has appeared in *Locomotive, Sequoia, American Review of Poets*, and *Tad Farley's Poetry Zine. [Or, if applicable*: My work has not previously been published.] I am submitting to *XYZ Poetry Journal* because I like your selection of poems that are written in traditional forms but concern contemporary problems and viewpoints.

Sincerely,

Chris Doe

Chris Doe
123 Elm Street
Anytown, CA 90210
(555) 555-1212
cdoe@aol.com

Figure 13-1:
Always
send a
cover letter
with your
poetry
submissions.

If you get rejected

Most editors do not have the time or the staff to send personalized notes to every poet whose work they reject. So you will often receive form-letter rejections or very brief notes (here's a favorite one: "Respectfully, no") enclosed with your SASE. If an editor takes the time to write a substantive, personalized rejection note, feel very, very good. It means you came close. The editor liked your work enough to take time to encourage you and tell you why you didn't make it this time. Pay close attention to such notes; they could help you get published in the future.

If you get a personal rejection note, wait a few weeks, send out a new batch of poems to the same editor, and in your cover letter, include some words of thanks to the editor, reminding him of the kindness of the rejection note. This constitutes a contact.

Don't flood responsive editors with huge gobs of new material. Meditate on the advice given in the note and think about what you want to send next, taking into consideration any comments made by the editor on your earlier submission.

We can't promise you won't sometimes get an editor who says something ill-mannered and cranky in a rejection note (such as "Consider auto mechanics"). But this is rare. If it happens, put it out of your mind, and forget that editor for a while.

Take one manila envelope, address it to yourself, and put postage on it. That's your SASE. Address another envelope to the journal and put the postage on. Make sure each has a return address. Fold the one addressed to you (leave it unsealed!) and slip it into the envelope addressed to the journal.

Gather your designated group of poems. Print them out with your name in the corner. Assemble them with their cover letter, *sign* the cover letter, affix a paper clip to the upper-left-hand corner, slip everything into the envelope, lick, close, kiss the whole package, and stick it in a mailbox. Done.

Keep a submission log. Note the titles of the poems, the journal to which you sent them, and the date sent.

Figuring out what to do next

After you send out your poems, start planning where to send this same group of poems if they return rejected. And start on the next batch.

We know poets who have groups of poems in stacks on one side, envelopes on another side. As the SASEs come back with rejections, these poets simply re-input the cover letters and ship the rejected stuff out to the next editor, like clockwork. They *make* themselves do it as a point of professional discipline.

Taking Advantage of Internet Publishing

Several Web sites invite people to post poetry. Some operate just as regular literary magazines do, with a rigorous editing and selection process. These are the ones we like the most, because rigorous editing teaches you about your poetry and about editorial standards.

But we also like the come-one-come-all sites. These invite everybody to post their poetry and to comment on the poetry of others. Being part of such a virtual writer's group has many advantages over other forms of self-publishing. The feedback from readers, although it may vary in quality, may at least give you the sense of being read and — who knows? — it may even give you some ideas about how to improve. You may strike up contacts with other poets and perhaps get e-mail correspondences going. You'll be in touch with people trying to do what you're trying to do, all in the public medium of the Web.

Web publication — especially on rigorously edited sites — is becoming more and more highly regarded. In fact, as of this writing, poets who apply for National Endowment for the Arts (NEA) grants may use Web publications to account for up to half the number of their published pages in their applications.

Another way to become virtually published is to create your own Web site. The downside is that there are a *lot* of these sites — and you'll have to find ways to get people to visit yours. The upside is that, with the Internet, you never know what will come your way. Creating your own Web site on which you can publish your poetry is certainly less expensive and less time-intensive than lugging cartons of books around to unenthusiastic buyers. Plus, you're going easier on the environment by not using paper.

If you create your own Web site, make sure that you do the following:

- ✔ **Install a counter, so you can tell how many hits you get.** A *hit* is Internet lingo for a visitor to your site; the more hits (the more visitors) the better.

- ✔ **Create a bulletin board or e-mail feature through which readers can leave their comments and invite your responses.** Another handy feature is "Recommend this site?" If a user clicks "Yes," it enables her to send your Web address by e-mail to other aficionados of poetry.

- ✔ **Find out about ways to cross-list your site with other poetry Web sites, so that folks browsing the Web for poetry may find out about yours and come grazing.**

- ✔ **Read other Web sites and pick up tips on construction, features, and publicity.** Some Web poets advertise on the Web or in print media; if you see an advertisement you like, you can try to create something similar for yourself.

Paying to get into a poetry book

Perhaps you've seen them — those ads that cry, "Get your poetry published today!" All you do is send in your poem with an application form and a fee ($25 seems a popular amount) — and, voilà! You'll be published . . . along with 1,249 other poets, in tiny type, all the poems jammed in, 30 to a page. And that $25 only gets you *in.* If you want to actually *own* a copy of the book, another check is required.

Paying to get your poem in print is not a good way to get published. Your poem isn't read or edited by knowledgeable professionals; it's merely printed. So you're denied the chance to learn anything about your poetry. Few people who read poetry take these books seriously. In fact, such books are widely regarded as a swindle. A legal swindle, yes — but a swindle nonetheless. They take advantage of people who don't really understand the nature of publication.

Our advice: Don't go this way.

Being Aware of Publishing Pitfalls

The biggest pitfalls of publishing involve one common mistake writers make: They think that getting in print is the same as getting published. Keep in mind the following when you're looking to publish your poetry:

- If anyone asks you to *pay* them to appear in a book of poetry, be very skeptical.

- Never pay a printer to crank out 100 books of your verse, unless you're ready to be the proud owner of these books — and are ready to lug cartons of them all over the place.

- Don't desktop-publish a book of your own unless you have strong reasons for doing so and you're ready to do all the work of distribution and publicity.

Self-Publishing Your Poetry

Getting published is difficult. There are thousands of poets and only dozens of spaces. Many writers try to get around the process by creating self-published books. Desktop publishing has made it easy to make your own books, and the results, as they say, "look great."

Should you publish your own book? The answer is yes, if you know what you're doing and you're doing it for the right reasons.

Self-publishing has a long and glorious history. (In the days before printing, self-publishing *was* publishing.) The Beat poets of the 1950s used to hand out mimeographed poems as the "daily news for the masses." Julia Vinograd, the "Bubble Lady" of Telegraph Avenue in Berkeley, California, has been self-publishing her poems in little books for years and has even made it into some anthologies published by others.

Self-publication often is *part* of the life of a poet. Self-published books can be useful as calling cards to give to fellow poets, to distribute or sell at open mikes and slams, or to send to poets you admire. And some poets have been able to establish presses of their own, assembling mailing-lists, creating Web sites, and reaching an appreciative audience. Writers such as Kathy Acker have moved back and forth between self-publishing and conventional publishing. From bookstore to bookstore, day after day, famed publisher David Godine drives boxes of the books he has published. A veritable one-man band of publication, he upholds the very highest standards of selection, editing, and printing.

The decision to self-publish or start a press often arises from communication with other poets who read one another's work and start magazines, journals, or presses. Poets who self-publish often do so because they have become part of a mutually-supportive circle of other poets and want to join the conversation about poetry here and now. What's nice about starting your own poetry press is that it lets you be a part of that conversation. When you publish yourself or other poets, you are in effect saying, "This poetry is worth your attention. What do you think?"

Self-publishing means self-publicizing, self-selling, self-stocking, and self-driving to local bookstores. Distributing your book, even in your locale, much less far and wide, requires a lot of time and effort. But it can have its rewards.

To publish is to send your words out into the world. It's an exciting endeavor, and sometimes you hit the jackpot: useful responses from readers. Don't rush into publication, but when you feel ready, be professional and patient about the quest, and you'll discover a great deal about yourself, the poetry world, and your own verse in the process.

Part IV
The Part of Tens

"This next poem is called, 'Never Try to
Milk a Bull'."

In this part . . .

This wouldn't be a *For Dummies* book without The Part of Tens. Here we tackle some of the misconceptions and myths that somehow have gotten stuck to poetry. Some are half-true, some are true only sometimes, and some are just plain bunk. We also suggest ten wonderful poems that will give you excellent practice in memorization, reading aloud, and interpretation, and ten love poems with which to woo your sweetheart.

If you have only a little time, but you want to fill it with all things poetic, you've come to the right part.

Chapter 14

Ten Myths about Poets and Poetry

● ●

In This Chapter

▶ Separating poetry fact from fiction

▶ Approaching the world of poetry with as little prejudice as possible

● ●

*T*he following ideas sometimes get in the way of people's enjoyment of poetry. Some of the ideas are just bunk, and others have a little truth in them. All, however, are myths.

Poetry Is Only for Intellectuals and Academics

True, sometimes scholars and academics have made it seem that poetry is their province and theirs alone. But colleges and universities are home to some excellent programs in reading and writing poetry. Thousands of interested writers flock to these programs, and many of them have had fine careers as readers and writers of poetry.

On the other hand, that's not everything. If a poem works for you, it works — and whether you or the poet went to college is, well, maybe nice to know, but it usually doesn't matter much.

Whenever a revolution in thought or culture happens, poets are usually the first to see it coming — and many people write about it, from all points of view and walks of life.

Not convinced? Here's a brief list of good poets who, as far as anyone knows, never earned a degree at a university: Homer, Sappho, Virgil, Basho, Dante, Geoffrey Chaucer, William Shakespeare, William Blake, Elizabeth Barrett Browning, Walt Whitman, John Keats, Charles Baudelaire, W.B. Yeats, Jorge Luis Borges, Dylan Thomas, Robert Frost, Carl Sandburg, Marianne Moore, and Maya Angelou. Not a bad list at all. Next time anyone says, "Poetry is for eggheads," you can immediately exclaim, "Well, what about *these* people?"

Poetry is not just for any one group. It's for you, no matter who you are or what your background.

Poetry Is . . . Well, Hard

Some poetry *is* difficult. Some of it takes patience and practice to appreciate. (So do snowboarding, computer science, French cooking, and almost anything else worth doing.) But most poetry is actually quite accessible, when you get into the habit of reading it.

Some poetry is authentically hard, and you're better off approaching it with a professional guide, like a teacher or an experienced reader. And some poems don't really *have* a meaning in the traditional sense. Some poets simply create a collection of words and sentences, not consciously trying to make it mean anything. They present this work to you, the reader, and you then become a collaborator in discovering what's happening in the poem.

Even the most difficult poems, if you dwell with them a while, tend to open up their riches generously. Most poetry, however, can be read and enjoyed with immediacy.

Now writing poetry — that takes work, practice, and devotion. Some poems just drop — plunk! — into your mind, as "Kubla Khan" evidently did into the mind of Samuel Taylor Coleridge. Other poems take years to write, as *Paradise Lost* took John Milton, or "Asphodel, That Greeny Flower" took William Carlos Williams. William Butler Yeats, certainly a hard worker, once complained of writing poetry that "nothing should be this hard." (His poem "Adam's Curse" is partly about how beautiful poetry is — and how hard to write!) Those who give writing poetry their best efforts have great satisfactions in store. Again, writing poetry is like any other skill: You get better the more you practice.

You Can't Make Any Money Writing Poetry

Okay, so you're probably not in it for the money. At least we hope you're not. Although few poets get rich on the sales of their books of poetry, some do. An extraordinary example is 8-year-old poet Sahara Sunday Spain, whose manuscript of poems landed her a five-figure deal with a major publisher (with the help of an agent).

Many of the big awards and prizes in literature come with some nice prize money. Cash prizes vary: The National Book Award currently awards its winners $10,000, as does the Lenore Marshall Poetry Prize. The average Guggenheim Fellowship Grants will set you ahead $33,800. MacArthur Fellowships not only give poets a lot of clout but also bring them a cool half million dollars (dispersed in five payments).

Most poetry contests you see in magazines offer the winner(s) smaller cash prizes along with publication. (You usually have to pay a fee, however, to enter such contests.) Even small sums of money are rewarding; you can say you are a paid writer, too.

Poetry slams and some open mikes almost always guarantee that one or more poets go home with cash in hand. (Again, there may be entrance fees — either to get in to the venue or to perform your poems.) Some regular slam winners do quite well, performing once or twice a week at different venues and bringing in hundreds of dollars a month in prize money.

Don't quit your day job to write poetry, though: Because there are only a small number of prizes out there compared to the number of people writing poetry, it follows that only a small percentage of poets make money writing poems.

No Poetry More Than 20 Minutes Old Can Possibly Have Anything to Say Today

We'll meet you halfway on this one. Older poetry in English can seem somewhat distant. It takes somewhat more effort to understand. Most of that work, however, is in getting used to slight differences in vocabulary and grammar. And very often, no work is necessary.

Read the following anonymous lines:

> Western wind, when will thou blow?
> The small rain down can rain.
> Christ, if my love were in my arms,
> And I in my bed again.

A couple of slight differences in spelling, but other than that, any problems? No? You just understood a poem from the Middle Ages.

Older poetry may demand that you sometimes uncover facts about history, biography, and mythology. (So can many new poems, too.) Luckily, ancient poetry exists in some very fine translations, and the translators take care of you. How about this one?:

> So soon. Today, love, we
> part. And our re-
> union — when
> will that time come?
>
> A bright lamp
> shines on an empty place,
> in sorrow and longing:
> not yet, not yet, not
> yet.

That's Jeanne Larsen's rendering of a poem attributed to the Chinese courtesan Tzu Yeh, said to have been written between A.D. 350 and 500.

Maybe human nature hasn't changed and maybe it has. But poems from 50, 500, and 5,000 years ago may still touch you today. The point is not to resist older poetry just because it's old. You may as well be prejudiced against the sun!

Poetry Is for Soft, Sensitive, Emotional Types

The stereotype of the poet — and the person who likes poetry — is of a weakling. Although you can find poets and poetry-lovers who aren't exactly linebackers, such a stereotype, like most, is unfair — and inaccurate. After Hamlet mistakenly kills a courtier, he decides to drag the body offstage. As he does, he lisps the following soft, sensitive, emotional line of poetry:

> I'll lug the guts into the neighbor room.

Poetry. No doubt about it. It's vivid and ugly — and much poetry is, because poetry often addresses the ugly side of life.

Poets are sensitive, all right — almost all poetry seeks to make readers more alive to the world. And we'll agree with *emotional* as well, because writing and reading poetry inevitably involve our strongest passions. But soft? Only sometimes, when soft is exactly right, like this passage from "Upon Julia's Clothes" by Robert Herrick:

Whenas in silks my Julia goes,
Then, then, methinks, how sweetly flows
The liquefaction of her clothes.

Otherwise, poetry is a vigorous challenge to the mind and body.

Rhyme Is So Ten Minutes Ago

Incorrect! As of the 21st century, rhyme is used in more ways than it ever has been used before. Far from abandoning rhyme, the last 150 years of poetry has celebrated it. Poets such as Emily Dickinson, Gerard Manley Hopkins, Wilfred Owen, Theodore Roethke, and Dylan Thomas found new resources for rhyme.

Today's poets use traditional end-of-the-lines rhyme, as well as a wide array of rhyming techniques, including inside lines and rhymes from within one line to another. You will find all sorts of chimes, echoes, and reflections in the work of contemporary poets and songwriters, including in the lyrics of rap artists like Snoop Doggy Dogg and Dr. Dre.

If you listen with your imagination, these imaginative writers will keep enlarging the world of rhyme for your ears.

There's No "Right" Way to Read a Poem

Sure, you can interpret a poem any way you want if all you want to do is read for yourself. But if you want to share your ideas with other people, you need to practice the art of interpretation — that is, make wise speculations about what the poem you're reading is trying to accomplish.

Here are two things to keep in mind about interpreting poetry:

✔ **Most poems have better and worse readings.** The statement "Shakespeare's play *Hamlet* is all about the Internet" is silly, impossible, and wrong. (Sure, you could have a production in which *Hamlet* takes place in cyberspace, and it's been done, but to claim that Shakespeare meant for the play to be about the Internet is a bit of a stretch.) The statement "*Hamlet* is about indecision and the terrible toll it sometimes takes" has a much better chance of hitting the bull's-eye.

✔ **People get better at feeling their way through poetry the more they do it.** Anything that requires feeling and awareness to do well — from interior decoration to swing dancing — requires a lot of patience and practice, because there's a lot in there no one can teach you. It's like Aristotle once wrote: "For some things, the only way to learn is to do."

Interpretation can actually help you improve both as a reader and as a writer. Interpretation is the art of educated, careful speculation about what's happening in the poem — not so much right or wrong, but more or less persuasive. Practicing interpretation helps you become more and more alert to the intricacies of poems.

Writing Poetry Is Essentially a Solitary Act

True, people tend to think of poetry as being the product of a single, inspired individual, passionately pouring out her soul at the behest of a fiery muse. And many wonderful poems appear to have been written in that way. But keep this in mind, too: Throughout all of history, the creation of a great deal of poetry has involved more than one person. That's right: Often, poetry is a *collaborative* affair.

Much ancient poetry — including the epic poems of the Sumerians, the Greek epic *The Odyssey,* the *Mahabharata* of the Aryans, and the Psalms — may be collections that more or less came together over the centuries until some literate person had the bright idea of writing them all down. Thus, they are collaborations.

In modern day, you can find many famous examples of teamwork in the verbal art. Surrealist poets tried to get away from the controlling conscious mind, so they composed poetry by means of elaborate party games that ensured that every player — but no *one* dominant player — had a hand in the production.

Perhaps the most famous such game became known as the "Exquisite Corpse," named after this line, generated during such a game: "The exquisite corpse shall drink the new wine." Here are the rules:

1. **Gather a group of people.**

   Three or more is preferred.

2. **Give each person a piece of paper and a pencil.**

3. **Decide on a sentence structure.**

   The structure article/adjective/noun/verb/adjective/noun resulted in the example that gave this game its name.

4. **In the first round, each person writes a word fitting the outlined sentence structure.**

   If you want to create new possibilities, ignore the prescribed structure.

5. **Fold the paper over to conceal the written word and pass it to the next person.**

6. **The next person writes a word, conceals it, and passes the paper to the next person.**

7. **When a round of sentences have been completed, open the paper and read the poetry thus created.**

So if the prescribed pattern was

> The [adjective] [noun denoting a concrete thing] of [abstract noun]
> Never [verb] a [concrete noun] until the [new noun] is [adjective]

you may get

> The sarcastic tractor of despair
> Never diagnoses a sunrise until the prison is ransacked

Poets today are working with one another, and with artists in painting, music, dance, and other arts, to extend the boundaries of what usually counts as poetry. Performance poetry, as in poetry readings and poetry slams, often includes the audience in the composition or creation of a poem. Whenever an audience is asked to recite a refrain, its members are helping to create the poem of the moment.

Poetry Is So Literary

When people say that poetry is "literary," they may mean that poetry involves a world of writing and reading, and that this world is sort of unto itself, hermetically sealed, with thousands of people reading silently to themselves. This myth has a germ of truth in it: Sure, the last 5,000 years have left us a great deal of written poetry, and some of it has gotten famous and become *literature*. And there's nothing wrong with that — nothing to be afraid of, certainly.

But poetry was *oral* millennia before it was written down, and much of it is still oral today: work songs, schoolyard songs, rap songs, the tales of itinerant bards. Yes, poetry is something the "literate" and the "educated" do — and something anyone can enjoy. So not all poetry is literary, especially lately.

Poetry also has always been something you see, feel, and hear, not just something you read as a written thing. It's often *extemporaneous* (done on the spur of the moment) and instantaneous. Think of the Beat poets, who improvised to the sound of jazz. That's not what most people mean when they say the word *literature.* The last 20 years of the 20th century saw a great deal of performance poetry, in hit recordings, in coffee shops from here to Bombay and back, and in poetry readings. Much of *this* poetry is improvised, brand-new, on-the-spot, once-and-never-again-quite-this-way. So poetry is not just a printed world. Poetry is a world about the world, and it takes all sorts of forms. It's what's spoken or sung as well as what is written or read. And no matter the form it's in, it's not just the letter — it's the spirit.

Anything You Want to Write Is Poetry

We like writing. Writing is good for you. But the idea that "if I write it, it must be poetry" is a trifle too easy.

Your signature on an everyday bank deposit slip is not going to be poetry — *unless* you can find some way to invigorate, energize, and renovate that mundane setting and make your readers experience the signature in a new way. (If you ever do all that, let us know.) Most of the time, however, all you're doing is signing the slip. Same with laundry lists, notes for a class, or other writings. All are forms of thinking, and some may be forms of feeling or expression or even exploration.

But to become poetry, you have to make something new happen somehow. Something has to happen in the language, or the presentation, or the form of the piece of writing, to give your readers some new awareness or emotional experience. That's your job as a poet, and it takes work — and patience. We firmly believe in getting great, surprising, startling, new ideas out of the blue. (Some people call it *inspiration.*) But we also firmly believe in this: It's the work that makes the art. We're not saying anything against spontaneity. Spontaneity is important, maybe even crucial. Many poets believe in the Beat poet Allen Ginsberg's notion of "first thought, best thought." And that philosophy certainly has led to some memorable poetry.

Think of the improvisational genius of a jazz soloist. The soloist improves through practice; he becomes more expert at his instrument, better at "finding the pocket" with a group of other expert players, better at thinking and feeling a way toward something new. He becomes expert at the process of improvisation.

Dizzy Gillespie, one of the great jazz improvisers, once said that to be great at jazz, the first requisite is "absolute mastery of the instrument" — and that goes for the "instrument" of writing, too.

Good poets of all kinds fill up journals with their observations and impressions. They know, however, that those things are just the very raw material, as different from poetry as a dozen eggs are from an omelet. So if you want to write poetry, don't cheat yourself out of the chance to explore the material you gather. Cultivate a patient work ethic. Take the time to shape your raw material. And revise and revise and revise again. You may never know when it's done — it may never be done. But it's the work that makes the art.

Chapter 15

Ten Poems Worth Memorizing

● ●

In This Chapter

▶ Stretching your mind by memorizing poetry

▶ Challenging your family and friends in a poetry-memorizing competition

● ●

In this chapter, we give you ten poems worth permanently installing in your brain. Practice reading them aloud. Have memorization parties. Give prizes to those who can memorize "Kubla Khan," the longest poem here. Give a grand prize to anyone who can memorize the whole list.

Sonnet 73 by William Shakespeare (1564–1616)

That time of year thou mayst in me behold
When yellow leaves, or none, or few, do hang
Upon those boughs which shake against the cold,
Bare ruined choirs, where late the sweet birds sang.
In me thou see'st the twilight of such day
As after sunset fadeth in the west;
Which by and by black night doth take away,
Death's second self that seals up all in rest.
In me thou see'st the glowing of such fire,
That on the ashes of his youth doth lie,
As the deathbed whereon it must expire,
Consumed with that which it was nourished by.
This thou perceiv'st, which makes thy love more strong,
To love that well which thou must leave ere long.

"A Crown Of Sonnets Dedicated to Love #1" by Lady Mary Wroth (1587?–1651?)

In this strange labyrinth, how shall I turn?
Ways are on all sides, while the way I miss.
If to the right hand, there in love I burn;
Let me go forward, therein danger is.
If to the left, suspicion hinders bliss;
Let me turn back, shame cries I ought return,
Nor faint, though crosses with my fortunes kiss.
Stand still is harder, although sure to mourn.
Thus let me take the right- or left-hand way,
Go forward or stand still or back retire.
I must these doubts endure without allay
Or help, but travel find for my best hire.
Yet that which most my troubled sense doth move —
Is to leave all, and take the thread of Love.

Psalm 23 (King James Version, 1611)

The Lord is my shepherd;
    I shall not want.
He maketh me to lie down in green pastures;
    He leadeth me beside still waters;
        He restoreth my soul.
He leadeth me in paths of righteousness
    For his name's sake.
Yea, though I walk in the valley of the shadow of death,
    I fear no evil,
For thou art with me;
    Thy rod and thy staff,
        They comfort me.
Thou preparest a table before me
    In the presence of my enemies.
Thou anointest my head with oil;
    My cup runneth over.
Surely goodness and kindness shall follow me
    All the days of my life,
And I shall dwell in the house of the Lord
    Forever.

Three Haiku by Chiyo (1703–1775)

After a long winter, giving
each other nothing, we collide
with blossoms in our hands.

Don't dress for it.
The moon will transfigure —
those darling rags.

Once my parents were older
than I, still children,
same cicadas.

"The Tyger" by William Blake (1757–1828)

Tyger, Tyger, burning bright,
In the forests of the night,
What immortal hand or eye
Could frame thy fearful symmetry?

In what distant deeps or skies
Burnt the fire of thine eyes?
On what wings dare he aspire?
What the hand dare seize the fire?

And what shoulder, & what art
Could twist the sinews of thy heart?
And when thy heart began to beat,
What dread hand? & what dread feet?

What the hammer? what the chain?
In what furnace was thy brain?
What the anvil? What dread grasp
Dare its deadly terrors clasp?

When the stars threw down their spears
And watered heaven with their tears,
Did he smile his work to see?
Did he who made the Lamb make thee?

Tyger, Tyger, burning bright,
In the forests of the night,
What immortal hand or eye
Dare frame thy fearful symmetry?

"Kubla Khan" by Samuel Taylor Coleridge (1772–1834)

In Xanadu did Kubla Khan
A stately pleasure dome decree:
Where Alph, the sacred river, ran
Through caverns measureless to man
    Down to a sunless sea.
So twice five miles of fertile ground
With walls and towers were girdled round:
And there were gardens bright with sinuous rills,
Where blossomed many an incense-bearing tree;
And here were forests ancient as the hills,
Enfolding sunny spots of greenery.

But oh! that deep romantic chasm which slanted
Down the green hill athwart a cedarn cover!
A savage place! as holy and enchanted
As e'er beneath a waning moon was haunted
By woman wailing for her demon lover!
And from this chasm, with ceaseless turmoil seething,
As if this earth in fast thick pants were breathing,
A mighty fountain momently was forced:
Amid whose swift half-intermitted burst
Huge fragments vaulted like rebounding hail,
Or chaffy grain beneath the thresher's flail:
And 'mid these dancing rocks at once and ever
It flung up momently the sacred river.
Five miles meandering with a mazy motion
Through wood and dale the sacred river ran,
Then reached the caverns measureless to man,
And sank in tumult to a lifeless ocean:
And 'mid this tumult Kubla heard from far
Ancestral voices prophesying war!
    The shadow of the dome of pleasure
    Floated midway on the waves;
    When was heard the mingled measure
    From the fountain and the caves.
It was a miracle of rare device,
A sunny pleasure dome with caves of ice!

    A damsel with a dulcimer
    In a vision once I saw:
    It was an Abyssinian maid,
    And on her dulcimer she played,
    Singing of Mount Abora.
Could I revive within me

Her symphony and song,
To such deep delight 'twould win me,
That with music loud and long,
I would build that dome in air,
That sunny dome! those caves of ice!
And all who heard should see them there,
And all should cry, Beware! Beware!
His flashing eyes, his floating hair!
Weave a circle round him thrice,
And close your eyes with holy dread,
For he on honeydew hath fed,
And drunk the milk of Paradise.

Poem 986 by Emily Dickinson (1830–1886)

A narrow Fellow in the Grass
Occasionally rides —
You may have met Him — did you not
His notice sudden is —

The Grass divides as with a Comb —
A spotted shaft is seen —
And then it closes at your feet
And opens further on —

He likes a Boggy Acre
A Floor too cool for Corn —
Yet when a Boy, and Barefoot —
I more than once at Noon

Have passed, I thought, a Whip lash
Unbraiding in the Sun
When stooping to secure it
It wrinkled, and was gone —

Several of Nature's People
I know, and they know me —
I feel for them a transport
Of cordiality —

But never met this Fellow
Attended, or alone
Without a tighter breathing
And Zero at the Bone —

"Spring and Fall" by Gerard Manley Hopkins (1844–1889)

To a Young Child

Márgarét, áre you gríeving
Over Goldengrove unleaving?
Leáves, líke the things of man, you
With your fresh thoughts care for, can you?
Áh! ás the heart grows older
It will come to such sights colder
By and by, nor spare a sigh
Though worlds of wanwood leafmeal lie;
And yet you *will* weep and know why.
Now no matter, child, the name:
Sórrow's spríngs áre the same.
Nor mouth had, no nor mind, expressed
What heart heard of, ghost guessed:
It ís the blight man was born for,
It is Margaret you mourn for.

"Sea Rose" by H.D. (1886–1961)

Rose, harsh rose,
marred and with stint of petals,
meagre flower, thin,
sparse of leaf,

more precious
than a wet rose,
single on a stem —
you are caught in the drift.

Stunted, with small leaf,
you are flung on the sand,
you are lifted
in the crisp sand
that drives in the wind.

Can the spice-rose
drip such acrid fragrance
hardened in a leaf?

"One Art" by Elizabeth Bishop (1911–1979)

The art of losing isn't hard to master;
so many things seem filled with the intent
to be lost that their loss is no disaster.

Lose something every day. Accept the fluster
of lost door keys, the hour badly spent.
The art of losing isn't hard to master.

Then practice losing farther, losing faster:
places, and names, and where it was you meant
to travel. None of these will bring disaster.

I lost my mother's watch. And look! my last, or
next-to-last, of three loved houses went.
The art of losing isn't hard to master.

I lost two cities, lovely ones. And, vaster,
some realms I owned, two rivers, a continent.
I miss them, but it wasn't a disaster.

— Even losing you (the joking voice, a gesture
I love), I shan't have lied. It's evident
the art of losing's not too hard to master
though it may look like (*Write* it!) like disaster.

Chapter 16

Ten Love Poems

In This Chapter

▶ Finding fantastic love poems worth knowing

▶ Inspiring your one true love with poetry

· ·

*L*ove is one of the most common themes in poetry. As long as poetry has existed, poets have used it to explore the passions, urges, surprises, and complications of this exalted feeling. Readers have turned to love poems for solace, a touch of beauty, or better understanding of their own situations. So in this chapter, we give you a selection of ten of the world's greatest love poems. Written by men and women from many different times and places (ancient Greece, 10th-century Japan, 20th-century Chile) and points of view, they explore all aspects of love, from lust to devotion to saying goodbye. These are great poems to memorize, to send to significant others, or simply to contemplate as lovely examples of what the meeting of great passion and great art can accomplish.

"He Is More Than a Hero" by Sappho (About 610–580 B.C.)

He is more than a hero

He is a god in my eyes —
the man who is allowed
to sit beside you — he

who listens intimately
to the sweet murmur of
your voice, the enticing

laughter that makes my own
heart beat fast. If I meet
you suddenly, I can't

speak — my tongue is broken;
a thin flame runs under
my skin; seeing nothing,

hearing only my own ears
drumming, I drip with sweat;
trembling shakes my body

and I turn paler than
dry grass. At such times
death isn't far from me

"If Someone Would Come" by Lady Izumi Shikibu (970–1030)

If someone would come,
I could show, and have him listen —
evening light shining
    on bush clover in full bloom
        as crickets bring on the night.

"Western Wind" by Anonymous (About the 15th Century)

Western wind, when wilt thou blow?
The small rain down can rain.
Christ, that my love were in my arms,
And I in my bed again.

Sonnet 61 from Idea by Michael Drayton (1563–1631)

Since there's no help, come, let us kiss and part —
Nay, I have done: you get no more of me;
And I am glad, yea, glad with all my heart
That thus so cleanly I myself can free.

Shake hands forever, cancel all our vows,
And when we meet at any time again,
Be it not seen in either of our brows
That we one jot of former love retain.
Now at the last gasp of love's latest breath,
When, his pulse failing, Passion speechless lies,
When Faith is kneeling by his bed of death,
And Innocence is closing up his eyes, —
    Now, if thou would'st, when all have given him over,
    From death to life thou might'st him yet recover.

"When I Heard at the Close of the Day" by Walt Whitman (1819–1892)

When I heard at the close of the day how my name had been receiv'd with
    plaudits in the capitol, still it was not a happy night for me that
    follow'd,
And else when I carous'd, or when my plans were accomplish'd, still I
    was not happy,
But the day when I rose at dawn from the bed of perfect health, refresh'd,
    singing, inhaling the ripe breath of autumn,
When I saw the full moon in the west grow pale and disappear in the
    morning light,
When I wander'd alone over the beach, and undressing bathed, laughing
    with the cool waters, and saw the sun rise,
And when I thought how my dear friend my lover was on his way coming,
    O then I was happy,
O then each breath tasted sweeter, and all that day my food nourish'd me
    more, and the beautiful day pass'd well,
And the next came with equal joy, and with the next at evening came my
    friend,
And that night while all was still I heard the waters roll slowly continually
    up the shores,
I heard the hissing rustle of the liquid and sands as directed to me
    whispering to congratulate me,
For the one I love most lay sleeping by me under the same cover in the
    cool night,
In the stillness in the autumn moonbeams his face was inclined toward me,
And his arm lay lightly around my breast — and that night I was happy.

Poem 640 by Emily Dickinson (1830–1886)

I cannot live with You —
It would be Life —
And Life is over there —
Behind the Shelf

The Sexton keeps the Key to —
Putting up
Our Life — His Porcelain —
Like a Cup —

Discarded of the Housewife —
Quaint — or Broke —
A newer Sevres pleases —
Old Ones crack —

I could not die — with You —
For One must wait
To shut the Other's Gaze down —
You — could not —

And I — Could I stand by
And see You — freeze —
Without my Right of Frost —
Death's privilege?

Nor could I rise — with You —
Because Your Face —
Would put out Jesus' —
That New Grace

Grow plain — and foreign
On my homesick Eye —
Except that You than He
Shone closer by —

They'd judge Us — How —
For You — served Heaven — You know,
Or sought to —
I could not —

Because You saturated Sight —
And I had no more Eyes
For sordid excellence
As Paradise

And were You lost, I would be —
Though My Name

Rang loudest
On the Heavenly fame —

And were You — saved —
And I — condemned to be
Where You were not —
That self — were Hell to Me —

So We must meet apart —
You there — I — here —
With just the Door ajar
That Oceans are — and Prayer —
And that White Sustenance —
Despair —

"A Negro Love Song" by Paul Laurence Dunbar (1872–1906)

Seen my lady home las' night,
　　Jump back, honey, jump back.
Hel' huh han' an' sque'z it tight,
　　Jump back, honey, jump back.
Hyeahd huh sigh a little sigh,
Seen a light gleam f'om huh eye,
An' a smile go flittin' by —
　　Jump back, honey, jump back.

Hyeahd de win' blow thoo de pine,
　　Jump back, honey, jump back.
Mockin'-bird was singin' fine,
　　Jump back, honey, jump back.
An' my hea't was beatin' so,
When I reached my lady's do',
Dat I could n't ba' to go —
　　Jump back, honey, jump back.

Put my ahm aroun' huh wais',
　　Jump back, honey, jump back.
Raised huh lips an' took a tase,
　　Jump back, honey, jump back.
Love me, honey, love me true?
Love me well ez I love you?
An' she answe'd, "'Cose I do" —
　　Jump back, honey, jump back.

"Leaning Into the Afternoons" by Pablo Neruda (1904–1973)

Leaning into the afternoons I cast my sad nets
towards your oceanic eyes.

There in the highest blaze my solitude lengthens and flames,
its arms turning like a drowning man's.

I send out red signals across your absent eyes
that move like the sea near a lighthouse.

You keep only darkness, my distant female,
from your regard sometimes the coast of dread emerges.

Leaning into the afternoons I fling my sad nets
to that sea that beats on your marine eyes.

The birds of night peck at the first stars
That flash like my soul when I love you.

The night gallops on its shadowy mare
shedding blue tassels over the land.

"The Business" by Robert Creeley (1926–)

To be in love is like going outside to see what kind of day

it is. Do not
mistake me. If you love

her how prove she
loves also, except that it

occurs, a remote chance on
which you stake

yourself? But barter for
the Indian was a means of sustenance.

There are records.

"A Kind of Loss" by Ingeborg Bachmann (1926–1973)

Things shared: seasons, books and a piece of music.
The keys, the teacups, the bread basket, sheets and a bed.
A dowry — of words, of gestures — brought with, used, used up.
House rules followed. Said. Done. The hand given, always.

I fell in love with winter, with a Viennese septet and with summer.
With maps of the country, a mountain hideaway, a beach and a bed.
Idolized days on the calendar, declared that promises last forever,
worshipped a something and was devout before a nothing

(— the folded-up newspaper, cold ashes, the scrap with some notes on it),
fearless in religion for this bed was the church.

My inexhaustible painting went forth from this view of the lake.
I saluted all peoples, my neighbors, down from this balcony.
By the fireplace, safe, my hair was its uttermost color.
When it rang, the doorbell sounded the alarm for my happiness.

I haven't lost you, I've lost
the world.

Part V

Appendixes

The 5th Wave   By Rich Tennant

"I appreciate the poetry of Lewis Carroll's 'Jabberwocky' too. But could you not call the Offensive End a 'frumious Bandersnatch' every time he makes a touchdown?"

In this part . . .

We finish this book with a few appendixes that you can turn to as a resource. You'll find a glossary of the major terms you encounter most often when you hear poetry being discussed, including concise definitions of those terms that you know but couldn't really define if your life depended on it. We also lay out the panoramic of poetry in a timeline sprawling across recorded history. We follow that with a resource section, telling you about books, Web sites, organizations, poetry events nationwide, and much more related to poetry.

Appendix A

Glossary

• •

accent: See *stress*.

allegory: A story in which all the characters and events symbolize truths about human life. Allegories make sense on at least two levels: a literal level and a symbolic level (which may be very different from the literal level).

alliteration: Repeated sounds in a passage of verse. The word *alliteration* often means repeated consonant sounds at the beginning of neighboring words (as in *doggy diner*). It also is used to mean the general repetition of a consonant sound, as in the repeated *m* sounds in Tennyson's famous lines from "Come Down, O Maid":

> The moan of doves in immemorial elms,
> And murmuring of innumerable bees.

allusion: A reference to something — a person, place, or historical event — outside the poem, usually as an illustration of the poet's point or as a metaphor.

analogy: A close, extended comparison between two things.

anapest: See *meter*.

Anglo-Saxon: Another term for *Old English*.

antihero: A hero who displays qualities that are different from or opposite to those you'd expect to find in a hero. See also *hero*.

apostrophe: Direct address to something you wouldn't ordinarily address, such as an abstraction ("Oh, love!") or an object in nature ("Oh, trees! Oh, rocks!"). Apostrophe is often a way to bring new life to things with which we are normally silent. It's a way to quickly become intimate with unexpected things.

archetype: This word can refer to the first, the original, or the model of a particular thing, character, or poet, as in "Odysseus is the archetype of the hero figure." It can also refer to a pattern running throughout a huge body of thought or poetry, as in, "This character is the archetype of the faithful lover in French troubadour poetry."

art ballad: See *ballad*.

assonance: Repetition of a sound; usually used to denote repetition or abundance of vowel sounds.

automatic writing: A practice in which the poet attempts to write but without conscious control. The aim is to give the subconscious freer rein, to loosen up the way the poet normally writes, producing (everyone hopes) new associations and new, unpredictable situations. Automatic writing is a practice central to the poetry of many Surrealist, Symbolist, and chance poets.

ballad: One of the most enduring forms of lyric poetry. Ballads are short, narrative songs, often with refrains. *Folk ballads* are anonymous ballads passed on orally. *Art ballads* are written by contemporary poets in imitation or reminiscence of the folk ballad.

blank verse: Poetry in iambic pentameter (see *meter*) that does not rhyme. (It isn't the same as *free verse,* which isn't supposed to be written in any meter at all.) A good example of blank verse is "Ulysses" by Alfred, Lord Tennyson.

caesura: The heaviest pause in a line of verse.

canon: The established or accepted list of the "best" pieces of art, painting, or poetry. Who establishes them? Well, lots of people — but usually scholars in the universities. Canons can help guide you to what's good, and they're a good way to introduce yourself to excellent poetry. But the other nice thing about them is that you can ignore them and make up your own canon — the pieces of art *you* think are best.

catalog poem: A poem based on a catalog or list. Two famous examples are Walt Whitman's "Song of Myself" and Allen Ginsberg's *Howl*.

chance poetry: See *open-form poetry.*

chapbook: A small book of poems, often published by a small press or self-published by the poet.

classical poetry: This term can refer to Greek and Roman poetry written between 600 B.C. and A.D. 200; poetry written in imitation of those writers; or any very famous or exemplary poetry. Many other cultures have "classical" periods. For example, Chinese poetry of the T'ang Dynasty, or other dynasties famous for the excellence of their verse, is known as *classical*.

comedy: A genre in which people mess up a lot but come out all right in the end. Comedy is really a celebration of how human beings, despite their foibles, manage to keep going in this crazy world.

conceit: A kind of metaphor in which two things thought to be very dissimilar are compared — as, for example, democracy and a wrecking crane. In Renaissance poetry, such as that of John Donne, conceits were often elaborate or extended.

concrete poetry: Poetry written to resemble the physical shape of its subject, as in a Coke-bottle-shaped poem about a Coke bottle.

convention: A widespread general agreement on how to do something. Poetry is full of such things. You could call rhyme a convention.

couplet: A pair of lines. Usually, but not always, a pair of lines written in the same form. Rhymed iambic pentameter couplets are called *heroic couplets*.

dactyl: See *meter.*

Dark Ages: A period of European history and culture extending from the fall of Rome in A.D. 476 to around A.D. 1000.

diction: Groups of words of the same social register, as in *high diction* (extremely formal or pretentious language) or *low diction* (slang or informal language). This term is also used to mean "word choice" in general.

dissonance: A combination of sounds that is displeasing to the ear.

dramatic monologue: A passage of verse written as if meant to be spoken by a single speaker on a stage. During a dramatic monologue, the speaker usually narrates events in his real or psychic life, thereby implying or revealing secrets about his viewpoint or psychological makeup. Also called *soliloquy.*

dramatic poetry: Poetry that's either meant to be put on as a play with actors, or poetry that could potentially be performed that way. Dramatic poetry has all the hallmarks of the drama, including plot, setting, character, and dialogue.

elegy: A poem of lamentation or sorrow. Poems that have these elements in them are often called *elegiac.*

end rhyme: See *rhyme.*

enjambment: The practice of running a phrase or sentence over the end of one line and into the next without a punctuated pause.

Enlightenment: A period of European art and history (about 1660–1798) characterized by a renewed interest in human reason (alongside or instead of such institutions as tradition or religion), clarity of thought and statement, and proportion.

epic poetry: Traditionally, poetry on a grand scale, which tells the story of the establishment of a nation or community, with an epic hero who carries that community's values into battle against anything that threatens it. The hero may descend into hell, battle monsters, or contend with evil forces.

epigram: A very unified, sharply pointed poem, often quite short.

epitaph: A poem either written on a tombstone or gravesite or written as though it were meant for such a place.

exact rhyme: See *rhyme.*

extended metaphor: A single, detailed, dominating metaphor that continues for a considerable way through a passage of poetry.

figure of speech: Any special use of language, including metaphor, simile, analogy, or pun. Figures of speech usually are not meant to be taken literally but imply more and other than what they say on the surface.

folk ballad: See *ballad.*

foot: A single rhythmical unit. See also *meter.*

free verse: Poetry in which the poet avoids repetition of the same line length, meter, or rhyme scheme from line to line. Individual lines, or short passages, may have these features, but the poem as a whole is constructed to avoid them. See also *blank verse* and *open-form poetry.*

genre: A kind of artwork or poetry, as in comedy, lyric, tragedy, satire, and so forth.

ghazal: A verse form practiced in Arabic and Persian poetry, as well as poetry in several of the languages of India. Ghazals became popular in English-language poetry in the late 1960s.

Global Period: The present period of literature and culture. The Global Period began around 1989, with the fall of communism in Europe.

haiku: A traditional verse form originally practiced in Japan and China. It was brought into American and European poetry in the 20th century and now is one of the most familiar of verse forms. As practiced in Western poetry, a haiku is composed of three lines, the first having five syllables, the second having seven, and the third having five. Haiku traditionally begin with a natural scene tied to a season.

hamartia: See *tragedy.*

Harlem Renaissance: An African American art and literary movement that flourished in the 1920s.

hero: The central figure in an epic, tragedy, or other tale. The hero usually undergoes or performs most of the important events in the tale. He causes the big changes that drive the story; his accomplishments have far-reaching meanings for the surrounding cast of characters. Not all heroes are successful or even clearly good. Heroes who don't act the way you'd expect heroes to act are often called *antiheroes.*

heroic couplet: See *couplet.*

high diction: See *diction.*

iamb: See *meter.*

image: Either (a) a vivid picture evoked through language, or (b) a particularly vivid evocation of the senses, especially sight.

internal rhyme: See *rhyme.*

inversion: In poetry, inversion is the practice of writing phrases or sentences out of their normal syntactical order. Compare "He isn't Leonardo DiCaprio" to "Leonardo DiCaprio he isn't." The second sentence is an inversion. Older poetry accepted inversion as a normal part of poetic expression. More recent poets use inversions for the sake of emphasis and surprise.

irony: Two kinds of irony are referred to most often. *Verbal irony* is the practice of saying one thing when you mean another. Such forms of irony include understatement, overstatement, *litotes* (created by negating a negative), and sarcasm. A second kind of irony is *situational irony,* which refers to events that happen at variance with or contrary to your expectations.

light verse: Poetry that is playful or humorous and usually rhymed. Ogden Nash and Dorothy Parker are two poets who wrote excellent light verse.

line: A row of words considered as a unit in poetry.

litotes: See *irony.*

low diction: See *diction.*

lyric poetry: Short, usually songlike or personal poetry, as contrasted with the longer, communal poetry of the epic.

lyrics: The words to a song. Song lyrics have been one of the major sources of world poetry.

metaphor: An implicit comparison between two things, as in "My love is a red, red rose" (as opposed to the comparison in Robert Burns's line, "O my love's like a red, red rose," in which the comparison is a simile because it uses *like* to make the comparison *explicit*). Metaphors are more intimate and more ambiguous than similes. Poets often speak of A in terms of B; it's one of the driving engines of all poetry — encouraging readers to think of familiar things in new and unfamiliar ways.

meter: The patterned repetition of strong and weak stresses in a line of verse. Much of English poetry is written in lines that string together one or more *feet* (individual rhythmical units). Feet are the individual building blocks of meter. Here are the most common feet, the rhythms they represent, and an example of that rhythm.

- anapest: duh-duh-DUH, as in, *Get away!*

- dactyl: DUH-duh-duh, as in, honestly

- iamb: duh-DUH, as in *alas!*

- trochee: DUH-duh, as in *pizza*

To build a line of verse, as mentioned, poets can string together repetitions of one of these feet. Such repetitions are named as follows:

- one foot: monometer

- two feet: dimeter

- three feet: trimeter

- four feet: tetrameter

- five feet: pentameter

- six feet: hexameter

Thus, *iambic pentameter* is a string of five iambs, as in Christopher Marlowe's line from *Dr. Faustus:*

> Was this the face that launched a thousand ships
>
> Duh-DUH-duh-DUH-duh-DUH-duh-DUH-duh-DUH

metonymy: The practice of replacing the name of the thing with the name of something associated with it, as when we say "the suits" when we mean "the executives."

Middle Ages: The historical period in Europe coming between the Dark Ages and the Renaissance, from about 1000 to about 1450.

Modern Period: The Modern Period in literature began roughly around 1910, when George V became King of England, and ended when the atomic bomb fell on Hiroshima and Nagasaki in 1945.

music: A catch-all term to cover the sum of all the sounds and rhythms in a piece of poetry; everything in a poem that strikes the ears.

myth: A story (fictional or true) told to set forth or explain the universe, history, or some enduring truth about human experience.

narrative poetry: Poetry that tells a story.

occasional poetry: Poetry written to observe an occasion or a meaningful happening in personal or national life, such as births, deaths, weddings, coronations, inaugurations, even the beginnings of seasons.

Old English: The earliest kind of English, spoken from at least A.D. 600 until about A.D. 1066.

onomatopoeia: The naming of a thing by imitating a sound associated with that thing. Onomatopoeic words include *moo, splash, blurt, zoom,* and *bang*.

open-form poetry: If you think of poems that are metered or rhymed as *closed* forms, you may call poems that reject those kinds of organization *open*. In open poetry (including chance poetry, Surrealism, and free verse), any of a wide variety of experimental techniques are used to blast open the possibilities of words on the printed page. The term also refers to the open use of language, theme, or subject.

oral poetry: Poetry that is primarily spoken rather than written. Also, poetry that is written but meant to recall the informality, rhythms, and surprises of oral verse.

overstatement: See *irony*.

oxymoron: A phrase that contains a contradiction but nevertheless makes sense, as in "aggressive modesty" or "quiet violence."

paradox: An apparently contradictory state that is nevertheless true to life. When the Roman poet Gaius Valerius Catullus writes, "I hate and yet I love," it seems contradictory, yet few of us will accuse him of lying.

parody: A poem that imitates or makes fun of another poem or a kind of poetry. Parodies take on the form of the poem they are ridiculing. So if you wanted to ridicule Shakespeare, you might write in mock-Elizabethan English.

periods: Spans of time in literary history. Scholars speak of periods as having characteristics that make them easy to group together. You may say, for example, that the Medieval Period (about 1000–1450) is characterized by religious belief, whereas the Postmodern Period (1945 to the present) is less so. Why do people make these distinctions? To help them make sense of the poetry and history of the past. Although they are arbitrary, periods can be very helpful in giving you a context for the poetry you read.

persona: (a) The identity assumed by a writer in a literary work; (b) a word sometimes used as a synonym for *speaker;* (c) a speaker with an especially complicated or involved personality or mental state. See also *speaker.*

personification: The act of treating a nonhuman entity as though it were human. You can personify concrete things (such as your car), natural events (such as the weather), or abstractions (such as love). When poets personify, they are creating a metaphor, a comparison between the thing personified (a car) and various human characteristics (the propensity to break down or disappoint).

pose: A very pronounced attitude struck by a character or speaker. A pose can be sincere but exaggerated, or it can be struck out of pretense.

Postmodern Period: A period beginning in 1945 and extending until about 1989 and the fall of communism in Europe. The word *postmodern* also denotes a kind of attitude toward art and history, one that seeks to create new, open ways of writing and thinking.

Pre-Homeric Period: The time preceding the Homeric era, which is reckoned to have begun about 1000 B.C. That's a long time, covering the very earliest existing poetry (about 3000 B.C.) and much of the poetry of the Egyptians.

prose poetry: Prose that is written employing the musical, rhythmic, and symbolic resources of poetry.

renaissance: Any vigorous rebirth of learning or artistic activity.

Renaissance Period: A literary and historic period extending from about 1450 to 1680. The Renaissance began and ended at different times in different European countries.

rhyme: The repetition of like sounds in a passage of poetry. The most familiar kind of rhyme is *end rhyme,* the repetition of the same (or nearly the same) sound at the end of consecutive lines, but there are several other varieties of rhyme, including

- internal rhyme: Rhyme that occurs within lines, as in this line from William Blake's "The Tyger": "Did he who made the Lamb make thee?"
- sight rhyme: Rhyme based on words that look as though they should rhyme perfectly, but in fact do not, as in

      the turkey bone
      says the turkey's gone

- slant, squint, or virtual rhyme: Various names for rhymes that are inexact or distant.
- vowel rhyme: Repetition of sounds based only on the vowel sounds in the rhyming words.

rhythm: The naturally occurring patterns of stressed and unstressed syllables in a passage of poetry. Different from *meter,* which is a repeated pattern of stresses.

romance: A genre of literature in which the characters and events are extremely fanciful or far from reality. Medieval romances may concern the activities of knights and dragons, whereas Shakespeare's romances, such as *The Tempest,* concern magic and the marvelous.

romantic: (a) Any aspect of literature having to do with the genre of romance; (b) any aspect having to do with love or amorous activity.

Romantic Period: A literary period (about 1798–1832) that saw an explosion of poetic activity across Europe.

sarcasm: See *irony.*

satire: A genre in which a social behavior, whether of individuals or groups, is held up to public ridicule in an attempt to correct that behavior.

scansion: The act of scanning (or examining) a line of verse for its weak and strong accents.

setting: The time, place, and physical environment in which a story takes place.

sight rhyme: See *rhyme.*

simile: An explicit comparison of two things, often using the words *like* or *as.* See also *metaphor.*

situation: (a) The circumstances or state of affairs at a given moment in a poem or story; (b) the circumstances a character finds himself in at a given moment.

situational irony: See *irony.*

slant rhyme: See *rhyme.*

soliloquy: See *dramatic monologue.*

sonnet: A poem of 14 lines, usually in iambic pentameter and usually rhymed. The two most familiar kinds of sonnet are the *Italian* (or *Petrarchan*) and the *English* (or *Shakespearean*).

speaker: The imaginary person who "speaks" the words in a poem. Some poems feature speakers as full-fledged characters with names and histories. But for the sake of discussion, people imagine all poems as having speakers. See also *persona.*

spondee: A metrical foot in which both syllables are long, as in "charmed lives."

squint rhyme: See *rhyme*.

stanza: A group of poetic lines that seem to belong together. In most traditional, rhymed verse, all stanzas have a predictable or regular form. In free verse, any sequential group of lines that appear to stand together may be considered a stanza.

stress: The emphasis or push given to a syllable in a word or a word in a line.

Surrealism: See *open-form poetry*.

syllabic poetry: In some poems, the number of syllables is the main structural element. For example, poets may write a poem in which each line has three syllables. Or poets can create a stanza in which the lines have different but fixed lengths.

symbol: Something that stands for something else, which in turn brings with it an intense world of meaning. In Christian religious symbolism, for example, the cross stands for the death of Jesus Christ, an intensely meaningful event.

symbolism: The sum total of a poem's symbols and their meanings; the way a particular symbol is connected to its meaning.

Symbolism: A poetic movement that began in France and Germany in the late 19th century and spread later to England, the United States, and beyond.

synecdoche: A figure of speech in which the poet names something by substituting a part of that thing for the whole, for example, when we call a runner "Legs."

tanka: A classical Japanese poetic form. As practiced by English-language poets, the tanka is a syllabic stanza with 5 lines, with syllable counts of 5-7-5-7-7. Many poets think of the tanka as a haiku (5-7-5) with two added 7-syllable lines.

tone: This word usually refers to the attitude of the speaker or the poet toward the subject of the poem. Thus, a poem's tone may be sincere, angry, ironic, jubilant, doubtful, or sad. *Tone* is also used to mean the attitude of the speaker or the poet toward the audience or the general emotional weather of the poem.

tragedy: A genre in which an admirable person is undone. Most tragedies contain the following characteristics:

✔ A tragic protagonist or tragic hero to whom most of the important events of the tragedy occur.

✔ A calamitous fall from good fortune by the tragic protagonist, usually ending in his or her destruction. Usually this fall is brought about by an error in the protagonist's judgment or character (called the *hamartia* or *tragic flaw*). This hamartia is

- An ending in which the protagonist's entire family line or nation is destroyed, to be succeeded by others who have learned from the protagonist's fall.

- Usually related to the protagonist's *hubris* or excessive pride.

- Ironically the best and most admirable thing about the protagonist.

tragic flaw: See *tragedy.*

trochee: See *meter.*

understatement: See *irony.*

verbal irony: See *irony.*

verse: (a) A line of poetry; (b) poetry in general. See also *light verse.*

Victorian Period: The historic and literary period occurring during the same time as the reign of Queen Victoria of England (1837–1901).

virtual rhyme: See *rhyme.*

visual rhythm: (a) The effect produced by the alternation of lines of varying length; (b) the total effect of the shape of a poem.

voice: The impression of a personality behind a piece of writing. Although the term *voice* is often used as synonymous with the word *style,* it's actually the impression that style leaves of the stylist's character.

vowel rhyme: See *rhyme.*

Appendix B

Poetry Timeline

Prehomeric Era

About 3000 B.C.	The first cities appear in the region between the Tigris and Euphrates rivers in what is now Iraq.
3000 B.C.	**Sumer:** The earliest recorded poetry is written, including *Gilgamesh,* a series of epic tales about the king of the city of Uruk. *Also:* Songs and tales about Ishtar, Enlil, and other Sumerian deities.
About 2350–2330 B.C.	**Mesopotamia:** Rule of Sargon, founder of Akkad. For 25 years, his daughter, Enheduanna, is high priestess of Nanna, the moon god, and writes hymns to her. Give it up for Enheduanna, the earliest poet whose name we know!
About 2600 B.C.	**Egypt:** Earliest verse inscriptions on pyramids.
About 2000 B.C.	**Egypt:** *The Book of the Dead* (a religious meditation on death and the afterlife) is compiled.
About 1850–30 B.C.	**Egypt:** Religious and personal lyric poetry.
About 1500–500 B.C.	**India:** The Vedas, a collection of hymns to the gods and goddesses, is compiled; it is the foundation of Indian literature.
About 1375–1358 B.C.	**Egypt:** Amenhotep IV (purported author of *Hymn to the Sun*) rules.
1028–256 B.C.	**China:** Zhou dynasty; compilation of the *Nine Classics,* a collection of tales, poems, and history.

Homeric Era

About 1000 B.C.	**Greek-speaking world:** *The Iliad* and *The Odyssey* compiled; tradition ascribes them to Homer.
	Middle East: Hebrew poetry enters its golden age (1000–400 B.C.) as the Psalms begin to be compiled. Around this time, the "Song of Songs" (also known as the "Song of Solomon") may have been written.
	India: The *Mahabharata,* the sacred poem of the Hindus, is compiled. More than 100,000 couplets long, it was passed on orally. It would not be printed for almost 3,000 years.
About 800 B.C.	**China:** The *Book of Songs* is compiled; it is the foundation of Chinese poetry.
770–256 B.C.	**China:** Eastern Zhou Dynasty; *Way of the Tao,* ascribed to Lao Tzu.
About 700 B.C.	**Greece:** Hesiod writes *The Works and Days,* an epic poem.

Classical Era

About 600–557 B.C.	**Greece:** Sappho of Lesbos, one of the earliest Greek lyric poets, lives and writes.
600–200 B.C.	**Greece:** Golden age of lyric poetry, including poetry by Alcaeus (about 600 B.C.), Anacreon (563–478 B.C.), Pindar (522–448 B.C.), Theocritus (316–260 B.C.), and Callimachus (310–240 B.C.). Great era of Greek drama — tragedies by Aeschylus (525–456 B.C.), Sophocles (496–406 B.C.), and Euripides (480–406 B.C.).
500 B.C.	**China:** According to tradition, China's first great poet, Ch'ü Yüan, writes *Nine Classic Songs* and *Li Sao* ("Falling into Trouble").
323 B.C.	**Babylon:** Death of Alexander the Great.
206 B.C.–A.D. 220	**China:** Han Dynasty. Buddhism spreads through China, influencing poetry. The imperial Ts'ao family produces several famous poets.

About 200 B.C.	**Middle East:** The Book of Daniel, the latest of the books of the Hebrew Bible, is written.
About 100 B.C.–A.D. 20	**Roman Empire:** Golden age of Latin poetry, including the epic poem *On the Nature of Things* by Lucretius (95–50 B.C.), the lyric poetry of Catullus (87–57 B.C.), the *Aeneid* of Virgil (70–19 B.C.), the work of Horace (65–8 B.C.), and the lifetime of Ovid (43 B.C.–A.D. 18), author of lyric poetry and the *Metamorphoses,* a myth cycle.
44 B.C.	**Rome:** Julius Caesar murdered.
About A.D. 3–35	**Middle East:** Life of Jesus Christ.
About A.D. 10–150	**Rome:** Second great period of Latin poetry, including the epigrams of Martial (about A.D. 40–100) and the verse drama of Seneca (A.D. 4–65) and Juvenal (A.D. 60–140).
About A.D. 300	**India:** The Sangam works, earliest collection of Tamil poetry.
A.D. 313	**Rome:** Emperor Constantine legalizes Christianity.
A.D. 322–550	**India:** Gupta empire; "Golden age" of India; much poetic activity. Includes career of Kalidasa (lived around A.D. 400), famous poet writing in Sanskrit.
A.D. 476	**Rome:** Last Roman emperor overthrown; thought of as the end of the Classical Era and the beginning of the Dark Ages in Europe.

Dark and Golden Ages

About A.D. 550	**Middle East:** Imr El-Qais, "The Wandering King," writes his influential odes in the anthology *Mu'allaqah* ("Necklace-Beads").
A.D. 570–632	**Middle East:** Lifetime of Muhammad, prophet and founder of Islam. The Koran, the holy book of Islam, is written. One of the great poets of the period is Al-Khansa, the major female poet in Arabic.
A.D. 618–907	**China:** The T'ang Dynasty, "golden age" of Chinese poetry; the work of Li-Po (A.D. 701–762), Tu Fu (A.D. 712–770), and Po Chü-i (A.D. 772–846).

A.D. 661–750	**Middle East:** The Ummayyad Dynasty, and beginnings of the "golden age" of Arabic poetry. Verse of Umar ibn Abi Rabi'a (A.D. 644–720). The ghazal is introduced and spreads throughout the Middle East and Asia.
About A.D. 670	**British Isles:** "Caedmon's Hymn," earliest extant Old English poem. *Beowulf,* an epic poem in Old English, probably written at this time (possibly in what is now Sweden). Also in Old English: Religious poetry, historical poems, riddles, and laments.
A.D. 685–784	**Japan:** Early literary period of court poetry, during which the *Manyoshu,* an important early anthology, helped establish the first great age of Japanese verse. Includes the work of Yamanoe Okura (about A.D. 660–733) and Kakinomoto Hitomaro (who lived between A.D. 680 and 700).
A.D. 750–1055	**Middle East:** Abbasid dynasty. Influences of Roman, Greek and Persian poetry. Great poets include Al-Mutanabbi (A.D. 915–965) and Abû 'l-'Alá al-Ma'arrí (A.D. 973–1057).
A.D. 784–1100	**Japan:** Early Classical Period: The anthology *Kokinshu* is compiled, including the work of Ono no Komachi (who lived around A.D. 850) and Ariwara Narihira (A.D. 825–80).
A.D. 800–1100	**Iceland:** Composition of the *Poetic Edda,* a collection of old Norse epic and mythological poems.
A.D. 960–1280	**China:** Sung Dynasty, during which new poetic forms were devised, as in the poetry of Hsin Ch'i-chi.
A.D. 974–1031	**Japan:** Life of Lady Murasaki Shikibu, author of *The Tale of Genji,* a long prose work that also included much influential poetry.

Middle Ages

1000	**Europe:** Observation of the end of the first millennium; thought to be the beginning of the Middle Ages or Medieval Period.

	France: *The Song of Roland,* an epic poem, is written; it is the foundation of French literature.
1000–1100	**Iberian peninsula:** Moorish and Jewish writers compose Mozarabic lyric poetry in a Spanish-Arabic-Hebrew dialect.
1034–1130	**Persia:** Life of Omar Khayyam, author of the *Rubaiyats.*
1066	Normans invade England.
About 1100	German epics *Tristan und Isolde* and *Parzifal* written.
1100–1200	**France:** Verse romances abound. These include the French *chansons de geste* (poems of action), Jean de Meun and Guillaume de Lorris's *The Song of the Rose,* and other works that became the foundation for tales of chivalry, leading ultimately to the Arthurian romances.
1100–1350	**South of France:** Great flowering of troubadour poetry. This includes the work of Bernart de Ventadorn (1130–1190) and Arnaut Daniel (about 1150–1200), who wrote some of the earliest love poetry in Western Europe.
1140	**Spain:** *El Poema del Cid,* an epic poem and the first major work in the Spanish language, is written.
About 1170–1230	**German-speaking principalities:** Life and poetry of Walther von der Vogelweide, one of the greatest practitioners of German courtly love poetry.
1177	**Middle East:** Death of the celebrated poet Muhammad ibn Ghalib al-Rusafi.
About 1200	**Northern Europe:** The German Nibelung cycle is written.
1165–1400	**Middle East and Persia:** Great era of Sufi verse, including the poetry of Ibn al-'Arabi (1165–1240) in Arabic and Hafez (1320–1389) and Rumi (1326–1390) in Persian.
1215	**England:** Magna Carta signed.

1265–1321	**Italy:** Life of Dante Alighieri, one of the greatest poets in history. His work includes *La Vita Nuova* (a book of love poems and prose commentary) and the epic religious work *The Divine Comedy,* in which the poet visits hell, purgatory, and paradise. His poetry is dedicated to his beloved, Beatrice.
1300s	**India:** Beginnings of Hindi poetry.
1300–1500	Collections of Italian, French, and English folk poetry compiled by scribes throughout Europe.
1304–1374	**Italy:** Life of Francesco Petrarca. His sonnets to his beloved Laura influenced poets throughout Europe for the next 350 years.
1345–1400	**England:** Life of Geoffrey Chaucer, the highpoint of medieval poetry in England. Includes the epic romance *Troilus and Criseyde* and the *Canterbury Tales,* a collection of stories in a variety of verse forms.
1375–1400	**England:** *Sir Gawain and the Green Knight,* an anonymous metrical romance, is written.
1431	**France:** Birth of François Villon, lyric poet.

Renaissance

1450	**Italy:** Florence under the Medici family becomes the center of a new flowering of arts and education; thought of as the beginning of the Renaissance.
	Caribbean Islands: Christopher Columbus lands.
1500s	**India:** Earliest written Bengali poetry.
1516	**Italy:** Ludovico Ariosto (1474–1533) publishes his epic romance *Orlando Furioso.*
	Germany: Martin Luther nails his 95 theses to the door of the cathedral at Wittenberg; beginnings of the Protestant movement in Europe.

1526–1857	**India:** The Mughal (or Mogul) Empire spreads Islamic ideas and aesthetics throughout the subcontinent. Arabic and Persian poetic forms have a huge impact on Bengali, Urdu, Tamil, and Hindi poetry.
1542–1591	**Spain:** Life and intense erotic-mystical poetry of San Juan de la Cruz (St. John of the Cross).
1549	**France:** Renaissance poetry reaches a peak with The Pléiades, an influential group that included Joachim du Bellay (1522–1560) and Pierre de Ronsard (1524–1580).
1558	**England:** Elizabeth I becomes queen.
1564	**England:** William Shakespeare is born.
1570–1620	**Europe:** Thousands of sonnets written by Renaissance courtiers in all major European languages.
1580–1640	**England:** Great period of English popular drama, the great bulk of which is written in verse. Playwrights include Christopher Marlowe (1564–1593), William Shakespeare (1564–1614), Thomas Middleton (1570–1627), Ben Jonson (1572–1634), John Fletcher (1579–1625), John Webster (1580–1625), Francis Beaumont (1584–1616), and John Ford (1586–1640). Coincided with a flowering of lyric poetry, in the work of Edmund Spenser (1552–1599), Sir Walter Raleigh (1552–1618), Sir Philip Sidney (1554–1586), Shakespeare, Jonson, John Donne (1573–1631), George Herbert (1593–1633), and many others.
1580–1660	**Spain:** Great period of verse drama, including the work of Lope de Vega (1562–1635), Francisco Quevedo (1580–1645), and Pedro Calderón de la Barca (1600–1681).
1588	**English Channel:** Defeat of the Spanish Armada by the English fleet.
1590	**England:** Spenser publishes first books of his epic romance *The Faerie Queene*. Publication of Sidney's *Arcadia* and *Astrophil and Stella*.

1600–1601	**England:** Shakespeare's *Hamlet* written and first performed.
1600–1700	**India:** First flowering of Urdu poetry in the courts of northern Muslim rulers.
1600–1867	**Japan:** Late feudal period and the rise of the haiku, including the poetry of perhaps the most famous of all Japanese poets, Basho (Matsuo Munefusa) (1644–94) and Kobayashi Issa (1762–1826).
1609	**England:** Shakespeare's sonnets published without his consent.
1611	**England:** Publication of the "authorized" King James Bible, one of the most influential publications in the history of the English language. Remains the best-known English translation of the Old Testament poets and religious writers.
1612–1672	**English colonies, North America:** Lifetime of Anne Bradstreet, first publishing poet in the colonies.
1614	**England:** William Shakespeare dies.
1616	**England:** The "First Folio," the collected plays of Shakespeare, published posthumously.
1620	**America:** Pilgrims arrive at Plymouth Rock.
1629–1691	**France:** Great period of French verse drama, including the tragedies of Pierre Corneille (1606–1694) and Jean Racine (1639–1699) and the comedies of Molière (1622–1673).
1632–1674	**England:** Poetic career of John Milton (1608–1674), who wrote lyric poetry and verse drama before writing his epics *Paradise Lost* (1667, 1674) and *Paradise Regained* (1671), as well as the verse drama *Samson Agonistes* (1671). Milton's work is recognized as the culmination and the end of the English and European Renaissance.
1648/51–1695	**Mexico:** Lifetime of poet Sor Juana Inés de la Cruz.
1649–1697	**England:** Career of satirist, dramatist, translator, and lyric poet John Dryden (1631–1700).

18th and 19th Centuries

1700–1800   **England:** An age of satirical and philosophical poetry, including the work of Jonathan Swift (1667–1745), Alexander Pope (1688–1744), Samuel Johnson (1709–1784), and Oliver Goldsmith (1730–1774).

1716–1783   **Japan:** Life of Yosa Buson, an eminent writer of haiku.

1749–1832   **Germany:** Astonishing life and poetic career of Johann Wolfgang von Goethe, whose poetry helped begin the Romantic era in European art and culture. He wrote massive amounts of lyric and philosophical verse, as well as the epic verse drama *Faust* (published in 1808).

1757–1827   **England:** Life and poetic career of William Blake. He published *Songs of Innocence* (1789) and *Songs of Experience* (1794), as well as a range of lyric, historical, philosophical, and epic poetry.

1780–1850   **Germany:** Great age of Romantic poetry. Lyric and philosophical work by Goethe, Friedrich Hölderlin (1770–1843), Friedrich Schiller (1759–1805), and Heinrich Heine (1797–1856).

1798   **England:** Samuel Taylor Coleridge (1772–1834) and William Wordsworth (1770–1850) publish *Lyrical Ballads,* an attempt to renovate and purify English verse. Their book instigates the English Romantic Period in earnest, an exploration of nature and human psychology with a new directness and power. Other Romantic poets include Scotland's Robert Burns (1759–1796), as well as England's John Keats (1795–1821), George Gordon, Lord Byron (1788–1824), and Percy Bysshe Shelley (1792–1822).

1802–1885   **France:** The life and writings of Victor Hugo mark the highpoint of French Romanticism.

1819–1824   **England:** Byron publishes his comic epic masterpiece, *Don Juan.*

1828   **Russia:** Alexander Pushkin (1799–1837) publishes the verse novel *Eugene Onegin.* Pushkin is considered the father of Russian poetry.

1832	**England:** Victoria becomes Queen of England, ushering in the Victorian Period.
1850	**England:** Alfred, Lord Tennyson (1809–1892) publishes *In Memoriam,* a long lyric elegy for his friend Arthur Hallam. It is one of the highpoints of Victorian poetry.
1855	**United States:** Walt Whitman (1819–1892) publishes the first edition of *Leaves of Grass,* his monumental lifetime work, written mostly in free verse. Along with the poetry of Emily Dickinson (1830–1886), Whitman's work marks the beginning of Modern American poetry.
1857	**France:** Publication of *Fleurs du Mal* (Flowers of Evil) by Charles Baudelaire (1821–1867). This book is thought to be the first book of Symbolist verse.
	India: British rule begins. English legal, cultural, and educational institutions spread throughout India.
1860–1910	**France:** Reign of the Symbolist poets, including Stéphane Mallarmé (1842–1898), Paul Verlaine (1844–1896), Arthur Rimbaud (1854–1891), Jules Laforgue (1860–1887), and Paul Valéry (1868–1955).
1867–1902	**Japan:** Life of Masaoka Shiki, great reformer and invigorator of Japanese verse, responsible for the modern understanding of the haiku form.
1868	**Japan:** The Meiji restoration opens Japan to the West, bringing with it a flood of influences, including French Symbolism; this led in the 1880s to a literary movement called the "New Style."
1888–1891	**Russia:** Within 18 months, 3 of Russia's greatest modernist poets are born: Anna Akhmatova (1889–1966), Boris Pasternak (1890–1960), and Osip Mandelstam (1891–1938).
1890	**United States:** First collection of Emily Dickinson's poems appears, four years after her death.
1891–1892	**United States:** "Deathbed edition" of Whitman's *Leaves of Grass* published.
1894–1930	**Russia:** Life of modernist poet Vladimir Mayakovsky.

20th Century

1905	**Nicaragua:** Rubén Darío publishes *Cantos de Vida y Esperanza (Songs of Life and Hope),* beginning the Modernist Era in Latin American poetry.
	England: Rudyard Kipling (1865–1936) receives the Nobel Prize for Literature.
1910–1940	**Russia:** Modernism. Poetry by Mandelstam, Akhmatova, Marina Tsvetayeva (1894–1941), Velimir Khlebnikov (1885–1922), and Mayakovsky.
1912	**United States:** Harriet Monroe founds *Poetry,* one of the century's most influential journals.
	England: H.J.C. Grierson's edition of the poetry of Renaissance poet John Donne leads to a rediscovery of Donne's work, which becomes quite influential among Modern poets.
1912–1922	**Germany and elsewhere:** Rainer Maria Rilke (1875–1926) writes his masterwork, *The Duino Elegies.*
1913–1914	**England:** American poet Robert Frost (1874–1963) publishes his first two books of poetry, *A Boy's Will* and *North of Boston.*
1913	**France:** Poet Guillaume Apollinaire (1880–1918) publishes *Alcools.* Apollinaire named both Cubism and the later movement known as Surrealism.
	India: Rabindranath Tagore (1861–1941) is awarded the Nobel Prize for Literature.
1914–1918	**England:** World War I inspires a generation of fine poets, including Siegfried Sassoon (1886–1967), Isaac Rosenberg (1890–1960), Wilfred Owen (1893–1918), Edmund Blunden (1896–1974), and David Jones (1895–1974).
1915	**England:** American poet Ezra Pound (1885–1972) publishes the influential anthology *Des Imagistes,* an important moment in the development of Modern poetry.

1916	**Switzerland:** Poet Tristan Tzara (1896–1963) and others found the Dadaist movement in art and literature, which rejects traditional methods of writing and making art. Dadaism led to the development of surrealism and other forms of modernist art and poetry.
1917	**United States:** William Carlos Williams (1883–1963) publishes his book *Al Que Quiere!*
1918	**England:** The poems of Gerard Manley Hopkins (1844–1889) are published in England, 29 years after his death. They influence poets in America and England for the rest of the century.
1919–1920	**France:** André Breton (1896–1966) and Philippe Soupault (1897–1990) begin collaborative projects that lead to the creation of the Surrealist movement. **England:** Pound publishes *Hugh Selwyn Mauberley: Life and Contacts.*
1920–1945	**Japan:** Growing influence of Western writers, which extends through the rest of the century; a proliferation of new verse forms, especially free verse.
1921	**England and Ireland:** William Butler Yeats (1865–1939) publishes "The Second Coming."
1922	**United States and England:** T.S. Eliot (1888–1965) publishes *The Waste Land.* **Russia:** Establishment of the Union of Soviet Socialist Republics (USSR), a federation of 15 countries.
1923	**United States:** Wallace Stevens (1879–1955) publishes *Harmonium.* **Ireland:** Yeats receives the Nobel Prize for Literature.
1924	**United States:** Frost receives the Pulitzer Prize for his book *New Hampshire.* It is the first of four Pulitzers for Frost. **France:** Breton writes the first manifesto defining Surrealism.
1925	**England:** Pound publishes *A Draft of XV Cantos.*

United States: Alaine Locke publishes *The New Negro,* a collection of poetry and fiction by African American writers, and a highpoint of the Harlem Renaissance.

1926   **United States:** African American poet Langston Hughes (1902–1967) publishes *The Weary Blues,* another milestone in the Harlem Renaissance.

Scotland: Hugh MacDiarmid (C.M. Grieve) (1892–1978) publishes *A Drunk Man Looks at the Thistle,* an attempt to write Modernist lyric poetry using the Scots dialect.

1930   **United States:** Hart Crane (1899–1932) publishes *The Bridge,* an influential Modernist-Romantic work.

1936   **Spain:** Federico García Lorca, the greatest Spanish poet of the century, is killed (as a civilian, but for political reasons) in the Spanish Civil War.

United States: Founding of the University of Iowa Writers' Workshop, with a gathering of poets and fiction writers under the direction of Wilbur Schramm. This, the first U.S. university writing program, would spawn a huge national movement after World War II.

1939–1945   World War II.

1941   **United States:** John Crowe Ransom (1888–1974) publishes *The New Criticism,* which influences writers and teachers for the rest of the century.

1942   **England·** Eliot publishes "Little Gidding," completing his masterwork, *The Four Quartets.*

1945   **Japan:** Atomic bomb falls on Hiroshima. End of World War II — and of the Modern Era.

France: Senegalese poet Léopold Sédar Senghor (1906–) publishes *Chants d'ombre (Shadow Songs).*

1946   **Japan:** Society and culture rebuild. Influence of Western Modernists.

1946–1958   **United States:** William Carlos Williams publishes his epic poem *Paterson.*

United States: University writing programs begin to flourish. In the next half-century, they will spread throughout the country, teaching tens of thousands of new poets.

1948 **England:** Eliot receives the Nobel Prize for Literature.

United States: Charles Olson (1910–1970) comes to Black Mountain College in North Carolina, of which he is rector from 1951 to 1956. He heads a group of poets, called the *Black Mountain Poets* or *Projectivists,* whose influence lasts the rest of the century.

1950 **United States:** Gwendolyn Brooks (1917–2000) wins the Pulitzer Prize for her book *Annie Allen.*

1952 **United States:** Marianne Moore (1887–1972) publishes *Complete Poems* and wins the National Book Award, the Bollingen Prize, and the Pulitzer Prize.

United States: First complete collected edition of Emily Dickinson's poems is published.

1955 **United States:** Allen Ginsberg (1926–1998) reads his poem *Howl* at the Six Gallery in San Francisco, beginning the Beat movement.

1956 **Spain:** Juan Ramón Jiménez (1881–1958) receives the Nobel Prize for Literature.

United States: John Ashbery (1927–) publishes his first book, *Some Trees.*

United States: After a court challenge charging obscenity, Ginsberg publishes *Howl,* the most important book of Beat poetry.

1958 **Russia:** Boris Pasternak (1890–1960) wins and declines the Nobel Prize for Literature.

1959 **United States:** Robert Lowell (1917–1977) publishes *Life Studies,* influential in the "confessional" poetry movement.

1960 **United States:** Publication of *The New American Poetry,* edited by Donald Allen, an influential anthology in the experimental poetry movement.

1961	**United States:** At the presidential inauguration of John F. Kennedy, Robert Frost reads "The Gift Outright."
1963	**England:** Death of Sylvia Plath (1932–1963).
1965	**United States:** Yvor Winters (1900–1968) publishes *Forms of Discovery,* an influential anthology and revision of English poetic history.
1966	**England:** Basil Bunting (1900–1985) publishes *Briggflatts.*
	United States: Death of Frank O'Hara (born 1926), perhaps the best-known poet of the New York School.
1967	**United States:** Anne Sexton (1928–1974) publishes *Live or Die* and wins the Pulitzer Prize.
1968–1969	**United States:** Black Mountain poet Ed Dorn (1929–1999) publishes *Gunslinger,* Parts I and II, a hip, epic poem about a metaphysical cowboy's quest through the universe.
1969	**Philippines:** First World Congress of Poets convenes.
1970	**United States:** Influential *Anthology of New York Poets,* edited by Ron Padsett and David Shapiro, is published.
1971	**Chile:** Pablo Neruda (1904–1973) receives the Nobel Prize for Literature.
1973	**United States:** Adrienne Rich publishes *Diving into the Wreck,* extremely influential in subsequent American poetry and in feminist culture.
1974	**United States:** Miguel Algarín and Miguel Piñero found the Nuyorican Poets Café, a venue on Manhattan's Lower East Side for performance poetry in a mixture of ethnicities, styles, dialects, and poetic practices. Ntozake Shange and Piri Thomas also play large roles in the dissemination of the new poetic style.
	Italy: Eugenio Montale (1896–1981) receives the Nobel Prize for Literature.

1978–	**United States:** Emergence of language poetry and performance poetries, including poetry slams, rap, and hip-hop.
1980	**United States:** Polish American poet Czeslaw Milosz (1911–) receives the Nobel Prize for Literature.
1984	**France:** Senghor becomes first black member of the French Academy.
1985	**United States:** Congress authorizes the position of Poet Laureate of the United States, replacing the office of Poetry Librarian for the Library of Congress.
1986	**United States:** First Chicago Poetry Slam held at the Green Mill bar, instigating a national craze for performance poetry. Other important venues include Boston (at the Cantab Lounge) and San Francisco (at the Café du Nord and elsewhere). By the 1990s, the poetry slam scene had gone international.
	United States: Robert Penn Warren (1905–1989) is chosen as the first official Poet Laureate of the United States.
1987	**United States:** Russian-American poet Joseph Brodsky (1940–1996) receives the Nobel Prize for Literature.
1990	**Mexico:** Octavio Paz (1914–1998) receives the Nobel Prize for Literature.
1991	**United States:** Vikram Seth (1952–) publishes *The Golden Gate,* a novel written in sonnets.
1992	**Trinidad:** Derek Walcott (1930–) receives the Nobel Prize for Literature.
1993	**United States:** At the presidential inauguration of William Jefferson Clinton, poet Maya Angelou (1928–) reads "On the Pulse of Morning." Publication of *Aloud! Voices from the Nuyorican Poets Café,* edited by Bob Holman and Miguel Algarín. *Also:* Publication of *Postmodern American Poetry*, edited by Paul Hoover, the first comprehensive anthology of American avant-garde poetry since 1960.

1995	**Ireland:** Seamus Heaney (1939–) receives the Nobel Prize for Literature.
	United States: First volume of the influential anthology *Poems for the Millennium,* edited by Jerome Rothenberg and Pierre Joris, is published.
1996	**Poland:** Wislawa Szymborska (1923–) receives the Nobel Prize for Literature.
	United States: First annual National Poetry Month in April.
	Russia: Nationwide celebration of the 200th anniversary of the birth of Alexander Pushkin.

21st Century

2001	*Poetry For Dummies* published.

Appendix C

Resources

● ●

Organizations

A variety of major literary organizations promote poetry and support poets.
Most are national, nonprofit organizations, and many offer membership.
Check out their Web sites or write or call them to find out more about their
programs and services.

92nd Street Y: For over 60 years, some of the world's best writers have taken
the stage at The Unterberg Poetry Center at the 92nd Street Y. In addition to
the Center's comprehensive annual series of readings by writers in poetry, fiction, nonfiction, and drama, they also offer special programs featuring the
spoken word. The Center's Web site has detailed information on upcoming
events as well as a comprehensive list of literary organizations across the
country. **1395 Lexington Avenue, New York, NY 10128; phone: 212-996-1100;
Web site:** www.92ndsty.org

The Academy of American Poets: Founded in 1934, the Academy is the largest
organization in the U.S. dedicated specifically to the art of poetry. The organization sponsors National Poetry Month (in April), the Poetry Book Club, and
the Online Poetry Classroom, an educational resource and online teaching
community for high school teachers. Its excellent Web site invites visitors to
"Find a Poet" for biographical information on major poets. The Web site also
offers a comprehensive list of literary links and a listening booth where you
can hear famous poets like Robert Frost, Sylvia Plath, H.D., Langston Hughes,
and William Carlos Williams read their own works. **584 Broadway, Suite 1208,
New York, NY 10012; phone: 212-274-0343; Web site:** www.poets.org

Audience for Literature Network (ALN): Self-described as "a growing group
of people who want to bring books and literature to more people in more
ways, everywhere," this new alliance of established literary centers creates
and presents literature programs in libraries, literary centers, community
centers, museums, bookstores, schools, on the radio, and on the Web.
Member organizations of ALN include: Just Buffalo (Buffalo, New York); The
Loft (Minneapolis, Minnesota); Florida Center for the Book (Ft. Lauderdale,
Florida); The Guild Complex (Chicago, Illinois); Washington Center for the

Book (Seattle, Washington); Woodland Pattern (Milwaukee, Wisconsin); Writers & Books (Rochester, New York); and The Writer's Center (Bethesda, Maryland). Visit the ALN Web site for more information including other literary events, organizations, publishers, and additional resources. **Web site:** www.wab.org/aln/alnweb/

The Center for the Book in the Library of Congress: This is a great place to start any search for information on programs — both nationally and internationally — focusing on reading, books, libraries, and literacy. Created in 1977 by an act of Congress, the Center works closely with other organizations on a wide variety of reading and book-oriented programming, and it includes over 40 affiliated state centers and dozens of other reading promotion partners. The Center sponsors such large programs as the Favorite Poem Project developed by Robert Pinsky (U.S. Poet Laureate, 1997–2000), and the River of Words project spearheaded by Robert Hass (U.S. Poet Laureate, 1995–1997). Their Letters about Literature annual contest invites students in grades 4 through 12 to enter a letter they've written to a poet or other writer describing how that writer changed the way they view the world; winners receive cash prizes. The Center's Web site offers extensive information on these programs, a calendar of literary events across the country, and much, much more. **101 Independence Avenue S.E., Washington, DC 20540-4920; phone: 202-707-5221; Web site:** lcweb.loc.gov/loc/cfbook/

National Poetry Association (NPA): Over the past 25 years, the NPA has reached over a half million people through its literary programs for live, broadcast, and Internet audiences. The NPA's extensive collection of over 500 cinematic-electronic poems or *Cinepoems* — video renditions of a variety of poems by everyone from Edgar Allan Poe to Allen Ginsberg — reaches hundreds of classrooms and cable channels worldwide. The NPA also produces the Annual Cin(E)-Poetry Festival, the Literary Television Project (L-TV), an online journal *(Poetry USA),* and hosts poetry slams and readings. **934 Brannan Street, 2nd Floor, San Francisco, CA 94103; phone: 415-552-9261; Web site:** www.nationalpoetry.org

PEN American Center: Part of PEN International, "the only worldwide organization of literary writers," the PEN American Center is a membership association of prominent literary writers and editors. As a major voice of the literary community, the organization seeks to defend freedom of expression, wherever it may be threatened, and promote and encourage the recognition and reading of contemporary literature. **568 Broadway, New York, NY 10012-3225; phone: 212-334-1660; Web site:** www.pen.org

The Poetry Center & American Poetry Archives: Founded in 1954 on the basis of a gift by the poet W.H. Auden, The Poetry Center is one of the most prestigious and nationally renowned literary arts institutions in the U.S. Located on the campus of San Francisco State University, The Poetry Center offers students and the public alike poetry readings and talks by some of today's most highly esteemed poets. You can attend The Poetry Center's readings throughout San Francisco, visit the center and its library of contemporary poetry books and journals, or join literature lovers around the world and attend the events — past, present, and future — via American Poetry Archive tapes. A full listing of titles and ordering information can be found on the online catalog at its Web site. **1600 Holloway Avenue, San Francisco, CA 94132; phone: 415-338-2227; Web site:** `www.sfsu.edu/~newlit/`

The Poetry Project: Founded in 1966 and housed in the landmark St. Mark's Church in the center of New York City's East Village, the Poetry Project offerings include a bimonthly newsletter, an annual literary magazine *(The World),* an annual New Year's Day Marathon Reading, tape and document archives, and general support for poets. Its Web site has a Web zine *(Poets & Poems);* the Tiny Press Center, a resource center for small publishers with reviews and interviews with writers; and links to other poetry sites. **St. Mark's Church in-the-Bowery, 131 East 10th Street, New York, NY 10003; phone: 212-674-0910; Web site:** `www.poetryproject.com`

Poetry Society of America (PSA): Founded in 1910, PSA supports a variety of poetry awards, seminars, and programs. Its Poetry in Motion program — a collaboration with the MTA New York City Transit — places large poem-placards in subway cars and buses in cities across the country (teachers, hospitals, and nonprofit organizations can receive free Poetry in Motion posters by writing to PSA). PSA's Web site offers an extensive list of over 200 poetry-related Web sites, including poetry journals, book publishers, MFA programs in poetry, conferences and festivals, literary organizations, and independent literary bookstores. **15 Gramercy Park South, New York, NY 10003; phone: 212-254-9628; Web site:** `www.poetrysociety.org`

Poets and Writers (P & W): Founded in 1970, P & W assists authors in their search for career-related information, outlets for their work, opportunities for professional advancement, and community with other writers. P & W provides a range of resources to the literary community, including the Readings/ Workshops Program, offering matching fees to writers for readings; Literary Horizons, helping writers advance professionally; and Publications Programs that include the information-packed *Poets & Writers* magazine. Its Web site offers writers an extensive array of resources, from information on grants and awards to publishing advice and news from the writing world to audio recordings of interviews and readings by notable contemporary poets. **72 Spring Street, New York, NY 10012; phone: 212-226-3586; Web site:** `www.pw.org`

Poets House: Founded in 1985, Poets House is a 40,000-volume, noncirculating poetry library of books, tapes, and literary journals. Its comfortably furnished literary center is open to the public year-round and has reading and writing space available. Poets House also presents over 30 public events each year, including readings, workshops, seminars, and poetic programs of cross-cultural and interdisciplinary exchange. Each April it hosts the Poets House Showcase, a comprehensive exhibit of the year's new poetry releases from commercial, university, and independent presses around the country, along with receptions, panel discussions, and seminars all open to the public. The Poets House Web site has information about its library, programs, and resources, as well as a calendar of literary events. **72 Spring Street, Second Floor, New York, NY 10012; phone: 212-431-7920; Web site:** www. poetshouse.org

Small Press Traffic (SPT) Literary Arts Center: For over 25 years, SPT has presented poetry and fiction readings, writing workshops, talks, panels, book parties, and theater productions, with a strong focus on innovative writing by authors outside of the mainstream. It offers reviews of small press publications, a newsletter, and membership opportunities. **Small Press Traffic at CCAC, 1111 Eighth Street, San Francisco, CA 94107; phone: 415-551-9278; Web site:** www.sptraffic.org

Teachers & Writers (T & W) Collaborative: Founded in 1967 by a group of writers and educators who believed that writers could make a unique contribution to the teaching of writing, T & W offers a plethora of resources for teachers and students and anyone interested in the ongoing learning process of writing poetry. It publishes a bimonthly magazine and books on teaching the art and craft of poetry and other genres. You'll find descriptions of these books, a writers' discussion group, links to other literary sites, and more on the T & W Web site or in its catalog. **5 Union Square West, New York, NY 10003-3306; phone: 212-691-6590; Web site:** www.twc.org

Events

Hundreds or even thousands of poetry festivals, conferences, gatherings, and shindigs take place throughout the U.S., and we simply couldn't list them all. So here is a list of some of the larger, national events that offer something for poetry lovers of all ages and persuasions. Participating in poetry events is a great way to meet other like-minded people, discover new poets and forms of poetry, get inspired about reading and writing poetry, and have fun!

Cowboy Poetry Gathering: This annual roundup is the granddaddy of cowboy poetry events and is sponsored by the Western Folklife Center in Elko, Nevada. At the end of every January, cattle people, rural folks, poets, musicians, gear makers, western enthusiasts, and urbanites gather in Elko for an extravaganza of conversation, singing, dancing, great hats and boots, stories, laughing and crying, big steaks, incessant rhymes, and a galloping cadence that keeps time for a solid week. Before you run out, buy a horse, put on a leather suede vest, and take a stage name like Chuck Roast, go to the official Web site of the Cowboy Poetry Gathering and round up all the information you need to join in on next year's festivities. You can also listen to poems from last year's Cowboy Poetry Gathering. **Web site:** www.westernfolklife.org

Geraldine R. Dodge Poetry Festival: The largest poetry event in North America, this biennial festival presents many of the country's top contemporary poets in a four-day poetry affair of concurrent readings, discussions, and workshops in the beautiful, rustic Village of Waterloo, New Jersey. Most events take place in tents outdoors at various village sites such as the sawmill, the gristmill, the gazebo, and the church, and last anywhere from 30 minutes to 2 hours and span all day from 9:00 a.m. to 9:00 p.m. Often, special events are held for teachers and instructors of poetry, as well as open mikes for all participants. **163 Madison Avenue, Morristown, NJ 07962; phone: 973-540-8442; Web site:** www.grdodge.org

National Poetry Month: The month of April, although considered the "cruelest month" by T.S. Eliot and U.S. taxpayers, has been declared a time of celebrating verse by the folks at the Academy of American Poets. This is not so much one event, but a national awareness program and general promotion of poetry. Many organizations, bookstores, and poetry lovers everywhere plan special events to celebrate National Poetry Month each year. Check the Academy's Web site for more information as well as for listings in your region for special poetry events in April. **Web site:** www.poets.org

National Youth Poetry Slam & Festival: An annual event in April hosted in a different city each year, this festival offers several days of slams, workshops, and gatherings for youths. The year 2000 slam shows in San Francisco sold out quickly. Over 2,500 audience members cheered for the 100 youths from 15 different regions (including young poets from London and Bosnia) who took part. To participate in a slam, poets must be between the ages of 13 and 19, in a group of four to six poets, and sponsored by an adult. Older and younger youths may participate in the other activities during the Festival. Participating is free; ticket prices for shows vary. For complete information on how to sign up, buy tickets, or get involved, go to their Web site. **Web site:** www.youthspeaks.org

Poetry Slam Nationals Annual Competition: This is the grandest of poetry slams, held in a different city each year. The first-ever national poetry slam, in which teams of four poets compete against one another based on random audience judges' scores, was held in 1990 in San Francisco. Growing by leaps and bounds each year, the past few Nationals have seen as many as 48 teams from regions in North America and Europe. For complete information, including the history of the National Poetry Slams, as well as slam rules and registration, go to the official Web site. **Web site:** www.poetryslam.com

Taos Poetry Circus: Each summer, The World Poetry Bout Association has presented this annual week-long event billed as "the nation's premier poetry festival." The Circus presents the work of locally, nationally, and internationally known poets in a unique and exciting performance series that includes readings, panel seminars, competitions, videos, slams, and daily open readings. The main event is the World Heavyweight Championship Poetry Bout. In the week preceding the Bout, the Taos Poetry Circus Education Project holds Mexican Bob's Poetics and Performance Camp, an 11-day intensive that focuses on students' work and performance as well as on the work of contemporary poets. **5275 NDCBU, Taos, NM 87571; phone: 505-758-1800; Web site:** www.poetrycircus.org

Magazines

Literary magazines have been popping up by the dozens in recent years, often showcasing new talent alongside established writers. With all the magazines out there, keeping up with them all is difficult. We've selected a sampling of literary magazines along with a couple of magazines filled with valuable information for aspiring writers. Many magazines now have sister publications on the Internet. You can browse a magazine's Web site, and, if you like what you read, subscribe to the traditional publication. Better yet, write and send a check to the magazine for a single sample issue. Many famous poets were first published in literary magazines. Who knows who *you'll* discover next?

The American Poetry Review: Since the early 1970s, this bimonthly tabloid has showcased new and emerging writers alongside some of America's top poets. Issues include poetry, reviews, interviews, and articles concerning poets around the world. Past issues have featured the poetry of James Tate, Alicia Ostriker, Edward Hirsch, and Ho Xuan Huong. The magazine also contains much information via its advertisers on creative writing programs and writing conferences across the country, as well as announcements of new poetry books and calls for submissions for many major poetry contests. *The American Poetry Review* boasts a worldwide audience. Single copies start at $3.95. **1721 Walnut Street, Philadelphia, PA 19103; phone: 215-496-0439; Web site:** www.aprweb.org

Conjunctions: A publication of innovative fiction, poetry, criticism, drama, art, and interviews by both emerging and established writers whose work challenges accepted forms and modes of expression, *Conjunctions* experiments with language and thought. Past issues have included writing by John Ashbery, Richard Powers, Joyce Carol Oates, Elaine Equi, Rick Moody, and Barbara Guest. Single issues start at $12. **21 East 10th Street, New York, NY 10003; Web site:** www.conjunctions.com

Drumvoices Revue: *Drumvoices Revue* doesn't just publish poetry; it celebrates poets, the spoken word, and the literary community with reports and photo-journals from poetry events such as the Langston Hughes Poetry Festival and the Peoples' Poetry Gathering. Consulting and contributing editors include Imamu Amiri Baraka, Maya Angelou, Janice Mirikitani, Gary Soto, Quincy Troupe, and Jessica Hagedorn. *Drumvoices Revue* is published twice yearly by the English Department of Southern Illinois University at Edwardsville in collaboration with the Eugene B. Redmond Writers Club of East Saint Louis, Illinois. Single issues start at $5. **Department of English, Box 1431, Southern Illinois University at Edwardsville, Edwardsville, IL 62026-1431**

Hanging Loose: This highly accessible magazine publishes established as well as new poets, and features poetry, short fiction, artwork, and, in every issue, writing by people of high-school age. It's published three times a year. Sample issues start at $9. **231 Wyckoff Street, Brooklyn, NY 11217; Web site:** omega.cc.umb.edu/~hangloos

The Hudson Review: For over 50 years, this quarterly publication has provided great reading and showcased the work of top-ranking poets and new American writers. Its 50th Anniversary Issue featured writing by poets Hayden Carruth, Maxine Kumin, Mark Jarman, Dana Gioia, and Emily Grosholz. *The Hudson Review* also publishes essays on literary and cultural topics, fiction, memoirs, book reviews, and chronicles covering film, theatre, dance, music, and art. Single issues start at $8. **684 Park Avenue, New York, NY 10021; Web site:** www.litline.org/hudson

New American Writing: Published in association with Columbia College Chicago and edited by Paul Hoover and Maxine Chernoff, this annual magazine publishes poetry and prose true to its name by many up-and-coming writers. A recent issue included translations of poems by 14 Brazilian poets. Sample issues start at $8. **OINK! Press, 369 Molino Avenue, Mill Valley, CA 94941**

The Paris Review: An international literary quarterly founded in 1953, known for presenting the *crème de la crème* of the literary world. Past issues have included poetry by such luminaries as John Updike, Sharon Olds, Mark Doty, and Carolyn Kizer, as well as fiction by Kay Boyle, Gabriel García Márquez, and Norman Mailer. The magazine also includes interviews with well-known writers such as A.R. Ammons and William F. Buckley, Jr. Single issues start at $10. **541 East 72nd Street, New York, NY 10021**

Parnassus: Poetry in Review: True to its title, *Parnassus* is one of the few higher-circulation magazines of criticism devoted exclusively to poetry. This publication is for serious poetry lovers who enjoy in-depth comparative reviews of books of poetry. Poems are also part of the magazine, and recent work published includes poems by Molly McQuade, Melissa Monroe, John Foy, and an opera by Anne Carson. Black-and-white art is placed throughout, including reproductions of paintings, mixed media pieces, and linocuts. Published semiannually. Single issues start at $12. **205 West 89th Street #8F, New York, NY 10024**

Ploughshares: A journal of new writing, *Ploughshares* is guest-edited serially by prominent writers who explore different and personal visions, aesthetics, and literary circles. Recent issues have included poetry by Yusef Komunyakaa, Toni Morrison, Susan Wheeler, and C.K. Williams; drama by Joyce Carol Oates; and fiction by Russell Banks, Claire Davis, and Edmund White. Single issues at the newsstand start at $9.95. Published three times a year at Emerson College. **Emerson College, 120 Boylston Street, Boston, MA 02116; Web site:** www.emerson.edu/ploughshares

Poetry: Founded in 1912 by poet Harriet Monroe, *Poetry* is published monthly by the Modern Poetry Association (MPA). A slim, unintimidating publication, typical issues offer no more than 20 poems by contemporary authors, as well as a selection of reviews on books of poetry. A recent issue included poetry by Billy Collins, Angela Shaw, Faye George, and Albert Goldbarth. Individual issues start at $3.50. **60 West Walton Street, Chicago, IL 60610; Web site:** www.poetrymagazine.org

Poetry Flash: Since the early 1970s, this tabloid of all things poetry has brought poetry news, reviews, essays, and interviews to an eager audience in the West and beyond. Past issues have included interviews with poet Philip Whalen by David Meltzer; a conversation between Gary Snyder and Peter Coyote; poetry reviews of books by Diane di Prima, C.K. Williams, Chana Block, and Bob Perelman; and a sprinkling of fiction reviews and interviews. *Poetry Flash* also carries the most comprehensive listing of literary events in the West. Its Calendar is an indispensable guide to the literary scene in all of California and offers Southwest, Pacific Northwest, and selected national event listings. *Poetry Flash* is distributed free to libraries, bookstores, community centers, and cafes, but you can subscribe to the publication from this tireless nonprofit. A one-year subscription (six issues) starts at $16. **1450 Fourth Street #4, Berkeley, CA 94710; Web site:** www.poetryflash.org

Poets & Writers: Published by the literary organization of the same name, *Poets & Writers* has become an industry standard. Each month, readers can expect jam-packed issues with articles on such topics as breaking through writer's block and submitting your work for publication, along with the most up-to-date information on grants and awards, deadlines, and conferences. Past issues have featured interviews with poets Lucille Clifton and Sapphire, as well as a profile of Frank McCourt. An essential source of information for serious poets and writers. Single copies start at $4.95. **72 Spring Street, New York, NY 10012; phone: 212-226-3586; Web site:** www.pw.org

The Poetry Project Newsletter: This newsletter is published five times a year and includes regular features and interviews, announcements, regional updates, poetry, short fiction, book and journal reviews, and literary-world gossip. Subscriptions start at $20 per year or are included with an annual membership to The Poetry Project at St. Mark's Church. **131 East 10th Street, New York, NY 10003; Web site:** `www.poetryproject.com`

Shiny: *Shiny* showcases cutting-edge poetry and prose from both living and dead writers of the genre. A recent issue included poems or other writing by John Ashbery, Carla Harryman, Jack Collom, Lyn Hejinian, Anselm Hollo, Kenneth Koch, and Emily Grenley. Single issues start at $15. **P.O. Box 13125, Denver, CO 80201**

Tin House Magazine: *Tin House Magazine* is a new, sexy, two-color literary magazine featuring poetry (including a section for new poets called "New Voices"), fiction, interviews, profiles, a literary acrostic, other writings of interest to literature lovers, and black-and-white art throughout. A recent issue included poetry by Marge Piercy, Yehuda Amichai, and David Lehman; fiction by Amy Hempel and Mian Mian; articles by Charles Simic and Lynne Tillman; and apple pie recipes from Alice B. Toklas, Erskine Caldwell, and Jane Austen. Published quarterly. **P.O. Box 10500, Portland, OR 97296-0500**

The Threepenny Review: *The Threepenny Review* is a tabloid quarterly featuring poems, fiction, art, films, essays, and articles of interest to poetry and prose lovers alike. Past issues include poems by Seamus Heaney, Jane Hirshfield, Thom Gunn, Yehuda Amichai, and Robert Pinsky; articles by Greil Marcus on Bob Dylan and James Ensor; and an article by Daniel Wolff on Elvis. Single issues start at $5. **P.O. Box 9131, Berkeley, CA 94709; phone: 510-849-4545; Web site:** `www.threepennyreview.com`

TriQuarterly: *TriQuarterly* is an international journal of writing, art, and cultural inquiry published at Northwestern University. For over 35 years, *TriQuarterly* has published the work of literary luminaries. Guest editors are frequently featured. A recent issue included letters from James Schuyler; poetry by W.S. Merwin, Barbara Guest, and Katharine Washburn; and prose writing from Louis Zukofsky. Sample copies start at $5. **Northwestern University, 2020 Ridge Avenue, Evanston, IL 60208-4302. Web site:** `http://triquarterly.nwu.edu`

Books

We recommend a number of good books of poetry throughout *Poetry For Dummies*. But here are a few more we think are particularly useful for readers and writers of poetry. These books can be found at most libraries and at new and used bookstores. You may want to use the library when it comes to the reference books that are updated annually; that way, you'll get the most up-to-date information. Consider these books tools of the trade.

American Poetry: The Twentieth Century, Volume 1: Henry Adams to Dorothy Parker **and** *Volume 2: E.E. Cummings to May Swenson,* **both edited by the Library of America.** This two-volume set was edited by acclaimed poets and critics Robert Hass, Carolyn Kizer, Marjorie Perloff, Nathaniel Mackey, and John Hollander, and is part of the Library of America's distinguished series on American poets and poetry. Here is the most comprehensive and inclusive attempt to assemble all the important poets of the 20th century. The poets are presented in chronological order by date of birth. Musicians and composers are also presented. The two volumes contain more than 1,500 poems by over 200 different poets, with excellent biographical notes.

A Book of Women Poets from Antiquity to Now: Selections from the World Over, **edited by Aliki Barnstone and Willis Barnstone.** This is a truly delightful anthology offering six millennia of poetry from women around the world. From Sumerian moon-priestess and poet Enheduanna (born ca. 2300 B.C.) to 17th-century Chinese poet Wang Wei, from 19th-century American poet Emily Dickinson to 20th-century African American poet Gwendolyn Brooks, the Barnstones have brought together an elegant collection of 300 women poets.

The Concise Columbia Encyclopedia, **by Paul Legasse.** An excellent one-volume encyclopedia for looking up facts, allusions, and chronologies. Includes black-and-white photos and maps.

From The Other Side of the Century: A New American Poetry 1960–1990, **edited and with an Introduction by Douglas Messerli.** This is an important anthology of innovative writers of the later part of the 20th century. Included are over 80 poets whose work has been some of the most influential and exemplary of Postmodern poetry. The poets are well represented in this collection, with often an offering of as many as a dozen poems by individual poets. This anthology takes up where the ground-breaking anthology, *The New American Poetry 1945–1960,* edited by Donald Allen, left off.

Handbook of Poetic Forms, **edited by Ron Padgett.** An easy-to-use guide to both traditional and modern forms written by 19 teaching poets, providing examples of 74 poetic forms. The *Handbook* succinctly defines the forms, summarizes their histories, quotes examples, and offers professional tricks of the trade on how to use each form.

Literary Terms: A Dictionary, **3rd Revised Edition, by Karl Beckson and Arthur Ganz.** As an adjunct to the short glossary in Appendix A of *Poetry For Dummies,* here is a resource book for word and term aficionados. Readers will find everything from the meaning of *abecedarius* (a type of acrostic poem in which the letters of the alphabet appear in order as the first letter of each line of the poem) to *zeugma* (a rhetorical figure in which a single word, standing in relationship to two others, is correctly related to only one). Other terms covered in this immensely informative guide include *macaronic verse* (it has nothing to do with pasta or cheese) and *feminine ending* (Shakespeare used this form, but not in the way you might guess he did).

The Merriam Webster's Collegiate Dictionary, **Tenth Edition.** Any reader worth his salt will have a good dictionary at his side at all times. This one is a favorite and known to be "The Voice of Authority," offering over 14.5 million examples of English words drawn from actual use. It also provides extensive cross-referencing, guidance on synonyms and usage, extensive definitions, and concise pronunciations.

The New American Poetry 1945–1960, **edited by Donald Allen.** This book has become one of the most influential anthologies published in the United States since World War II. Originally published in 1960, it is considered prophetic by critics, because so many of the writers included here have gone on to produce works that are signatures of Postmodern writing. Allen delivered the first taste of these remarkable poets, and the book has since become an invaluable historical and cultural record, as well as a guide for new readers to Postmodern poets.

The New Princeton Encyclopedia of Poetry and Poetics, **edited by Alex Preminger and T.V.F. Brogan.** The standard source for information on the history and criticism of poetry and poetic technique and theory, including discussions of 106 national poetries. This comprehensive reference work deals with all aspects of its subject: history, types, movements, prosody, genre, rhetoric, and critical terminology. An indispensable guide for poets and readers of poetry.

The Norton Anthology of Modern Poetry, **2nd Edition, edited by Richard Ellmann and Robert O'Clair.** Spanning a period beginning with Walt Whitman (born in 1819) to Cathy Song (born in 1955), and including 1,580 poems, this anthology shows the variety and depth of modern poetry, with an introduction and footnotes for each poet.

The Norton Anthology of Poetry, **4th Edition, edited by Margaret Ferguson, Mary Jo Salter, and Jon Stallworthy.** Not just for the classroom, this anthology is an essential guide for the ongoing student of poetry. The book offers 1,800 poems by 300 poets, including 72 women poets. This edition features a diverse selection of work by African American, Hispanic, Native American, and Asian American poets, as well as 37 poets from Australia, New Zealand, Ireland, Scotland, Wales, the Caribbean, South Africa, and India.

Poems for the Millennium, Volumes I and II, **edited by Jerome Rothenberg and Pierre Joris.** These two books survey the 20th century from an angle different than that of most other anthologies. The editors are looking for the experimental, the alternative, "with an emphasis on those international and national movements that have tried to change the direction of poetry as a necessary condition for changing the ways in which we think and act as human beings." The Rothenberg-Joris view is a retelling of the whole century of poetry. The result is surprising, challenging, and refreshing.

Poet's Market. This annual guide to places that publish poetry is an indispensable resource for beginning poets who want to get their poetry published. The current directory includes over 1,800 listings, including large and small magazines, literary journals, electronic publications, small presses, and trade book publishers. Listings are coded with easy-to-reference indexes and symbols so you can find the type of publications you are looking for quickly. You can also find information on grants, contests, conferences, workshops, and organizations. The book also offers articles on such important topics as poetry submission etiquette, the value of participating in public poetry readings, and the pros and cons of self-publishing.

Postmodern American Poetry: A Norton Anthology, **edited by Paul Hoover.** This is the first major anthology of avant-garde American poetry since 1960. Here is the definitive guide to the poets of the 20th century whose work characterizes the Postmodern Era, beginning with John Cage (1912–1992) and concluding with the youngest poets in the book, Amy Gerstler (1956–) and Diane Ward (1956–). The book concentrates on poets and theorists who resist the mainstream ideology, with essays on poetics from Charles Olson, Allen Ginsberg, Lyn Hejinian, Victor Hernández Cruz, and Robert Creeley.

Roget's 21st Century Thesaurus, **edited by The Princeton Language Institute.** This thesaurus boasts 500,000 synonyms, a unique concept index for the fastest access to scores of new choices, and hundreds of recently coined and common slang terms.

Shakespeare For Dummies, **by John Doyle and Ray Lischner.** A true must for Shakespeare lovers and anyone who longs to gain a better understanding of the great bard and his legendary plays and poems.

Webster's New World Rhyming Dictionary, **by Clement Wood, edited by Michael S. Allen and Michael Cunningham.** An essential handbook for poets who use rhyme in their poetry. This volume offers over 60,000 modern American English words categorized in over 1,500 phonetically rhyming groups. You'll need this when trying to find a word that rhymes with *orange.*

World Poetry: An Anthology of Verse from Antiquity to Our Time, **edited by Katharine Washburn, John S. Major, and Clifton Fadiman.** This indispensable volume contains more than 1,600 poems drawn from dozens of languages and cultures, and spans a period of more than 4,000 years from ancient Sumeria and Egypt to the late 20th century. *World Poetry* encompasses the many realms of poetry — poetry of all styles, eras, and tongues — and brings to the reader the best that all the world's cultures have to offer. More than 80 percent of the book is poetry originally written in languages other than English and expertly translated.

If you're interested in making poetry a part of your life for years to come, you may enjoy membership in the Poetry Book Club (PBC). PBC is a program of The Academy of American Poets and is the first book club devoted to poetry in the U.S. Six times a year, the PBC mails a catalog to its subscribers, offering the best of contemporary and classic poetry, delivered right to your doorstep. Currently, the PBC is available only to residents of the United States. You can find more information on the PBC Web site at www.poetrybookclub.org

Teachers of poetry may find Story Line Press (www.storylinepress.com) and Teachers & Writers Collective (www.twc.org) particularly helpful. Both publish a number of titles on teaching poetry.

Internet

We encourage you to go out and get involved in the poetry community by going to literary centers, libraries, bookstores, and cafés. But when that midnight urge hits to find your favorite book of poems, chat with other poets, or even send in your recent masterpiece, the Web is where you'll need to be. While you're surfing the Internet, you just may bump into poetry from the Old Testament, the Greeks, Shakespeare, Whitman, and Emily Dickinson — much of the world's great poetry can be found on the Web. Here are just a few poetry-related Web sites to get you started.

Electronic Poetry Center (epc.buffalo.edu): The Electronic Poetry Center is brought to you by the State University of New York (SUNY) at Buffalo and offers extensive links to other poetry sites, including sites for e-poetry, authors, magazines, books, and other literary sites. A great place to begin your exploration of poetry and poetic sites available on the Web.

Favorite Poem Project (www.favoritepoem.org): Discover the Favorite Poem Project, past Poet Laureate Robert Pinsky's project to record Americans reciting their favorite poems. You can read the poems as well as watch video clips from the Project's Archive created for the Library of Congress.

How2 (www.departments.bucknell.edu/stadler_center/how2): At *How2*, you'll find "poetry's renegade path, as practiced by Twentieth Century women writers and scholars." *How2* focuses on innovative writing by women and publishes new poems, essays, reflections, letters, journals, research, translations, and more. Published twice a year.

Jacket (www.jacket.zip.com.au): This award-winning site for *Jacket,* a leading literary e-zine, is published quarterly on the Internet from Sydney, Australia, and is free. *Jacket* publishes poetry, interviews, reviews, and articles on photography and type.

Magnetic Poetry Kit (www.magneticpoetry.com): Here's your chance to play with magnetic poetry — without a refrigerator! Create poems on your computer by clicking and dragging different words and/or letters from the list onscreen. Be careful though, because even if you create the next *Howl,* you won't be able to print it out. You can check out the anthology of poems all created by people using poetry magnets, and browse the Poetry Magnet company's line of kits and other cool stuff.

Poetry Daily (www.poems.com): Get your poem a day at this site. *Poetry Daily* offers a vast and continuously updated anthology of contemporary poetry and brings news from the poetry world to its readers. You can also subscribe for free to its weekly newsletter, which features presses that publish poetry books, interviews with poetry leaders, and more.

Readme (www.jps.net/nada/): *Readme* is a quarterly online journal of poetics featuring interviews, essays, and reviews relevant to contemporary poetry. Poetry is published only in tandem with author interviews and/or critical prose, except in cases of poem-as-reading/critique. The site also features 20th-century author links and other literary links.

Web del sol (www.webdelsol.com): Web del sol is a collaboration on the part of dozens of dedicated, volunteer editors, writers, poets, artists, and staff whose job it is to "acquire and frame the finest contemporary literary art and culture available in America and abroad, and to array it in such a manner that it speaks for itself." The site has links to many online magazines, and it also publishes a monthly newsletter, the Electronic Literary Arts Newsletter (ELAN).

The Zuzu's Petals Literary Resource (www.zuzu.com): The Zuzu's Petals Literary Resource site offers over 10,000 organized links to helpful resources for writers, artists, performers, and researchers. Its mission is to "expand the influence of poetry beyond its traditionally academic audience and to make quality writing an everyday craving." We like that.

Permissions

Abū-l-`Alā' al-Ma'arrī. *See* Timpane, John.

Adonis (Ali Ahmad Sa'id). *See* Hibbard, Allen and Osama Isber.

Antin, David. Translation of "A Man and Woman Absolutely White" by André Breton. Reprinted by permission of David Antin.

Barnard, Mary. Translation of Sappho, "He is more than a hero." From *Sappho: A New Translation.* Copyright © 1958. The Regents of the University of California. Renewed 1986 by Mary Barnard. Reprinted with permission of the University of California Press.

Bachmann, Ingeborg. *See* Damion Searls.

Barnstone, Willis. Translation of "Mother's Song" ("If snow falls"). Reprinted with permission of Willis Barnstone. Excerpted from *A Book of Women Poets from Antiquity to Now: Selections from the World Over*, edited by Aliki Barnstone and Willis Barnstone. New York: Schocken, 1992.

Bei Dao. *See* Finkel, Donald.

Bernstein, Charles. Writing exercises from http://epc.buffalo.edu/authors/bernstein. Reprinted by permission of Charles Bernstein.

Bishop, Elizabeth. "One Art," from *The Complete Poems 1927–1979* by Elizabeth Bishop. Copyright 1979, 1983 by Alice Helen Methfessel. Reprinted by permission of Farrar, Straus and Giroux LLC.

Breton, André. *See* Antin, David.

Carter, Steven D. Translation of Lady Izumi Shikibu, "If someone would come." Reprinted from *Traditional Japanese Poetry: An Anthology*. Translated, with an Introduction, by Stephen D. Carter. Reprinted with permission of the publishers, Stanford University Press. Copyright © 1991 by the Board of Trustees of the Leland Stanford Junior University.

Césaire, Aimé. *See* Davis, Gregson.

Chernoff, Maxine. Writing exercises. Reprinted by permission of Maxine Chernoff.

Chilam Balam. *See* Sawyer-Laucanno, Christopher.

Chiyo. *See* Ray, David.

Corbett, William. "Vermont Apollinaire." Copyright © 1995 by William Corbett, from *New & Selected Poems*. Zoland Books, Cambridge, Massachusetts.

Creeley, Robert. "The Business." From *Collected Poems of Robert Creeley, 1945–1975*. Copyright © 1983 The Regents of the University of California. Reprinted by permission of University of California Press on behalf of the author.

Cummings, E.E. "in Just-." Copyright 1923, 1951, © 1991 by the Trustees for the E.E. Cummings Trust. Copyright © 1976 by George James Firmage, from *Complete Poems: 1904–1962* by E.E. Cummings, edited by George J. Firmage. Used by permission of Liveright Publishing Corporation.

Davis, Gregson. Lines from "Since Akad, Since Elam, Since Sumer" by Aimé Césaire. Excerpted from *Non-Vicious Circle: Twenty Poems of Aimé Césaire*, translated, with an introduction and commentary, by Gregson Davis. Reprinted with the permission of the publishers, Stanford University Press. © 1984 by the Board of Trustees of the Leland Stanford Junior University.

Dickinson, Emily. Lines from Poems 214, 621, 640, 986, 1732. Reprinted by permission of the publishers and The Trustees of Amherst College from *The Poems of Emily Dickinson*, Thomas H. Johnson, ed., Cambridge, Mass.: The Belknap Press of Harvard University Press, Copyright © 1951, 1955, 1979 by the President and Fellows of Harvard College.

Eliot, T.S. Excerpt from *The Waste Land* from *Collected Poems, 1909–1962*, copyright 1930 and renewed 1958 by T.S. Eliot, reprinted by permission of Faber and Faber Ltd.

Enheduanna. *See* Hallo, William W. and J.J.A. van Dijk.

Feinstein, Elaine. Excerpts from translation of Marina Tsvetayeva, "Poem of the End." From *Selected Poems*. Reprinted by permission of Carcanet Press Limited.

Ferlinghetti, Lawrence. Excerpt from "Constantly Risking Absurdity" (*Coney Island of the Mind*, #15) from *A Coney Island of the Mind*. Copyright © 1958 by Lawrence Ferlinghetti. Reprinted by New Directions Publishing Corp.

Finkel, Donald. Excerpts from translations of Bei Dao, "Answer," from *A Splintered Mirror: Chinese Poetry from the Democracy Movement*, translated by Donald Finkel. Translations copyright © 1991 by Donald Finkel. Reprinted by permission of North Point Press, a division of Farrar Straus & Giroux, LLC.

Francis, Robert. "Silent Poem." From *Collected Poems* by Robert Francis. Copyright © 1976 by Robert Francis. Reprinted by permission of University of Massachusetts Press.

Fraser, Kathleen. "Vanishing Point: Third Black Quartet" from "Wing." From *il cuore: the heart* © 1997 by Kathleen Fraser, Wesleyan University Press. Reprinted by permission of University Press of New England.

Frost, Robert. "Nothing Gold Can Stay." From *The Poetry of Robert Frost*, Edited by Edward Connery Lathem. Copyright 1916, 1923, © 1969 by Henry Holt and Co., copyright 1944, 1951 by Robert Frost. Reprinted by permission of Henry Holt and Company, LLC.

Glück, Robert. Translation of "Departure" by Pierre Reverdy. Reprinted by permission of Robert Glück.

Graham, Jorie, Lines from "In What Manner the Body Is United with the Soule," from *Erosion* by Jorie Graham. Copyright © 1983 by Princeton University Press. Reprinted by permission of the publisher.

Guest, Barbara. Lines from "Red Lilies." Reprinted by permission of Barbara Guest.

Hallo, William W. and J.J.A. van Dijk. Translation of *The Exaltation of Inanna*, "Antiphonal Hymn in Praise of Inanna" by Enheduanna. Reprinted by permission of Yale University Press.

H.D. (Hilda Doolittle). "Oread" and "Sea Rose." From *Collected Poems, 1912–1944*. Copyright © 1982 by The Estate of Hilda Doolittle. Reprinted by permission of New Directions Publishing Corp. and Carcanet Press Limited.

Hibbard, Allen and Osama Isber, excerpt from translation of Adonis (Ali Ahmad Sa'id), "A Desire Moving Through the Maps of the Material." Reprinted by permission of Allen Hibbard and Osama Isber.

Hoffman, Roald. Excerpt from "Deceptively Like a Solid." Reprinted with permission of David Moore, Managing Editor, Society of Glass Technology.

Holt, Kelly. Writing exercises. Reprinted by permission of Kelly Holt.

Homer. *See* Timpane, John.

Howe, Fanny. "About Face." Reprinted by permission of Fanny Howe.

Imr El-Qais. *See* Timpane, John.

Issa, Kobayashi. *See* Timpane, John.

Jarkesy, Linda. "The Bed," "Bed," and narration of revision. Reprinted with permission of Linda Jarkesy.

Index

• *H* •

• *1* •

● *K* ●

● *L* ●

Notes

Notes

Notes

Notes

Notes